D0614445

THE CHOSEN PEOPLE
in an
ALMOST CHOSEN NATION

THE CHOSEN PEOPLE

in an

ALMOST CHOSEN NATION

Jews and Judaism in America

Edited by

Richard John Neuhaus

WILLIAM B. EERDMANS PUBLISHING COMPANY
GRAND RAPIDS, MICHIGAN / CAMBRIDGE, U.K.

© 2002 Wm. B. Eerdmans Publishing Co.
All rights reserved

Wm. B. Eerdmans Publishing Co.
255 Jefferson Ave. S.E., Grand Rapids, Michigan 49503 /
P.O. Box 163, Cambridge CB3 9PU U.K.

Printed in the United States of America

07 06 05 04 03 02   7 6 5 4 3 2 1

Library of Congress Cataloging-in-Publication Data

The chosen people in an almost chosen nation: Jews and Judaism in America /
edited by Richard John Neuhaus.
p.   cm.
ISBN 0-8028-4929-6 (pbk.: alk. paper)
1. Jews — United States.   2. Judaism — United States.
I. Neuhaus, Richard John.

E184.355.C56   2002
973′.04924 — dc21

2002023819

www.eerdmans.com

Contents

CONTENTS

Contents

Introduction

That the Jews are God's chosen people should be beyond dispute for Christians, and it is for most Christians. The Bible is unmistakably clear: "The Lord has chosen you to be a peculiar people for himself" (Deuteronomy 14:2). Yet there is no denying that there are still Marcionites among us. Marcion, it will be recalled, was the second-century heretic who taught that Jesus came to establish an entirely new religion. Obedience to his God of Love required a total rejection of Judaism and its God of Law. The Creator God of Israel, said Marcion, was the evil Demiurge, and it was the mission of Jesus to overthrow the Demiurge in the name of the God of Love whom he called the Father. According to Marcion, it is not only that the Old Testament is not part of Holy Scripture; the Old Testament is the very antithesis of the New. Further, in order to accommodate his teaching, Marcion proposed a truncated list of writings to be included in what came to be called the New Testament, the canon of which was still much disputed at that time.

The condemnation of Marcion and his teachings by the Great Tradition was one of the most monumentally important decisions in the history of the Church. The "what if" questions of history are always enticing, but of course they are unanswerable, since we cannot know what would have happened if what happened had not happened. We can be reasonably sure, however, that over these two thousand years the relationship between Judaism and Christianity, and between Jews and Christians, would have been very different if Marcion had prevailed. In view of what has been the tortured nature of that relationship, some might think that almost any other history would have been preferable. That is, I believe, quite thoroughly wrongheaded. We cannot know what would have been the human consequences of a different and hypothetical history, but we do know that Marcion's proposal was set against the Divine intention revealed in the history of salvation that there should be one covenant and one people gathered in obedience to the God of Israel — the God of Abraham, Isaac, Jacob, and Jesus.

When I say that there are still Marcionites among us, I do not mean that there are Christians today who endorse the entirety of his heresy. But there are many Christians for whom Jews and Judaism properly belong to the past. They are the people of Bible history, meaning Old Testament history, and the continuing existence of living Judaism is an embarrassing anachronism. Such Christians subscribe to "supersessionism" in which the New Testament not only fulfills the Old but displaces it. In this view, the continuing existence of Jews and Judaism makes no sense in terms of God's purposes; it is in fact something of a scandal. The scandal is either to be overcome by the conversion of the Jews to Christianity, or to be politely evaded. It is politely evaded by ignoring the reality of living Judaism as a *religious* question posed to Christianity, and it is politely evaded by escape into the relativistic acceptance of all religions certified as equally valid by the American Way of Life. Lingering Marcionism takes many forms.

The essays and commentaries in this book are selected from pieces published in *First Things* and include a wide range of subjects, viewpoints, disputes, and different ways of telling the story of Jews in America. Most of the items in this book are not theological in the ordinary sense of that term, and some are not explicitly religious in character, and yet the book has theological and religious undergirdings about which a word might be in order. *First Things* and its publisher, the Institute on Religion and Public Life, have been from the beginning a Jewish-Christian enterprise. That is because — for reasons made amply and sometimes painfully clear in this book — it is not possible to speak of the role of religion in American public life without paying close attention to Jews and Judaism. It is also because the thinkers and writers who launched this enterprise include Jews and Christians who over the years have come to trust one another, forming that good and rare thing, a company of mutual criticism and encouragement. Above all, however, *First Things* is a

Jewish-Christian enterprise because of the constituting conviction that our engagement with one another is part of our personal and communal vocation in obedience to the God of Israel.

For Christians, *First Things* hopes to play a part in exorcising the ghost of Marcion. The prospect of such an exorcism is also welcomed by many Jews. Not all Jews, of course. Some among the Orthodox agree with Marcion that Christianity is an entirely new and radically different thing; it is "other" and, for the most part, it is a threatening "other" that is to be kept, as much as possible, at safe distance. In addition, there are many Jews who are thoroughly secularized and could not care less about whether Christians think Marcion was right or wrong, except as it might have a bearing on the increase or decrease of anti-Semitism. Whatever Jews may variously think of it, the exorcism of the ghost of Marcion is a matter of urgency for Christians. If St. Paul is right — notably in the profound ponderings of chapters nine through eleven of the letter to the Romans — the mystery of living Judaism is at the root of what Christians believe, or should believe, about God's redemptive purpose in Christ and his Church. "Remember it is not you that support the root, but the root that supports you" (Romans 11:18).

I have been variously involved for more than thirty years with the Jewish-Christian dialogue. Usually referred to simply as "the dialogue," that conversation has undergone many changes, and today is reaching a new level of maturity, as is indicated by, for instance, the statement included in this book on how Jews understand Christians and Christianity. In my case, involvement started at Concordia Theological Seminary, St. Louis, when Rabbi Sol Bernards, then director of interreligious affairs for the Anti-Defamation League of B'nai Brith, was a traveling evangelist, so to speak, for the new thing called Jewish-Christian dialogue. That involvement was immeasurably deepened through my years of intense conversation and argument in my cherished friendship with the great Abraham Joshua Heschel, until his death in 1972. In 1989, I wrote with Rabbi Leon Klenicki, Sol Bernards' successor at ADL, *Believing Today: Jew and Christian in Conversation* (Eerdmans). Over the last ten years and more, the conversation has been sustained with many Jewish interlocutors, of whom I should mention in particular Matthew Berke, for many years the managing editor of *First Things,* and Rabbi David Novak, now of the University of Toronto and, in my judgment, the Jewish thinker who is today making the most substantive theological contributions to our understanding of the Jewish-Christian connection.

I have written here about the theological dimension of that connection in order to explain the relationship of *First Things* to Jews and Judaism. It would be a mistake, however, to assume that the essays and commentaries of this book are mainly about theology. Some of them are. For instance, the exchange between David Novak and Isaac Rottenberg on what it means to be a "Jewish Christian." But this book takes up the broad array of questions and disputes embroiled in the ongoing experience of "the chosen people in an almost chosen nation." Philosophy, law, psychology, history, anti-Semitism, proselytism, intermarriage, public policy, the State of Israel, and whether Christians can be trusted — all these and other questions are addressed in lively, diverse, and frequently provocative ways. Almost all the authors are Jewish, and most of them are religiously observant Jews.

For many Christian readers, this book will be an introduction to a Jewish world of discourse marked by energy and intelligence inexhaustibly engaged with the anxieties and aspirations that make this people, in the many senses of the phrase, a peculiar people. For Jewish readers, the book is an invitation to join in arguments that are ever old and ever new, and on which the last word will not be said until the coming — or as Christians must insist, the return — of the Messiah. For all readers, the book intends to be an instructive, spirited, and sometimes entertaining reflection on the distinctive experience of a people providentially living in an almost chosen nation.

For the happy trope, "an almost chosen nation," we are, of course, indebted to Abraham Lincoln, who knew something about providence, redemption, and judgment.

RICHARD JOHN NEUHAUS
New York City

Judaism or Jewishness?

ELLIOT ABRAMS

Jewish life in America began, at least for the vast majority of Jewish families, in the decision of European Jews to leave their parents, their synagogues, and their homes to go to America. That decision was part of a process their descendants now continue: the confrontation between Jews and life in the modern age. Their decision to come to America brought them the challenges that Jews today have inherited: how, and indeed whether, to live as Jews in a society that is overwhelmingly Christian and increasingly secular; what parts of Judaism to cling to, and what parts to abandon; and whether the community would define itself as Jewish by faith or ethnic inheritance.

The earliest Jewish settlers in America were Sephardim, descendants of Jews who had been expelled from Spain in 1492 and had fled to places such as the Ottoman Empire, Holland, and Brazil. They arrived in Dutch and British colonial America, driven to emigrate there by the same forces that propelled other early settlers. In America they soon lived not as poor immigrants in separate neighborhoods, but as respected and often prosperous, influential citizens. And they not only mixed with but very often assimilated into the Christian gentry, who accepted them as fellow members of the upper reaches of society. In the South in the early 1800s, according to historian Frederic Cople Jaher, "marriage with prominent gentile clans was extensive." In the North, says Leonard Dinnerstein, it was the same story: "Every Jew who settled and remained in colonial Connecticut before the Revolution married a

I

Christian. Similarly, large numbers of Jews in New York and Philadelphia married, raised their children in the community's dominant faith, and sometimes became Christian themselves."

What was to be the place of Jews in America, as independence approached? These early communities eagerly supported the Revolutionary ideals of individual rights and freedom of conscience, which American statesmen learned from the Enlightenment. Viewing themselves not as a community apart but as Americans of Jewish faith, they fought for full citizenship rights and the disestablishment of Christianity as a state religion. At the national level, they shared the victory when the First Amendment to the Constitution was adopted, prohibiting an establishment of religion and guaranteeing them, and all others, the free exercise of their faith. The Jews did not seek to separate religion and society, nor did they argue that the government could not support religion in general. Rather, they demanded that it be absolutely neutral *among* religions. And the Constitution was a great advance toward this goal.

At the state level, however, Jews continued to suffer from disabilities that must have reminded these Sephardim of their experiences in less enlightened regions of Christendom. The constitutions of nine of the thirteen original states contained a reference to Christianity, and four allowed tax assessments for church support. Under the early constitutions of Massachusetts, New Hampshire, New Jersey, North Carolina, Georgia, South Carolina, and Maryland, only Protestants could hold public office. In fact, not until the Civil War was full political equality for American Jews achieved.

The public agenda of American Jews was, then, the demand for equality, and they defined the religious liberty guaranteed in the Constitution as meaning nothing less. They pressed not for a secular state or society, but for treatment of Judaism no less favorable than that accorded Christianity. This would be a historic achievement and a sharp break with the past experience of Jew and Christian alike. The strategy of the Jewish community for gaining a secure place in the new United States, then, may be described as insisting on government neutrality among religions. But soon, when many new immigrants from Germany arrived, this strategy began to seem inadequate.

The emancipation of Europe's Jews began in Europe itself — in the aftermath of the French Revolution and in the swirl of ideas and actions we call the Enlightenment. For Jews, the Enlightenment, the *Haskalah,* meant throwing off the patterns of life and thought with which they had bound themselves for centuries. It meant a new way of dealing with Christian neighbors and a new relationship with the government, which in many places began to grant Jews more rights as citizens. The first step had been to leave the Jewish settlements and head for the heart of Europe's great cities. This was a physical action for some, coming from shtetls and small towns, and a psychological change for others, who emerged from urban ghettos.

In small towns, in rabbinical courts, and in cities renowned for Jewish learning, Jews in Europe had lived for centuries next to, yet apart from, their Christian neighbors. The Jewish community had not only its own religion, but its own Yiddish language, its own economy, its own system of justice. It had never been entirely cut off from Christian society, and Jews had sold their merchandise to Christians and bought from them the products of the land Jews were forbidden to own. But the Jewish community had enveloped its members and Judaism set the pattern of their days. Its autonomy and its inner peace were broken by the violence of Christian neighbors and Christian princes, seeking taxes and, on occasion, blood.

But in the nineteenth century Jews began to join the social and political, and more of the economic, activities of the people among whom they lived. From the Jewish community emerged philosophers and composers, businessmen and financiers, whose lives were played out not within the walls of a ghetto, but in the wider life of the country they inhabited.

The first waves of Jewish immigrants from Central and Eastern Europe arrived from Germany in the 1840s. There had been just a few thousand Sephardic Jews here in the early 1800s, but the German immigration increased their ranks to fifty thousand by 1850, and again to three times that number by 1860. They were escaping the disappointments of a Europe where, especially after the revolutionary hopes of 1848 were dashed, Jews still faced great danger and discrimination. They were also escaping their own pasts, leaving traditional communities governed by Orthodox authorities. It is not surprising that these enterprising and youthful arrivals were drawn from less, rather than more, religious elements of the German Jewish community.

In America, they sought what they could not fully obtain back home: true civil equality for Jews, and a new, more modern kind of Juda-

3

ism free from the control of Orthodoxy. How could this be achieved? The now enlarged community of American Jews, most originating in Germany, began to envision a new strategy: rather than stand apart as a visibly distinct group and demand government neutrality among religions, it would be wiser to Americanize and assimilate as quickly as possible and insist that government must not support religion at all. So they abandoned German for English and, as Melvin Urofsky notes, "deliberately downplayed any tendencies that might set them apart from their fellow Americans" in language, dress, and manners. Meanwhile, absolute separation of church and state, not benevolent government support of all religious groups, gradually became the community consensus on public policy.

Their argument for absolute separation was strong. The country they saw before them, and the memories they carried with them, made this seem the logical course to increasing numbers of Jews and their leaders. To begin with, they had experienced government support of established churches in Europe. They did not believe that government would actually remain neutral in any country where the vast majority of citizens were Christian. How would this be possible when many in the populace, the government, and the churches feared and hated Jews? Any government in a Christian country was certain to propound the "true faith," they believed, if it involved itself in religious matters at all. And if government support for religion must mean support for Christianity, the only way to stop it — to reduce the influence of Christianity on public life and on their lives — was to separate church from state.

This issue arose in disparate areas of life. While full political rights had been won by the time of the Civil War, other battles continued. Must Jews who closed their shops on Saturday close them on Sunday as well? Would there be Bible reading in public schools, and if so, whose Bible? Were Jewish children to be preached to from the New Testament each morning? The only practical answer seemed, again, to keep religious matters out of any contact with the government — and vice versa.

Second, this conclusion was further reinforced by the arrival, just as the German Jews were reaching America, of large numbers of Catholics from Ireland and Germany. Given the historic link between the Catholic Church and anti-Semitism in Europe, it was predictable that Jews would fear to see Catholicism strengthened in America. Far better, again, to ensure that government would do nothing to assist the Church.

Third, Jews who wanted to see reforms of their own faith in Germany had often had to contend with official support for the Orthodox rabbinate. Separation of church and state meant that the government would leave them to themselves to sort out Jewish community affairs. If the Orthodox authorities had no civil power over Jews, Jews would be free to be irreligious or to define new religious practices they felt more fitting for the modern world. So the popularity of Reform Judaism among the German immigrants also argued for keeping the state out of religious affairs altogether.

Finally, the German Jews arrived here when the goal of previous generations, government neutrality, was already ensconced in the Bill of Rights. They did not have to fight for toleration or legal rights, at least from the national government. They could raise their sights and ask for more: a society where religion played no public role. For, as they became more and more American in their ways, religion alone was what separated them from their fellow citizens. To minimize this divisive factor seemed the safest path.

Moreover, as Naomi Cohen, a leading historian of American Jewry and professor of American Jewish History at the Jewish Theological Seminary, has suggested, as the German Jewish community weakened — in faith, in ritual observance, and in cohesiveness — this very weakness led it to hope that the new strategy could substitute for the security Jews no longer obtained from membership in a tightly knit and to some extent self-governing group. Jews were coming to believe that their community might be weaker internally, yet safer nonetheless, if the separation between church and state were strengthened while that between Christian and Jew disappeared.

Besides, the Jewish community of the early 1900s was now filled with immigrants who, whatever their level of ritual observance, spoke Yiddish, lived among themselves, and were Orthodox at least in their religious training and education. What is more, community solidarity was reinforced by pressure from without, by anti-Semitism. The lynching of Leo Frank by a Georgia mob in 1915 reminded Jews that, even in America, anti-Semitism could bring violence and death.

Given the extremely high levels of prejudice and anti-Semitism prevalent then, the foreignness of the newly arrived Jews, and their intense desire to become part of American society, the risk of assimilation evoked far less concern than the challenge of achieving full participation in this new society.

By the early twentieth century, the Jewish community was rapidly being swelled by yet a new immigration: in the decades between 1880 and the First World War, millions of poor Jews from Russia and elsewhere in Eastern Europe began to reach New York and other East Coast ports. By the end of World War I, four million Jews lived in America. While their arrival transformed much in American Jewish life, it only reinforced the view that a secular American society was the safest one for Jews.

For most American Jews, the story begins here — with the arrival, three or four generations back, of a relative from Eastern Europe. Like the German Jews, these newcomers were escaping not only government oppression, but sometimes family and religious authority as well. For a young Jewish man or woman, the Tsar was a distant tyrant; there were often others closer at hand. The vast majority came from religiously observant, indeed Orthodox, families. Here, in America, their Orthodoxy crumbled.

From a religious point of view, the transition from a shtetl to life in an American city was devastating. In his famous book about the immigrant experience, *The Rise of David Levinsky,* Abraham Cahan's hero explains that "If you are a Jew of the type to which I belonged when I came to New York and you attempt to bend your religion to the spirit of your new surroundings, it breaks. It falls to pieces. The very clothes I wore and the very food I ate had a fatal effect on my religious habits."

My own maternal grandfather arrived here just before the First World War, from the town of Tlumatch in Galicia — then belonging to Austria-Hungary, now part of Ukraine. He and my grandmother had an entirely Orthodox upbringing, and to the day they died their household remained strictly kosher. But when employers required that he work on the Sabbath, he complied. The synagogue, and religious law, took second place to the need to feed five children. A chain smoker until his death, he was soon smoking on the Sabbath, too, and by the time I knew him he confined his visits to the synagogue to the High Holidays.

The society operated to Christian rhythms: Christmas and Easter were work and school holidays, not Rosh Hashanah and Yom Kippur.

6

Sabbath closing laws shut stores on Sunday, not Saturday. The food, as David Levinsky said, violated Jewish dietary laws, not those of Christians. Toward the end of the nineteenth century a famous European rabbi declared (in Yiddish, of course) that America, which so many Jews call the promised land, was in fact a *"trefe land,"* an unkosher country. Abraham Cahan knew what the rabbi meant. For the Puritans, the New World had provided the opportunity to practice their religion more freely than had the Old, and they saw themselves as the successors to the ancient Hebrews striking out into the wilderness. For the descendants of those Hebrews, life in America, far from reinforcing their religious practices, eroded them.

In addition, the very individualism of the Enlightenment philosophers subverted the spirit of Jewish peoplehood. The free individual choice of which those thinkers wrote, and which was sanctified in the American Constitution, was absolutely contrary to the Jewish idea of covenant and commandment. Jewish law was about the collective, inherited obligation to God of an entire people. Could anything have been further from the modern notion that each individual must freely choose his faith? And could anything have been more subversive of the idea that Jews were by birth bound to 613 commandments than a philosophy suggesting that men were free at birth from any religious obligations whatsoever?

But there is more: something special about Judaism that rendered Jews less able to cope with America than were members of other old-world religions. Nathan Glazer, professor emeritus of sociology at Harvard and author of the classic study *American Judaism,* wisely described the problem:

> Judaism is even more vulnerable to the unsettling influence of modernity than is Christianity. Judaism emphasizes acts, rituals, habits, a way of life. . . . Once one had found — as so many immigrants did — that it was more convenient to work on Saturdays or to shave or to abandon traditional dress, one had no body of doctrine to fall back upon that could explain what remained *really* important in Judaism — indeed, the question was whether *anything* was really more important than the rituals established by God's word. Under these circumstances, an entire way of life disintegrated.

Professor Glazer was suggesting not that there are no doctrines in Judaism, but that East European Jews had tended to concentrate on ritual far more than on doctrine. And the East European Jews who came to America — the grandparents and great-grandparents of most American Jews — were usually, to say it again, not the most devout people in their communities. Some came for economic opportunity, some to escape the draft, and many to escape oppression, but they did not come to pray. And when they did come to America for religious freedom, very often they were seeking the freedom to be irreligious.

In Europe they had performed the rituals, for there was parental and social pressure to do so, and it was easier to live as a Jew than to violate community norms. But in New York, the reverse was true. There was pressure to grab a (probably non-kosher) sandwich, to work on the Sabbath, to skip a prayer here and there. And as the ritual pillars began to collapse, they brought down with them the whole structure of faith for many new American Jews.

Finally, the American Jewish community cannot have been unaffected, in its religious behavior, by its own argument that a secular society was a safer one for Jews. If religious divisions within the society threatened Jews, how could it be helpful to stress them by ritual practices that set the Jew apart from his neighbor? In the mid-1880s, the East European poet J. L. Gordon, a champion of the *Haskalah,* told his community that the Enlightenment now allowed Jews to join civil society. The formula was to "Be a Jew in your tent and a 'mensch' [man] when you go out." But Gordon did not foresee that those who stopped being Jews in the street and on the job almost inevitably would stop being Jews in their tents as well. An end to rituals that interfered with the rhythms of American life might soon undercut faith as well, for who could wish to believe that he was shirking and doing wrong? Far easier, and more natural, to shirk not only the practice but the beliefs that required it. To enjoy the bounty of America fully, to mute the distinctiveness that had always brought danger to Jews, and to contribute to the building of a secular society where Enlightenment values would be safer, all seemed to lead away from traditional Judaism as it had been practiced for a thousand years.

Away from traditional Judaism, and into the melting pot. For nothing was more American than the steady diminution of old-world traditions among the new immigrant groups, and especially among their children. It was nearly unthinkable, and surely un-American, for any group to wall itself off, rejecting the fabulous opportunities of this new land because it preferred self-segregation and absolute fidelity to its past. True, the Amish and a few other sects did this and ultimately earned the admiration of the society at large for their resolute refusal to integrate. But these were rare exceptions, and the vast sea of immigrants — Jew and Christian alike — embraced the American ethos. Far from segregating themselves from America as the Amish did, the majority of Jews sought the "social invisibility" that alone would protect them and permit them to thrive here.

By the 1920s there were millions of Jews in America, and they constituted 3.7 percent of the population. Yet there is another way to see that number, and it is the way most Jews, and their leaders, saw it: America was still over 96 percent Christian. The leaders of the most important Jewish organizations wondered what public policies would best protect American Jews, and faced again the choices that had once been before their predecessors. They could insist that Judaism be given an equal place with Christianity in a deeply religious America, or seek a more secular America where religion's role was diminished.

They chose the latter path. Their choice is not in retrospect surprising — nor, even when viewed in the light of today's demographic crisis, was it necessarily wrong. They did not believe that even in America, even in the twentieth century, Christians would grant Judaism equal dignity. If there were no religious tests for public office by the late 1800s, American society remained pervasively Christian. Moreover, there were repeated efforts by Christian clergy and activist laymen to push through Congress the so-called "Christian state" amendment, which would push aside the neutrality mandated by the First Amendment and make America an officially Christian country. Judaism would be relegated to a permanently inferior position, and the ability of Jews to succeed in America would suffer enormous damage. How could an officially Christian nation ever be home to Jews? Jews strongly opposed and resisted the "Christian Staters" and even became suspicious of other causes dear to the Christian clergy, such as the temperance movement.

Most American Jewish leaders came to believe that security in America would be found by insisting that this country's Constitution be secular and that Jewish pressures to diminish the role of religion were based not on self-interest but on faith in law and the Constitution. For most of them, there must have seemed to be no alternative to this approach. For what else could they do? Accept permanent inferiority, or assault Christianity and hope to change its view of Jews? The first was morally unacceptable, and the second implausible and dangerous.

The universalism of the Enlightenment attracted Jews because it offered them a way out of the ghetto. The two great secular movements that won the support of European Jews after the Enlightenment — socialism and Zionism — had something of Jewish messianism in them. Zionism thought to save the Jews, and socialism to save all mankind, and on one question both agreed entirely: it was dangerous for Jews to live as a distinct minority in a Christian state. Dividing religion from state and society, and relegating it exclusively to the area of private life, had been seen by Jews in Europe as the beginning of their emancipation. America was no different from Europe in this respect, for here too a society where individuals could make their way without being segregated according to group origins would be better for Jews.

A more secular, more tolerant, more open society would be more just, benefit all minorities, and be truer to the nation's fundamental principles. Those principles were not specifically American but rather universal values such as liberty and equality — precisely the values of the Enlightenment. There was, according to this view, a complete identity among Enlightenment, American, and Jewish values.

To this mix was added a new version of the ancient Jewish respect for "the Law," as Jerold S. Auerbach explains in his brilliant work *Rabbis and Lawyers*. A reinterpretation of Judaism's commitment to the Law became a critical element of American Jewish adaptation to life in this country, he argues. In essence, Jewish immigrants became American Jews by redefining Judaism and submerging it in Americanism, itself newly defined by the Jewish lawyers who came to lead the community.

In the nineteenth century, rabbis had usually been the community's most influential leaders; but early in the twentieth century lawyers such as Louis Marshall, who served as president of the American Jewish Committee, and Louis Brandeis, the first Jew to serve on the Supreme Court, took their place. "As they redefined Jewish legitimacy in American legal terms," Auerbach recounts, "they fused Torah and Constitution as the sacred texts of a Judeo-American legal tradition." A key conduit was America's Puritan heritage, which permitted connecting ancient Israel and America "to a common democratic tradition whose origins could be found in the Hebrew Bible." The Puritans looked back to ancient Israel, and the Jews used that reference to affirm their own new American identity. The "new synthesis" that Marshall and Brandeis developed between 1906 and 1916 was based on the importance of law and justice in both the American and the Jewish traditions. The result was "the identification of Judaism with Americanism. . . . The prophetic teachings of 'brotherhood and righteousness' . . . had become the modern liberal ideals of democracy and social justice."

As Brandeis put it, "the highest Jewish ideals are essentially American," for "America's fundamental law seeks to make real the brotherhood of man. That brotherhood became the Jews' fundamental law more than twenty-five hundred years ago."

Under the leadership of Marshall and Brandeis, Auerbach concludes, "the rule of law that governed American Jewish life came to depend upon the Constitution, not the Torah." This sacralization of the Constitution joined Judaism and Americanism, and the immigrant Jew was now able to embrace a synthesis that allowed him to be a patriotic American as well as an observant Jew — observant, that is, of the newly defined requirements and responsibilities of the Jew in America.

Safety through secularism, integration rather than separatism, and life under the new sacred Law of the Constitution rather than the old Law of the Torah became the American Jewish ideology, and the institutions of the community pursued it with zeal. By the 1960s the battle to disestablish Christianity as the nation's public religion had largely been won. Great public occasions required clergymen from all three denominations, Protestant, Catholic, and Jewish, and the inadmissibility of using state power to advance Christianity was well established. Still the Jewish community pressed on, as Naomi Cohen reports in her history of the American Jewish Committee: "Jewish insistence on the sanctity of separation persisted. . . . As a pluralistic society accepted Jewish assertiveness more readily, the Jewish minority sharpened its attack against any entering wedge, no matter how innocuous in itself, which might breach the wall of separation."

Over the decades, as East European Jews became dominant in American Jewish life, the major Jewish organizations changed from being creatures of the rich, assimilated German-Jewish elites who saw themselves as stewards of the community. But the ideology of these organizations, which was secularist and non-Orthodox, did not change as their leadership passed from civic-minded laymen to a new generation of professionals. The members of this new group, like their more elitist predecessors, were highly secular in their own private lives and unenthusiastic about the role of religion in American society. As Cohen argues, "They spoke for a religious community, but . . . their actions in opposition to public religion reflected their own indifference if not hostility to religion itself."

Originally, for example, the Jewish defense organizations had fought to remove Christian prayers from the public schools on the grounds of discrimination against Jewish children. But when specifically Christian prayers were gone, these organizations carried on the fight, hoping to exclude any prayer (even voluntary and silent prayer), any observance of religious holidays, any benediction at graduation ceremonies, or any use of school facilities by religious groups. In one celebrated case, Jewish organizations sided with a school administration that permitted all voluntary student organizations, except a Bible club, to use school facilities after school let out. This, the Christian students argued, was discrimination against only one form of voluntary student activity. But the school administration resisted, and the major Jewish organizations supported it and sought to bar even this after-hours and unofficial religious activity. The principle they backed was absolutism in the separation of church and state, for fear that any link of religion to a public institution would eventually endanger American Jews.

Soon, however, that principle was extended from church and state to religion and society. Separation of church and state, as the late social critic Christopher Lasch put it, is "nowadays interpreted as prohibiting any public recognition of religion at all." While the Supreme Court has been rethinking these questions recently, the major Jewish organizations continue faithfully to promote the absolutist dogma.

This continuing effort is perfectly illustrated by the 1994 case involving the Kiryas Joel school district. Kiryas Joel is a town in New York State established in 1977 and populated by twelve thousand members of the Satmar sect of Hasidic Jews. The problem they faced when they established their private religious school system was the burden of educating emotionally and physically disabled children. When the sect's leaders concluded that they lacked the resources to educate these children, they tried to arrange for their education at the expense of the state, invoking a right common to all New Yorkers. The children were, for a time, educated in secular subjects by licensed public school teachers on premises within the town. Later, state authorities said this solution violated separation of church and state, and insisted that the disabled children be transported to public school premises outside the town. Claiming that the trip away from familiar surroundings upset the children, and that the other students who crossed their paths mocked their distinctive clothing and appearance, the parents convinced the state legislature to establish the town as a separate school district so that their handicapped children could be educated at a public school within it. The only schooling offered by this new school district was a secular special education program for handicapped children, and the teachers, therapists, and district superintendent were not Satmar Hasidim and did not reside in the town. Still, the state superintendent of schools brought suit, arguing that this new school district was set up solely to help the Hasidim and as such constituted an unconstitutional establishment of religion.

As might be expected, the major Jewish organizations (with the exception of the Union of Orthodox Jewish Congregations, Agudath Israel of America, and the National Council of Young Israel — all Orthodox groups) lined up uniformly against the Hasidim. An amicus curiae brief was filed by the Anti-Defamation League, the American Jewish Committee, and the National Council of Jewish Women, together with the American Civil Liberties Union, the Unitarian Universalist Association, and Americans United for Separation of Church and State; another brief was joined by the Union of American Hebrew Congregations, the American Jewish Congress, and the National Jewish Community Relations Councils with People for the American Way. Besides Orthodox Jews, the only organizations that sided with the Hasidim were the National Association of Evangelicals and the U.S. Catholic Conference. The deep religious faith of the Kiryas Joel Hasidim was for the major Jewish organizations outweighed by their fear that some conservative or fundamentalist Christian groups might conceivably benefit from a Kiryas Joel victory.

Thus separation of church and state was here taken another step, for now it appeared that any state action whose effect is to help parents keep their children faithful to their religious beliefs could be struck down as unconstitutional. The major Jewish groups all argued that to assist Orthodox Jews in making their children Orthodox was *by defini-*

tion unconstitutional. Several members of the Supreme Court agreed. New York's law went beyond constitutional bounds, Justice John Paul Stevens wrote in his opinion, because it "provided official support to cement the attachment of young adherents to a particular faith" and in this sense "affirmatively supports a religious sect's interest in segregating itself and preventing its children from associating with their neighbors."

This language is a far cry from the ways in which the Court used to talk about religious obligations and the parental role. In the famous 1925 case of *Pierce v. Society of Sisters,* the Court spoke of "the rights of parents to direct the rearing and education of their children," and in a 1944 case it added that "It is cardinal with us that the custody, care, and nurture of the child reside first in the parents, whose primary function and freedom include the preparation for obligations the state can neither hinder nor supply." If these decisions do not speak to the issue of public aid to parochial schools, they do demonstrate how the Court's attitude toward parents who seek to bind their children into obligatory religious commitments has changed from respect and even admiration to outright hostility. And in this journey the Court had the support of most American Jewish organizations.

Judaism, because it is an all-embracing way of life — intended to govern or at least influence one's thoughts and behavior from waking until sleep, and from birth until death — cannot be entirely private, in that it affects one's behavior in society. Nor is it entirely voluntary, for the Jew is born into a covenantal community with obligations to God.

But the view of the Jewish agencies — and to some extent of the Court majority, which decided against the Hasidim — is very distant from this understanding: It is that religion is not a way of life, but rather a private opinion. As Nathan Lewin, an Orthodox Jew who was the attorney for the Kiryas Joel Hasidim, noted, the Justices "do not see religion as an individual lifelong condition, like poverty or disability. They view it as a temporary personal preference — a possession that one may choose to keep or discard." Far from being a network of obligatory actions that must be taken to follow God's commandments, religion becomes just another "lifestyle choice." Any adjustment to that personal preference, then, is an unconstitutional favoring of religion, and Justice David Souter called the Kiryas Joel law unconstitutional "religious favoritism."

Far from demanding that the government grant some leeway to facilitate the practice of a demanding faith, in this case their own, the Jewish groups insisted that such an accommodation is not only unwise but unlawful. The elements of the Jewish community having the greatest difficulty keeping their children Jewish used the courts to attack the practice by which the elements having the greatest success keeping their children Jewish were doing so.

In 1995, the Supreme Court stepped back from the ever more absolute separationist position it seemed to be embracing in *Kiryas Joel*. In two cases, *Capitol Square Review and Advisory Board v. Pinette* and *Rosenberger v. Rector and Visitors of the University of Virginia*, the Court refused to read an endorsement of religion into official actions treating religious activity no better and no worse than other forms of private conduct.

In these cases the Court took a clear step back from the extremes of separationism, provided a bit more space for religious views in the public square, and clarified a point it had previously made — that the Establishment Clause does not require barring religious viewpoints from expression in neutral government programs. But the major Jewish organizations refused to take that step back. They fought the Court's conclusions, once again joining with the absolute separatist groups submitting briefs.

To this day, the major non-Orthodox Jewish organizations reject any deviation from absolute separationism. They still see the expression of religious convictions as a danger to Jews. Whatever may be the nature of their commitment to Judaism, their faith in separationism is absolutely intact.

Thus the official views of the Jewish community in the 1992 Rhode Island benediction case, *Lee v. Weisman,* where the Supreme Court found that it was unconstitutional for a rabbi to read a prayer at a high school commencement. The case was brought by a nonreligious Jewish family, the Weismans, whose daughter Deborah was a graduating senior. A majority of five justices found that her objections to the prayer were enough to make it impermissible as a matter of government coercion. She might be made to feel uncomfortable by this prayer reading, and might feel peer pressure to stand during the prayer or in some other way show a belief in God that she did not have. This was the "coercion" that rendered the prayer unconstitutional. Justice Anthony Kennedy wrote, in the opinion of the Court, that "the undeniable fact is that the school district's supervision and control of a high school graduation ceremony places public pressure, as well as peer pressure, on attending students to stand as a group or, at least, maintain respectful silence during the Invocation and Benediction." This could not be allowed because "research in psychology supports the common assumption that adolescents are often susceptible to pressure from their peers towards conformity."

So the benediction was barred, because it was too much to ask Ms. Deborah Weisman to stand quietly or sit silently when others prayed. The support of Jewish organizations for her cause, and their jubilation at her victory, were the product of their assessment of American society and the Jewish place in it. The tradition of benedictions at great public events, from a presidential inauguration to a high school commencement, goes back to the founding of the Republic, but they found it an offensive and unconstitutional practice. In their arguments to the Supreme Court, they once again remained true to the strategy that has motivated them for decades. In other words, they continue to believe that a secular America is the only safe America for Jews and to oppose any practice that may force American Jews to acknowledge their religion in public, or permit Christians to do so. They continue to believe that these results are compelled by sacred Law, in this case the Constitution.

The foregoing cases provide striking evidence of what is actually a shift in the thinking of America's Jewish leaders. They see religion not as the guarantor of civic virtue, but as the source of civic strife — and of danger for Jews. From the original Jewish insistence that Judaism be treated with the respect accorded to other religions, and even beyond the subsequent belief that any form of government support for religion was barred by the Constitution and potentially harmful to American Jews, their position presently stands revealed not merely as fear of government support for religion but *fear of religion itself.*

How this came to be is a long and complicated story. One key element is the history of Christian anti-Semitism, which made Jews fearful of any display of Christian religiosity. A second element is the sense among Jews that Jewish religiosity and ritual observance would prove to be an insuperable barrier to assimilation and success in America. And a third is the sad fact that most of the American Jewish community has abandoned *Judaism the religion.* The old Judaic commandments to keep the Sabbath day, to observe the dietary laws, even to worship God regularly and to keep Him at the center of one's life, have given way.

It is not that American Jews or their leaders wished to abandon being Jewish. Rather, they adopted an elaborate system of substitute faiths that were supposed to keep people Jewish — from commitment to "prophetic Judaism" (read, left-wing politics), to Israel, to the memory of the Holocaust, to a generalized ethnic "Jewishness." But the newest demographic data show that these substitute faiths are all failing. It is not possible to transmit this irreligious "Jewishness" successfully, as the Hebrew prayers have it, *l'dor vador* — from one generation to the next. Such "Jewishness" is a counterfeit faith, a passing phenomenon that will outlast the immigrants by only a few generations. There is within the American Jewish community an increasingly widespread conclusion that it is so, and with it a growing sense of crisis. The critical question facing the community today is whether it will acknowledge and act upon the disturbing truths that, as always in Jewish history, substitutes for Judaism are idols; that following them is a path to ruin; and that Judaism — centered on the worship of God and fulfillment of His commandments — must be returned to the center of Jewish life.

A Jew in Anti-Christian America

MIDGE DECTER

To speak of something called "Christian America," as both the advocates and the opponents of this idea are nowadays at high levels of passion wont to do, is by itself evidence of how un-Christian the country has become. Many Christian activists, especially the most innocent and high-minded among them, seem not to understand the true nature of their underlying predicament. We are, for instance, constantly being reminded by those who have an interest in declaring the robustness of Christianity in America today that such-and-such a high percentage of Americans are to be found in church each Sunday and that an even higher percentage profess to believe in God; and while such numbers surely do not mean nothing, the very fact that the Christian party so often needs to invoke them is evidence that the religious enterprise, for all its vaunted majority status, is in a deeply defensive mode.

When I was young — which, at least as history reckons these things, is after all not all that long a time ago — everyone, Jew and Christian alike, would in fact have been puzzled by the term "Christian America," puzzled in much the same sense as a fish might be puzzled by the idea of "ocean." What other America was there? Christians did not think about it, and Jews imagined no alternative. (Islam, of course, and Buddhism were in those years strictly the Arabian Nights to most Americans: for one thing, oil was cheaper than water, so who really cared about Islam? and the fascination of the young of the 1960s with exotic spirituality was still quite beyond imagining.) There were only two religious possibilities, Christianity and Judaism, and no honest person on either side of this divide was in any doubt about the status of the latter as a minority on sufferance. On the whole benignly treated, to be sure, but in need of tolerance nonetheless.

Back in the period I am talking about, the 1930s and 1940s, Jews living in the major population centers of American Jewish life — New York, Philadelphia, Chicago, and so on — might at least in some part of their daily lives have experienced a sense of cultural dominance: in their neighborhoods, on their blocks, most people lived as they did, and spoke as they did, and viewed the world as they did. Thus the shock of recognizing their status as a drop in a bucket might have come to them a bit later than to others of their fellow Jews living more scattered throughout the country. In any case, for the timid and the wounded of the ghettoized big-city Jewish community, the home enclave could always be a safe haven to remain in; and indeed many then did (and to this day some still do) remain there.

But for many other Jews, who, like me, grew up in what has come to be called the American heartland — namely, small to medium cities in the Middle West — there was never a safe haven; as children we pretty much sank or swam, socially speaking, among the majority. At least, that is, until some point in middle-to-late adolescence, when thoughts of marriage began to intrude — in those days most people married at a sensible early age before too much consciousness set in — and one way and another Jewish boys and girls, whether by instinct or external pressure, joined together in a kind of separate social entity. (I do not speak here about Jews in the South, who lived perpetually between the hammer and the anvil and who must have been so constricted by the experience that to this day not a single serious Jewish novelist has risen from that literature-soaked land to tell us about it.) For us as children, Christmas and Easter, to take only the gaudiest and most public examples, were not only major events in school, undertaken with full and unselfconscious panoply — and, be it noted, without even a hint of a glance at Hanukkah and Passover — but even more important, they were events in the households of all those among whom we lived day to day, our neighbors and our neighbors' neighbors, as well. Christian observances were part of our street life and part of the civic life of our communities.

My own home town, St. Paul, was a predominantly Catholic city, with a sizable minority of Scandinavian Lutherans. Just across the river was our "twin" city, Minneapolis, which back then touted itself among other things as the capital of the Bible Belt and whose radio stations, in earnest of this claim, carried a more than modest number of fundamentalist preachers. (You might have thought that the Bible Belt was actually somewhat to the south of Minnesota, but that didn't bother the Minneapolitans, who staked their claim all the same, just as travelers to my own city across the river were greeted by a sign that read "Welcome to St. Paul, Gateway to the Great Northwest.") I offer these data about the respective religious compositions of the two cities with the consciousness of now; back then distinctions of this kind would have largely escaped me and, I think, most of my fellow twin cities Jews as well. In other words, they, the others, Catholics, Protestants, were truly one big "they" — some more agreeable than others; some truly one's friends, some not — and it was unmistakably their terrain on which we were living.

If all this added up to certain kinds of discomfort that would have seemed somewhat peculiar to our Eastern big-city cousins — childhood friendships, for example, that unspokenly and mysteriously evaporated in adolescence — in some respects we were also far more at ease than they. A few years ago someone published a book about Brooklyn in the early years of the century, and in this book is to be found a positively gripping photograph: a group of Jewish boys and girls, say about eight or nine years old, from their dress clearly the children of immigrants, standing in a line that stretches down what looks to be a whole city block. They are waiting, the photo caption tells us, to get into . . . the neighborhood public library. How much venturing away from the warm comforts of home and into the far-off precincts of American, and beyond American, Western, civilization that photograph speaks of — how much fearful striving, how much passion, how much longing to get out and get away, are these children to be letting themselves in for! (For some, of course, there would be reward beyond measure; and for others, there would be only a lifetime of a kind of chronic, low-grade disaffection.)

But we out there in our heartland cities, we did not have to venture to find America — we were living totally, if not without a certain self-consciousness, in it. And because we were not driven, so to speak, to find our way to the library, like most of the middle Americans among whom we lived we tended to be a little smug and more than a little provincial. The boosterism once so grossly though alas not altogether unrecognizably caricatured by Sinclair Lewis was no less a besetting sin of St. Paul's Jewish than of its Christian inhabitants. And as for provinciality, that is a quality of being best illustrated for me by the story of my introduction to Mr. Roy Wilkins (for many long years, before its descent into shame, the wise and sturdy leader of the NAACP). We met at a dinner party, and as we sat sipping martinis and seeking, as people do, some way into conversation, we discovered that we had grown up in the same city. He was quite a bit older than I, and when I sought to discover if we nevertheless had any acquaintances in common, I asked him what street he had lived on. He told me the name of the street and of the school he had gone to, and when he did so, I realized that I had never once in all my life set foot on that street or laid eyes on that school — this in a city whose population when I lived there was not much more than 200,000!

Meanwhile, as the old song has it, back in the jungle — which was in this case a land called Germany — there were Hitler and his minions, revving up among other things to alter the course of Jewish history forever. In the comfort of our American existence we were aware that Hitler was doing evil things to Jews, first in Germany and next in Central and Eastern Europe; we would not for a few years — in some cases not till the end of the war in Europe — know just exactly how evil, but what we already knew by the late 1930s was bad enough.

Now, though our lives were pleasant, we were not, of course, growing up entirely ignorant of the experience of anti-Semitism. The preachments wafted through the airwaves from Minneapolis, for instance, were more than liberally salted with reminders of Jewish malfeasance, some of which I found rather difficult to grasp (and do to this day, I might add). There was Father Coughlin of Detroit, to whom we sometimes listened and whose accusations against us were considerably less arcane than those of our fundamentalist radio interlocutors. And then, of course, there were the boys from Nativity School, just a block from our own, who would now and then spice up their boyish tauntings on our common way home with the charge that I had murdered their Lord and other such pleasantries. But public humiliations, beatings and dispossessions, and unspeakable concentration camps — all this certainly had nothing to do with us and seemed more akin to those old stories of Eastern Europe offered in explanation of why our forebears came here to this promising land in the first place.

21

There was, however, one difference between the fate of our parents and grandparents and that of those 1930s and 1940s Jews of Europe: and that is, that the doors of the United States were no longer wide open. Some of the Jews of Germany and Austria got out while the getting was good and one way and another were taken in here. But when the Blitz-krieg moved East, engulfing in its murderous maw not only millions of innocents but a whole rich, thick, various, and teeming Jewish culture — "hurling into silence," as Harold Rosenberg once put it in an essay on Adolf Eichmann, "so many of the subtlest and most humane minds of Europe" — there would be no escape. (But what would we do with a million Jews? was the response of the British foreign office when an in-termediary brought an offer from Eichmann to exchange the lives of a million Jews for some trucks and materiel.) So though the war would be over before we knew, or admitted to ourselves, just how bad things had been with our European cousins, we were not for a moment permitted to be unmindful that the world had become a murderous place for a large proportion of its Jews.

I realize that I am here touching upon what has become to our friends the most nagging and tiresome of all Jewish points of reference, namely, the Holocaust. But it is impossible to understand what has be-come of America's Jews, culturally as well as politically, without under-standing our experience of those immediately prewar and wartime years — without, to put the case in far too crude but convenient short-hand, understanding the role played by Franklin D. Roosevelt in our communal fantasy life.

Though the New Deal was itself certainly of major importance to the political formation of what has come to be known as the organized Jewish community, for many if not most Jews Roosevelt's greatness lay not so much in the fact that he was a liberal in opposition to conserva-tives as it did in the fact that in the face of Nazi Germany he was an in-terventionist in firm and successful opposition to the isolationists. The isolationist party, best known by the name of America First, was in fact a jumble of people with a whole variety of agendas: there were those who believed that the United States should have no truck with Europe and its wars, there were socialists who found nothing to choose among the imperialists on both sides, and there were those who believed that Germany's was not necessarily the wrong side to be on, this latter group itself being a kind of odd amalgam of Anglophobes, anti-Semites who said that the war against Hitler was merely a Jewish war, and immigrant German patriots. Except for a tiny handful of, to put it mildly, deracinated radicals, American Jews knew World War II to be overridingly a moral war and they were entirely certain that Roosevelt knew it too.

There were of course other sources of the Jews' loyalty to Roosevelt: primarily, I think, that Jews, even those originally from the remotest villages in Eastern Europe, were in their inmost cultural being an urban people, and Roosevelt was the President of the cities: patrician and alien of background though he might be, he somehow managed to create the illusion for the teeming city folk that he spoke their language. But most of all, Roosevelt was to the Jews one of the major heroes of that great and good war. And when the war was over, not only was their fealty to the Democratic party now graven in stone, anything that smacked of the old order or of the forces of America First was simply unthinkable — out of the question — anathema — to them.

At war's end, something would begin to happen to the rest of America, too: something that would take more than a decade to manifest itself but that had probably been brewing — as Norman Mailer might say, in the American psychic underground — since the first heady days of victory. And that was the acquisition of a newfound sense of vast power and unending possibility. To be sure, the war against the Axis, followed almost immediately by the Cold War, had introduced a new recognition of evil, with its concomitant sense of human limitedness and imperfectibility, into American political-philosophical discourse. This new understanding was, of course, an inherently religious one, and was most prominently associated with the influence of Reinhold Niebuhr. (It ought to be remembered, however, that Sigmund Freud, too, had a hand in it, through the offices of some of the influential intellectuals who had subjected themselves to his much misunderstood and much distorted discipline.) But in the culture at large, such a view of the human condition could not stand for long against the almost overwhelming tide of wealth and innovation and freedom of movement and the sensation of moving toward . . . sheer limitlessness.

In my own life, this new sense of possibility was given its first expression by my leaving home and moving to New York City. I would not have thought of it — and would not to this day quite think of it — as leaving Christian America, but I was certainly getting away from what felt to me to be the prospect of a restricted and over-prescribed life. (In any case, as it would turn out, Christian America was itself coming to manifest signs of leaving home: Minneapolis, for example, quondam self-styled capital of the Bible Belt, was growing far more dedicated to art and theater than to preachments and country music, both of which had just about disappeared from local radio. Indeed, Minneapolis was plighting its troth to metropolitanism, with all the high pretension and low adventure that implied. And the same process would, though some-what later and with considerably less success, also overtake my own home town, as it would, at least superficially, just about every American city of more than minimal size.)

As a Jew in the newly post-Holocaust period, and as someone who had come with adulthood to loathe the Soviet government and its apologists, I too for a time, that much-libeled time known as the fifties, professed to derive my ideas of the world from a deep commitment to the doctrine of human imperfectibility. But though I would never cease to harbor the altogether illiberal belief in the existence of unmitigated evil, something else, which continued as always to lie in wait for American intellectuals, was also lying in wait for me.

Before I begin to describe what this something else was, it is important to understand that the postwar transition years — the years, say, from 1945 to 1965 — were very good years for American Jews. For after the shock of discovering just how completely the entire civilized world had averted its gaze from what was happening to their fellow Jews in Europe, they would find not only that they were now being welcomed to hitherto restricted precincts but that all the traditional expressions of hostility to Jews had been banished from polite, and even largely from impolite, society. Beyond this, in some considerable degree as a result of the primary system, Jews began to exercise a new degree and new kind of political influence. And above all, Jews were now at ease culturally: not only were they being let in, but what they were being let into was more and more losing any definable character as Christian.

Now, what I have referred to before as the something, the force, just waiting to spring on the American Zeitgeist would in the early sixties be given throaty articulation by the courtiers surrounding John F. Kennedy, who, while clearly doing little more than making rhetorical gestures, nevertheless managed to hit the cultural nail squarely on the head.

What I am talking about is summed up in the famous question of Robert Kennedy: "Why not?"

The question "Why not?" requires as its first premise great wealth and even greater expectations — conditions that for the American educated middle class came to be ever more taken for granted as the postwar years wore on. Beyond that, as we know, this question is and has ever been the introduction to sweet and irresistible seduction. "Why not?" turns out to be the means by which virtuous societies no less than virtuous ladies are led in pleasure down the path of self-destruction.

To be sure, many influences beyond sheer wealth led to the sense of being unshackled, prominent among them a number of literary and intellectual ideas and attitudes whose power over the country's culture was being vastly increased by the massive spread of higher education. In addition the country was beginning to experience a burst of just plain old political restlessness, the outgrowth of boredom — ever a possibility in the life of any democracy. Be these influences as they may, the sense of open-endedness came upon me and, I would say, a decisive number of my contemporaries with the force of a new revelation: life need no longer be constrained.

It was not so much that we actually lived our day-to-day lives according to this revelation; our households and our work proceeded pretty much as they would have had we still been living in the old society in which we had been brought up. We worked hard, for instance, and were for the most part and perforce reasonably prudent. We led fairly steady lives, and if there were certainly much more libertinism and many more divorces among us than there had been, say, in our parents' generation, they tended still to be very costly and painful and for the most part not light-mindedly undertaken.

When it came to politics, asking "Why not?" led us to disdain the old-style liberals, who for all their declared intention to make the country a more expansive place were in our view too smug of spirit and too banal of mind to be truly open to the new. Thus many of us declared ourselves to be radicals; but despite a few feeble efforts in the direction of play-acting at social transformation, our radicalism was to be found not in our lives, not even our political lives, but in our heads.

And in our heads was precisely the place where the radicalism of "Why not?" could, and did, do the maximum amount of damage, primarily to our own children. For if our 1930s nervous systems did not

25

permit us, as they say, to "act out" the liberation of our minds, our children were to become its perfect foils. One of the things that to this day few people understand about the famous young of the 1960s is that far from rebelling, most of them were in fact being deeply obedient to the demands and expectations of their elders. That these demands and expectations were largely unspoken is little to the point. The sixties generation's inordinate self-regard; their demand to be given, without striving for it, all the goodies their society had to offer, including, of course, easy sex; their recourse to the instant and unearned sense of power and comfort supplied by drugs; their refusal to serve their country; their general ingratitude, expressed most of all in their declared intention to lead lives in no respect like those of their forebears — all these were translations of the hubris that, partly unconsciously but entirely influentially, constituted the basic underpinning of their upbringing.

And if "Why not?" proved in the end to be an invitation to sin against one's children — not to speak of an invitation to one's children to do some further considerable sinning against themselves — this question carried in its wake a second, even more lethal, one. That second question was, "So what?" — two words that in combination have the power to wither growing things on the vine. In our own time, for instance, this question is the intellectual shrug that lies behind the institution of multicultural education, the social shrug that lies behind a race-based double standard of conduct, and the moral shrug that lies behind the permission to teach techniques of anal and oral sex to schoolchildren.

In any case, these two questions — "Why not?" and "So what?" — would in the end prove to be among the most lasting legacies of our escape from the bounded, and limiting, view of life that had been our natural birthright, Jews and Christians, separately and together. Obviously, neither serious Judaism nor real Christianity can cohere with a sense of life that has banished all need for prayer, humility, and submission — three things that depend precisely on the recognition of human frailty and finitude. "Why not?" in its arrogance and "So what?" in its nihilism were thus to set the stage for a kind of nationwide drama of moral paralysis.

Many people who are shocked and repelled by the decadence that has so widely overtaken Western societies are now prepared to join the theorists who have traced our troubles all the way back to the Enlightenment. Theirs is a view of things that can be, and indeed has been, most persuasively argued, but it seems to me at once too convenient and too iniquitously ungrateful for either a Jew or a Christian to entertain. For Jews, certainly, the Enlightenment was the beginning of the hope, if not at all times and all places the reality, of liberty — a hope that it would be criminal for people like me to dare to make light of. And I would presume to say that the same is true for Christians: freedom of choice has after all been given to us by God, as have the mighty and humane benefits of science and technology. This is, let us remember, His universe, constituted as He has seen fit to constitute it and offering itself up to our scrutiny and management as He has chosen to offer it.

The same goes for the currently far too careless animadversions against humanism on the part of many conservatives. We are after all the heirs of giants who have lived on earth through the ages, many of whose ideas we may reject but whose genius and whose arts, be they of thought and language or of color and representation, both inspire and civilize us. Surely it was not meant for us to cut ourselves off from such an inheritance. So rather than calling on ancient and modern history — illuminating as they may be — to provide us with the source of our present threatening condition, let us just in all simplemindedness agree to recognize that our deepest troubles are of our very own making. They do not stem from enlightenment or from humanism; they are the troubles of our very own, very contemporary, self-generated atheism, the atheism, precisely, of "Why not?" and "So what?"

But to return to my story: there is no more efficient way to recover from the ungodly temptations of radicalism than to become conscious of the traps it has set for one's children. For if we, as I indicated before, still had moral and emotional capital to draw on from that other, that earlier, call it Judeo-Christian (a usage I am not crazy about) world, our children had only our reserves of "Why not?" and "So what?" to depend upon. I don't have to go into all the characteristics of the failure of that particular account; it can most aptly be summed up by the fact that in the late sixties and especially the early seventies there was a marked and sudden increase in the adolescent suicide rate. (That rate, by the way, persists, and may if anything have increased in recent years.)

In any case, there were basically two ways to respond to the admission, which became harder with each year to evade, that the young were in deep trouble. The first of these, the liberal way, was to assert that the sorrows of the young arose from the fact that the revolution had not yet been completed. Their demands for freedom and justice were still a long way from being met: there was as yet, for example, no justice for blacks or women or homosexuals; and as for freedom, regardless of how much of it was being wrested from courts and legislatures, no one had yet succeeded in putting an end to the continuing pressure from a group of the so-called "troglodytes," mainly small-town Christians, who, it was said, wished to return the country to the dark ages of censorship and intolerance. Not to mention the persistence of yet a different group of "troglodytes," in this case more sophisticated ones, who with their invention of the Cold War were constantly endangering the country and its young citizens with their longing to engage in jingoistic military exercises. No wonder, said the liberals, "the kids" were restless and unhappy. (I have referred to this reading of the young as liberal rather than radical because by the mid-seventies the former had in fact become entirely interchangeable with the latter.)

The second way was the way that came, not without considerable resistance, to surrender to the sobriquet neoconservative. Neoconservatives came with varying degrees of alacrity to see that it was the revolution itself and not the basically just and free country against which this putative revolution was being made that was responsible for the social ill-health of the young — responsible in one sense for the indisposition of the privileged among them and in another, far more permanently damaging, way for the ever more inescapable pathology of young blacks in the inner cities.

What we had here, then, was no mere difference of opinion, but rather a deep, and to this day ever deepening, schism. What had once been the liberal community was now split asunder; the metaphor of civil war would not be an entirely exaggerated one. In any case, the neoconservatives believed that justice and freedom as defined by the young and their middle-aged camp followers were at best caricatures and at worst outright perversions of those terms, properly understood.

Properly understood: there's the rub. From whence such proper understanding? Lenin once declared that he who says a must say b. Despite what happened to be the murderous nature of his own particular a, Lenin was of course right. The neoconservatives came to a new recognition of freedom (I do not, of course, mean to suggest that this recognition was in any sense theirs alone — God forbid — it's just that it happens to be their story I am telling here), and this view of the nature of freedom had, for the reasons I have cited and others, ceased to be the ersatz liberation of "Why not?" It had become rather the freedom meant by the term "free will" — which is to say, the taking of responsibility for what one does and what one is.

There you have the essential neoconservative a. And the b? The b — what else can it be? — is God. Beyond that, as the old Jewish saying has it, the rest is commentary. Rationalists find it interesting to debate whether or not God exists. Theologians seek to understand His attributes. But for Jews the real questions are not, or rather ought not to be, does He exist, and if so, who is He, but rather only, what is it that He wants of us? He has, to be sure, answered this question, not only in His Scripture but in the very constitution of our natures: to choose life, to be fruitful and multiply, and to walk in His ways, which means among other things to understand that life makes sense and that human fulfillment resides in resisting the ever-present temptation to return to *tohu wavohu* — the primordial chaos and void.

Such an understanding, of course, goes beyond politics and can never be satisfied by politics, but it does inevitably have a political dimension. It requires one to renounce the arrogant rejection of God's world that many liberals, particularly young ones, call by the name of idealism. What follows from this is one's commitment to a whole host of ideas and proposals which, despite the fact that they represent a major departure from what has been the dominant American ethos for more than half a century, are called conservative. (Alas, so far have things gone that many of the things that conservatives say they are out to conserve will in fact have to be rebuilt from scratch.)

The slowly dawning process of realization that brought the neoconservatives from a to b — the discovery or in some cases perhaps rediscovery of God — was for most of us more like a long climb up a steep hill than like a flash of lightning. And among other things it was to bring us into a new and largely unfamiliar community of conservative fellows. It would be hard to say who was more surprised, nonplussed, and possibly to some extent also amused by this new association, the old conservatives or their new neoconservative allies.

Now, most of the journalists who have assigned themselves the task of trying to describe or explain — or simply give vent to their hostility toward — this new development called neoconservatism have identified it as being primarily a Jewish phenomenon. This is most certainly not the case; many neoconservatives are Christian. Nevertheless, this misapprehension does make a certain perverse sense. For Christians in America, however far and for however long they may have strayed, the journey from liberal culture to conservatism is essentially a journey back home, where, so to speak, there are a multitude of loving arms to enfold them. For the Jews involved in this phenomenon, the case is rather different: conservatism for them represents an estrangement from not one but from two of their former communities, from the Jewish community as well as from that of the liberal intellectuals.

Thus they have found themselves in a kind of no-man's-land where they have been engaged in constructing for themselves a cultural home for which there has been neither precedent nor blueprint. In an alliance with Christian conservatives against the atheism that has made a sick and paltry joke of each of their respective and joint traditions and that has begun like a swarm of termites to eat away the underpinnings of this democratic republic, the new Jewish conservatives have come to understand that any alienation they felt as children in Christian America is as nothing compared with the danger they sense to themselves and their progeny, along with their uncomprehending coreligionists, in atheist America. Even less than others, they know, can America's Jews afford to indulge themselves and others in the reckless endangerment represented by the various movements that have swept unresisted through liberal society: prominent among them, the movement for a woman's right not to be a woman; the movement for homosexuals to be considered merely heterosexuals with a somewhat different erotic taste; the movement to dehumanize blacks by exempting them from ordinary moral demands.

School prayer? This is what organized Jewry finds threatening? As it happens, I am no devotee of school prayer, on the ground that it is a distraction, a kind of trivializing surrogacy for truly weighty issues this society must find the courage to face and deal with. Nevertheless, there is something unholy in the Jewish argument that the reintroduction of the acknowledgment of God into the schools will in some way be discriminatory of and psychologically harmful to their children when these schools as they are represent so many real dangers to them: the danger of the coarsening of their sensibilities, for one, and of the snuffing out of their normal youthful longing to grow up, as well as the danger of leaving them utterly cynical about their society and their country and the rightful demands on them of both. Prayer, indeed; it is Jewish liberals, more than children, who should be doing the praying.

There are other unholinesses as well. One need not spell out each and every aspect of the participation of the organized Jewish community in the liberal culture. It is enough to say that that participation involves a kind of heedless assurance of being in the right that sits particularly ill on people whose very existence depends on a mere stroke of luck — the luck of someone's having immigrated to the United States. Such people ought to be the first rather than the last to be found each day on their knees in gratitude to God. And such people ought to be the first rather than the last to understand the anxieties of the devout Christians — evangelicals, fundamentalists, orthodox Catholics and Protestants — about, precisely, the growing chaos in a country from whose public life religion has not so much disappeared but been banished. Thus have the neoconservative Jews sought — so far, to put it mildly, with mixed success — to convince their mainstream fellow Jews that the growing political strength of Christian believers is not a danger to them, that, on the contrary, in the long run it will conduce far more to the security and well-being of their children and grandchildren.

And yet, and yet . . . While the new Jewish conservatives may quarrel with their fellow Jews about conservatism and Christianity, there are occasions, too, when they wish they could make their Christian fellow-conservatives a little slower to temper against Jewish liberal stiffneckedness. It is true that the mainstream American Jewish community has egregiously, and I believe suicidally, conflated liberal atheism — radical feminism, gay rights, promiscuous abortion — with the Jewish interest. And it is true that the mainstream Jewish community, priding itself on its concern for social justice, has on the whole been almost professionally insensitive to the many valid complaints of social injustice on the part of believing Christians, particularly the evangelical fundamentalists. But now and then those of us who wish to turn our fellow Jews from the path of liberal suicide come up against a certain crackpottedness — and sometimes worse — from the right that appears to be reminiscent of that old 1930s Bible Belt, Coughlinite, America First damnation of the Jews. And when that happens, it is not ideas we are left to deal with but nervous systems.

The late Lucy Dawidowicz, distinguished historian of the Holocaust, declared that there should be a moratorium on the very use of the word "Holocaust" — that it has become a crutch and an excuse and a cheapener of memory — and what she said is undeniably right and healthy. Moreover, if the twentieth century witnessed a horror beyond all the horrors of Jewish history, it also witnessed a new redemption, the return to our ancient land. Still, we remain testy about our security, in the United States as well as in the ever-threatened Israel — testy in a way that others perhaps do not understand.

The "Why not?" and "So what?" of present-day liberalism are thus a special temptation to Jews, who entertain themselves with the idea that they can escape what has for so long been God's seemingly difficult, and for them often particularly cruel, decree. And if anything, these questions are proving more dangerous to Jews than to anyone else, undermining as they do the foundations of the kind of free society on which the twentieth century has taught them that they must depend for their very continuation. As between the old Christian America, which did, it cannot be denied, visit the Jews with certain discomforts, and the new atheist America, which goes straight for the jugular of their children and their children's children, how can America's Jews feel there is even any choice? And yet, of course, they do most unsentiently continue to feel exactly that.

Still, there are many Christians, too, who suffer from that age-old Hebraic malady that the Lord once diagnosed as stiffness of the neck and who, I like to think, cause Him a certain worry, as they do me.

Let me explain. Last year I sat one evening in late spring on a veranda in Jerusalem, looking across at Mount Zion, from whose wonderfully lighted nightscape loomed the dome of the Dormition church. It was a beautiful evening, balmy, heavy with the scent of jasmine. And as I sat there I thought: Why do not the world's Christians celebrate the return of the Jews to this city? They have tended it so lovingly, burnished its ancient beauty, planted it with flowers and trees, made it so pleasant and been so tender and so mindful of its holiness. For nineteen years the eastern half of Jerusalem, including the much hallowed Old City, languished under the Jordanians, who not only desecrated Jewish holy places and graveyards but left the whole area in a dirty and threadbare condition. Why, then, do the Christians not celebrate the salvation of Jerusalem made possible by the Israeli military victory in 1967? Why do Christian institutions take part in pressuring the Israelis to place themselves once again in mortal danger and throw the history- and faith-laden parts of the city back into wretchedness? The answer is that the evangelicals do indeed celebrate, both the return of the Jews to the holy land and their rescue of old Jerusalem. But others, many, many others, do not — for reasons that, no matter how often they are articulated, simply make no sense to me.

In any case, as I sat there that evening, I understood with my senses instead of merely with my head how truly dependent on one another Jews and Christians nowadays really are — in a world in which they are both so dangerously surrounded by barbarians, Christian and Jewish barbarians among them. The little girl from St. Paul has come a long way and so, I keep hoping and believing, have at least some of the boys from Nativity.

The Modern Jewish Condition

ALAN L. MITTLEMAN

Autonomy means to live under one's own law: to discover the norms of a lawful life, a nomos, by or within oneself. Thus it is not, in principle, anarchic or anomic. Autonomy and authority are, as etymology suggests, paired concepts. Autonomy means that the self becomes its own authority, that authority per se is conditional upon the consent of the self. Autonomy takes self-directedness as its governing principle.

How does self-directedness come to have credibility as a moral concept? Its origins lie perhaps in the logic of responsibility; in the conditions under which we can attribute blame or praise to an agent. To be fully responsible, an agent must have freely chosen his course of action. The idea that we are responsible only if we can be said to have chosen or consented willingly to a course of action is certainly an old one. The great German Jewish philosopher, Hermann Cohen, attributes its discovery to the prophet Ezekiel, who, in contradiction to the exiles' belief that "the fathers have eaten sour grapes and the children's teeth are set on edge," asserted that every man suffers for his own sin. Ezekiel appears to have displaced the older biblical notion that God will punish the children for the sins of their fathers for several subsequent generations. Blame and punishment are neither collective nor hereditary. They are merited by individuals on a basis of personal desert. If Cohen is correct, the concept of autonomy in the sense of having to take responsibility for one's own destiny — of having, on one's own, to recognize what is right and to act accordingly — is not new.

What is new is the idea that the discovery of what is right is an idiosyncratic self-discovery. The self, as the field and the agent of moral discovery, acquires a whole new weight. The process of the self ratifying what it has discovered, that is, of consent, takes on a new prominence. Thus what is new is the construction of the self now held to be capable of aiming at an ideal of autonomy. Autonomy as an ideal renders the relation of the autonomous self to other selves, to community, to nature, and to divinity enormously problematic. The ethics and the anthropology of the autonomous self represent a departure from prior traditions of Western thought and religion.

The theme of autonomy has been of defining significance for modernity. Indeed, the major intellectual architects of the modern project have put the individual at the crux of their thought. Modern philosophy begins with the individual. For Descartes, often held to be the first modern philosopher, reality per se is discovered in self-reflection. Being depends upon the solitary, thinking ego for its self-disclosure. The little "I," which was at best a microcosm of a vast, created (or, for Aristotle, eternal) macrocosm, now becomes the only open window onto the world of being. We cannot know, hence we cannot trust in, anything that is beyond what we can think. The little "I" has now become the arbiter of all that is.

If premodern men and women feared such radical independence, such excision from the context of an environing universe, moderns exult in it. Despite all of the modern talk of loneliness and alienation, the modern soul shrinks from attachments that are not of its own choosing. The modern soul, as Edward Shils put it, has a dread of metaphysical encumbrances. This dread is systematically expressed in the modern traditions of ethical and social thought. The newly definitive individual, stripped of constitutive attachments to primal groups and faiths, is an arbiter not only of what is but of what ought to be.

Although autonomy is not antithetical to authority per se, it is antithetical to traditional, heteronomous authority. Autonomy regards claims to authority that cannot be validated by, or in principle discovered within, the self as suspect. Traditional authority is based on claims to a superior wisdom, to divine revelation or to the accumulated and refined legacy of the ancestors. The modern ideal rejects this as so much paternalism. No prophet, philosopher-king, or historical collectivity knows better than the individual what the individual's good is. No human arrangement affecting our lives and destinies that does not rise from, or merit the consent of, the individual so affected ought to exist. Furthermore, this consent is a private matter. No one can tell us what we ought to consent to. Society should not prescribe our good for us. Only we who know ourselves best, as John Stuart Mill argued, can decide what is our special good. There are as many goods as there are persons. Autonomy implies that we are epistemic and ethical worlds unto ourselves.

Traditional authority is enfeebled by modernity because it has become increasingly difficult to speak persuasively about the good as such: the human good, the good of man qua man, the common good in which all humans share. Tradition speaks about human beings in broad, species-wide categories: for example, "It is not good for man to be alone." But what if some humans prefer solitude to sociality? Who is to say? As the postulate of a higher human nature lost ground, the good has been atomized into a near infinity of particularities. The old version of a common human nature which both Jews and Christians developed from Greek thought during the Middle Ages, namely, that man is a thinking being whose telos is found in the perfection of intellect which is also *communio* and *imitatio dei,* became incredible with the rise of modern science. The teleological universe of Aristotle was replaced by the mechanical universe of Newton. Nature was a gigantic machine, not a purposive process leading back and up into divinity. The heavens do not speak the glory of God, they speak the theorems of the calculus. Without a divinely directed, providentially purposive nature, human nature lost its human purpose. Man came to be defined increasingly by what had earlier been held to be his lower nature. As modernity progressed, it was the only nature that science could know.

The "scientization" of nature, that is, the triumph of the quantitative methods of the new physics and of the technological goal of mastery, as well as the loss of a Judeo-Christian anthropology of man as a being with a higher nature, not only atomized the concept of the good into an infinity of particularities, it also shifted the concept of the right, of *justice,* into a different framework. Formerly, justice was a matter of the conformity of human institutions and practices with an inherent natural standard: of *nomos* with *physis* where *physis* was understood to strive toward the divine. Nature, in the earlier thought, implied an immanent natural law, which linked the mundane, the transcendent, and the human. In a more theistic key, nature was the field in which divine providence engaged in shaping human destiny. While these concepts of nature are not equivalent, they share a common horizon vis-à-vis the modern one. In modernity, by contrast, talk about justice need not appeal to a transcendent norm. What is just is what the individual consents to.

Raising consent to the chief, or at least to a chief, criterion of justice shifts the framework within which we understand justice from ontology to history. Justice does not seek ontological legitimation. Appeals to the way of things or the will of God do not matter. Even worse, they signal antimodern reaction. What matters is the history of the society in which institutions of justice are found. Suttee would be intolerable for Jews and Christians, but it is more than just, one might argue, for Hindus.

Moderns (at least those quintessential moderns, the Enlightenment founders of the modern project) have tried to avoid such culture-dependent relativism by positing a universal and primitive attribute of man qua man that could replace the now enfeebled natural law: namely, rights. Human rights are held to be culturally invariant human possessions that guarantee basic claims to life, freedom, and dignity for all. Yet there is no doubt that the discourse of rights derives from the prior traditions of biblical anthropology. It is a secularized, sanitized version of *bĕtselem 'elohim bara' 'otam:* in the image of God He created them. Can one doubt that should this historical link between rights and biblical monotheism be lost, rights discourse will collapse as well? There is no reason to doubt this intuition: the process is already well advanced. In many quarters, foremost among them the old USSR, rights discourse was, or was thought to be, a parochial, Western, Judeo-Christian language game. One can well imagine that an Indian devoted to suttee would resent an argument opposed to the practice based on rights no less than an argument based on the Bible. Both, especially at this end of modernity, appear to be so much cultural imperialism.

It is as if there were a law of the conservation of skepticism: that which was designed to replace biblical faith becomes as vulnerable to rational assault as biblical faith. Human rights are no less jeopardized by the intellectual climate of the world that first gave them systematic articulation than they are by governments who abuse and destroy their citizens.

What we are exploring here is how weak claims of authority are in the modern context. As the case of rights shows, modern reason is not able to sustain itself. The modern project of securing a universal human dignity irrespective of tribe, clan, race, or religion founders on its own parochialism. Having abandoned a belief in significant natural right, modernity sought its own anthropology of rational, enlightened man. But such a man proved to be nothing but parochial. The enlightened, autonomous self was nothing more or less than a European, a Western, self. Even Germany, where the Enlightenment had originally found great advocates, by the early nineteenth century had rejected central tenets of Enlightenment as too French. Thus modern reason, having rejected the old religious absolutes, tried to innovate its own absolutes only to discover that relativity, that cultural particularity, continued to haunt them. Without belief in revelation or in natural right we seem necessarily to be thrown upon the shifting fashions of history. And history, Hegel notwithstanding, is not the history of reason. History is the struggle of wills.

The autonomous self of modernity has put will at the center. It is will, the idiosyncratic will of the autonomous self, that chooses a course of life, that decides what is good and right for itself. Yet what is it that illumines the will which chooses? The once unquestioned light of revelation grew dim. It became an *'or ganuz,* a hidden light. In principle, it is a light that cannot be lost in questions, only in too certain answers. Modernity was quick to foreclose the questions and to believe that its answers, tentative as they were, were the only answers. Thus revelation could illumine the self only if the self still sensed the openness of the questions: that is, if the will, in its sublime privacy, consented to such illumination. Of course, there are always such selves, but in modernity they sense, more than ever before, their aloneness. To read great works of mysticism such as the *Cloud of Unknowing* is to hear what the aloneness of the devout was like in a "religious age." Yet there is a difference. That age at least recognized the cultural salience of the contemplative. His virtuosity, while surely not for everyone, made sense to everyone. Radical religious seriousness, while always entailing aloneness, was a publicly intelligible and valued phenomenon.

Modernity, however, was born in the retreat of revelation from the light of day, from the public world. The men and women who lived revelation — and the religious authorities that spoke in its name — became culturally solitary voices competing for a hearing at the door of modern reason. Thus the religious communities are no longer thought to be primal. They are derivative, voluntary: they derive from volition. They are not called into being by God, but by consent. Their authority, to the extent that they have any authority, is a matter of voluntary obligation. One consents to it within the framework of autonomy.

How does this consent work? For thinkers in the social contract tradition such as John Locke, community, including the communities formed in the name of revelation, arise from the decision and choice of individual humans. We band together to secure advantages that we are unable to secure by living singly. Community is no longer an organic and a priori condition of our humanness, as it was for Aristotle. Man is no longer a *zoon politikon,* a being for whom sociality is a condition of soteriology, for whom community opens onto the horizons of both virtue and transcendence — rather, he is Homo sapiens, a thinking being who arranges his life in light of his calculations of gain and loss. Community is made, not found. It is not the condition of our being, but a consequence of it. Thus, the norms of community, including the communities of revelation, bind us only insofar as we consent to them, that is, only insofar as we continue to associate our lives with them through choice.

Why should we consent to the norms of the social order that we ourselves (or at least our social contracting ancestors) have allegedly made? It seems hopelessly crude to say that we should consent to them only if in the calculation of gains and losses we stand to gain more than we stand to lose by the association. A horde of self-interested, calculating, potential nomads could never amount to a society. How does one proceed from a radical doctrine of individual autonomy to sociality, to human solidarity? Those too, at least in sanitized, rationalized form, constitute a modern ideal. An early answer to the problem of consent and the origin of normative solidarity, i.e., political obligation — Locke's answer — continued to borrow from medieval tradition. Locke did not make consent dependent on strict and arbitrary autonomy. Rather, consent is consent to what is right. What is right is determined by natural law. We ought to give our consent to what is right. We ought not to consent to what is wrong. Suicide, which Locke, for example, believes contravenes natural law in a fundamental way, is never something one could rightfully choose. Nor is slavery. Such consent is no consent at all. Thus Locke, writing in a religious culture in early modern times, heavily qualifies autonomy. A transcendent order of norms limits the range of moral possibilities that the will to consent may select.

As modernity progresses, however, these limitations weaken. Consent is shorn of its normative horizon and simply becomes an act of will illumined, if at all, by tastes and preferences. This possibility was glimpsed, or perhaps preached, by David Hume, who offered a radical critique of the social contract tradition. He saw in consent not a rationally informed moral act of affirmation, but a passional surrender to inherited, irrational prescriptions. Consensual affirmation of the authoritative norms of social life was a myth, an old wives' tale for those who still thought that reason governs the life of man.

Kant sought to rescue autonomy and consent from Hume's bleak vision by tying them firmly to reason. Yet for Kant, too, the authority that still resided in Locke's natural law receded. Natural law as a source of authority is replaced by an ideal of a self-sufficient, solitary individual governing himself according to formulas of reason. The lawfulness that we discover in the logic of our own moral self-reflection is the only authority worthy of consent. Autonomous reason is the source of its own law. If one can will a course of action — a maxim — such that all other rational agents could also will it without self-contradiction, then that maxim passes muster. Formal criteria of universality, discoverable by practical reason reflecting on the experiences of moral life, set the parameters for what is right.

Such attempts to ground or justify autonomy all return to a calculation of gains and losses. For Locke, one has more to gain by living in society than in the state of nature. For Kant, one has more to gain by living under the universal moral law, discovered by individual reason, than by living under the partial and particularistic codes imposed by an external agency. One gains freedom, which, for Kant, appears as a kind of summum bonum.

Yet, there are other versions of individual gain and advantage. The most radical version, which modernity produced as a dialectical reaction to the stress on autonomous individuality, is the nullification of individuality altogether. Modernity offers the total absorption of the individual into a collectivity, usually a society or nation-state, as a putative version of a human good. Modernity has produced leviathans more terrible than Hobbes could have imagined or approved of.

The possibility of surmounting and transcending the autonomous individuality that modernity has itself unleashed in the form of absorption in a collectivity strengthens in proportion to the decline of biblical faith. The religious communities, Jews and Christians, continued to represent a social order that claimed ontological legitimation for itself: the Church as the body of Christ, the Jews as the chosen people. With the retreat of the public legitimating function of transcendence, society represented itself to itself as a more or less immanent affair: the product of decision, choice, consent. These, as we have seen, are relatively vulnerable grounds for social order. Given the modern idea that society is made, not found, that the human world is a product of volition, not nature, the way was cleared for radical experimentation, for inventing new, rational versions of social order. As biblical understandings of transcendence retreated, rival versions of transcendence filled the vacuum. The state could become an ersatz divinity offering salvation for those who sacrifice themselves to it. The strains and terrors of modern autonomy spawned a solution that both rejects modern autonomy and derives from it. This "solution" has not yet run its course.

Jews and Christians, as representatives of forms of community far older than modernity, have not a common, but a related, task: to model a way of life, both private and public, that is demonstrably superior to both the culture of radical autonomy and to its totalitarian antithesis. To do this, Christians and Jews need to recover the essential lineaments of their archetypal communities from the mass of adaptations they have made in the course of secularization. I am unable to say precisely what this might imply for Christians, but let me conclude with what it implies for Jews.

Modern Judaism has been pulled between two poles: the confessional and the national. Judaism has been constructed as nothing-but-religion and as nothing-but-ethnicity. The nineteenth century reinvented Judaism as the "Mosaic faith" of German or American or British Jews, and deemphasized the national and ethnic elements implicit in the tradition. Zionism and other secular movements, by contrast, rejected this confessionalization of Judaism, but substituted no less modern a construction of the ethnic and national elements. Secular peoplehood is no less a distortion of traditional sacral peoplehood than is sacred religion without peoplehood at all. With the success of Zionism, secular constructions of Judaism became dominant, either marginalizing the confessional model or creating a new form of confessionalization: Jewish religion as a civil religious appendage to Jewish national identity.

For Jews to reach a new/old self-representation of their communal reality entails the rediscovery of the Jewish *polity*. Community is rather too weak a term to describe the sociality of the Jews. Jewish historical being is *both* chosen, voluntary, consensual and primordial, natural, and transcendent. One is born a Jew and one chooses Judaism. Judaism is found in oneself, not made. Yet one must also make one's Judaism, that is, one must make oneself into a Jew. The law precedes one, yet one must make it one's own. The massive, public otherness of the law becomes personal, intimately one's own.

The resolution of this apparent paradox has been a major concern of modern Jewish theologians. Throughout modernity, Jewish thinkers have been simultaneously drawn to and deeply agitated by Kant. Kant's stress on ethics, inner purity, and on the dignity and ennoblement of man through righteous will and action seemed like a convincing and a compatible statement of Judaism's own ideal. Yet Kant's uncompromising rejection of heteronomy seemed fully incompatible with Judaism's revealed Law. Indeed, Kant called for a "euthanasia of Judaism" (Judaism represented pure heteronomy for him) as a condition of the moral development of mankind. Thus the Kantian version of autonomy became a persistent challenge to modern Jewish thought.

The time has long since arrived for modern Jews to free themselves from the Kantian dialectic of autonomy vs. heteronomy. It is a true dialectic only if we accept its metaphysical presupposition that human beings are or ought to be radically individuated beings; that community is derivative, not primal; that self and other are mutually exclusive. Judaism (and, it would seem, Kant himself — at least the Kant of the *Critique of Judgment*) rejects these premises.

The primary Jewish reality is not the individual agent but the historic polity in which the individual discovers his or her Jewishness. "Polity" is stronger than "community" because it resonates with the sense of obligation that characterizes the political. It entails as well a sense of continuity, primordiality, and objectivity that community has come to lack. On the other hand, polity must not be confused with "state" or any other political category where the emphasis is on sovereignty and the monopoly of legitimate violence. Polity refers to forms of social life more binding than community yet more decentralized than the modern state.

To belong to the Jewish polity means to live in a network of duties, obligations, rights, and privileges that has worldwide range and temporal depth. The ground of this order is the covenant: a binding intimacy of a human group with God that is characterized by both love and law. Two parties chose one another. The human party must still, in every generation, choose. This stress on consent as a condition of covenantal participation, that is, of life within the polity, satisfies the modern orientation toward autonomy. On the other hand, the divine partner clearly expects that the Jew will "choose life" and ratify, in both an individual and a collective way, the terms of the covenant, not the least of which is the halakhah, the Jewish way of life. The Jew ought to consent to what is right. Consent is not directed by radical autonomy, but by a bounded autonomy. Such autonomy is conditioned by a vision of the human good that claims ontological legitimation. This vision is at once both private and public. Just as the individual stood at Sinai only as a member of the Jewish polity, so too the individual stands before Torah today. Torah is both the law of the Jewish heart and the constitution of the Jewish polity.

With appropriate qualifications, Christianity's understandings of polity bear resemblance to Judaism's. The distinctions are of crucial significance, but so are the commonalities. Jews and Christians can moderate the excesses of the modern dialectic of autonomy by modeling legitimate authority within their polities. Such authority is neither sovereign nor arbitrary. It recognizes God as the only sovereign and so circumscribes its own reach and tendency. Such authority seeks consent, but asks that consent be illumined by a persuasive ideal of the common good. Such authority speaks the language of rights but never without the correlated language of obligation. Such an authority should renew our sense of relatedness to the natural world without denigrating or distorting the uniquely human. Here, Jews and Christians, either in dialogue if they are willing, or by cultivating their own gardens if they so choose, can become a *nes 'amim,* a sign for the peoples, of a human life worthy of the name.

The Orthodox Jew as Intellectual Crank

DAVID SINGER

My subject is "The Orthodox Jewish Intellectual as Crank," and it would be best if I began with some definitions. My dictionary defines a crank as an "ill-tempered, grouchy person," as an "eccentric person who is overzealous in his advocacy of a private cause." By these standards, Baruch Kurzweil and Yeshayahu Leibowitz, two Israeli Orthodox thinkers, certainly merit the label "crank." Both men — Kurzweil died a suicide at age 65 in 1972, while Leibowitz is still active at age 87 — have well-deserved reputations as intellectual wild men, as ferocious polemicists, no-holds-barred critics, and fevered champions of the unconventional and the outrageous. Is there a reader even slightly familiar with the writings of Kurzweil and Leibowitz who would not recognize "ill-tempered," "eccentric," and "overzealous" as suitable descriptive terms for these men?

The question I want to raise is this: is the crank element — what I shall hereafter refer to as "crankitude" — that manifests itself in the work of Kurzweil and Leibowitz merely a reflection of personal idiosyncrasy or does it point to something more significant? To be sure, the personal element is there: Kurzweil and Leibowitz come by their crankitude honestly and naturally. At the same time, one cannot help but notice that being a crank helps them to function more effectively as Orthodox thinkers — crankitude provides them with nothing less than a full-fledged intellectual stance. In short, my thesis is that Kurzweil and Leibowitz have elevated personal idiosyncrasy into a stylized cultural response — a response that permits them, at once, to take modernity with full seriousness, but also to reject modernity in the name of Jewish faith. The excesses that one associates with these men — excesses of style, of rhetoric, and of substance — all play a part in this process. Kurzweil and Leibowitz are not Orthodox intellectuals who just happen to be cranks; rather, they are full-fledged "Orthodox intellectual cranks" — i.e., crankitude goes to the very heart of their enterprise as Orthodox thinkers.

To better appreciate the nature of the enterprise that Kurzweil and Leibowitz engage in as Orthodox intellectual cranks it would be useful to consider the categories employed by sociologist Peter Berger, the leading academic analyst of the modernization process. Berger argues that religious thinkers have available essentially three types of response to the challenge of modernity: "cognitive retrenchment," "cognitive bargaining," and "cognitive surrender." Cognitive retrenchment is the sectarian option, calling for a conscious rejection of modernity as a dangerous heresy. The thinker taking this position in effect states, as Berger puts it: "The rest of you go climb a tree; we believe this, we know this, and we are going to stick to it. And if this is irrelevant to the rest of you, well, that is just too bad." In cognitive bargaining, in contrast, "there are two conflicting views of the world and they start to negotiate with each other"; an "attempt is made to arrive at a cognitive compromise." Finally, there is cognitive surrender, in which, in Berger's terms, "one simply accepts the fact that the majority is right, then adapts oneself to that point of view."

Most Orthodox thinkers operating in a modern framework — a tradition stretching from Samson Raphael Hirsch in the early nineteenth century to David Hartman in the late twentieth century — have engaged in one form or another of cognitive bargaining. In sharp contrast, Kurzweil and Leibowitz offer us the model of Orthodox intellectuals managing to combine — in equal measure no less — cognitive surrender and cognitive retrenchment. This, to put it mildly, is an astonishing intellectual feat, and crankitude is the form of its expression. Kurzweil and Leibowitz, at one and the same time, embrace and reject modernity. They exhibit, on the one hand, a radical openness to key aspects of the modern experience, and, on the other, a radical rejection of basic tendencies of modernity. Moreover, all this is carried out in the name of a radicalized version of Orthodox faith, a version that presents itself as the one true way. Small wonder then that Kurzweil and Leibowitz come across as intellectual wild men, that their work is characterized by high-voltage tension and extreme formulations. Such are the pressures — personal and psychological, no less so than abstractly intellectual — that come to bear on the Orthodox intellectual crank.

Rather than embarking on an extended discussion of what Kurzweil and Leibowitz have to say, I want to put forward a limited series of propositions that relate to their work in its typological aspects. After all, it is the Orthodox intellectual crank as a type that engages our attention. First, however, some biographical and bibliographical notes are in order.

Kurzweil and Leibowitz belong to the same generation — the former was born in Pirnice, Moravia, in 1907 and the latter in Riga, Russia, in 1903 — and emigrated to Palestine during the same period — Kurzweil in 1939 and Leibowitz in 1935. They differ sharply, however, in their fields of scholarly pursuit and the trajectories of their careers. Kurzweil was the very model of the Central European intellectual, specializing in the study of literature, aesthetics, and philosophy at the University of Frankfurt. While he eventually attained the post of professor of Hebrew literature at Bar-Ilan University and wrote a regular column for *Haaretz,* he remained a permanent outsider to the Israeli intellectual establishment. Leibowitz, in contrast, was oriented toward the sciences, studying chemistry and medicine, although he also showed a strong interest in philosophy. Upon settling in Palestine, he became associated with the Hebrew University — an institution that Kurzweil detested — first as a professor of organic and biochemistry and neurophysiology, and later as a professor of the history and philosophy of science. Leibowitz's extreme dovishness with regard to the Arab-Israeli conflict, as well as his harsh attacks on institutionalized Orthodoxy — the latter element also appears in Kurzweil's writings — have made him something of a darling to many secular Israeli intellectuals.

On the bibliographical side, it is important to note that only a very small sampling of the writings of Kurzweil and Leibowitz are available outside the Hebrew language. This fact underscores the point that the work of these two Orthodox thinkers, in its origin — though certainly not in its reach — is inseparable from the Israeli context. Indeed, until quite recently, Kurzweil and Leibowitz were virtually unknown beyond the borders of Israel. This has begun to change, however, with the appearance of James Diamond's very fine English-language study *Baruch Kurzweil and Modern Hebrew Literature* and David Hartman's English-language writings on Leibowitz. Within Israel itself, of course, both men have received considerable scholarly attention. The secondary literature on Kurzweil, including *The Baruch Kurzweil Volume,* a series of memorial essays, is quite massive, while that on Leibowitz — including *The Yeshayahu Leibowitz Volume,* a *festschrift,* and *Negation for Negation's Sake,* an anti-*festschrift* — is also substantial.

Let us now get down to cases by describing some of the key typological features of the Orthodox intellectual crank.

Proposition 1: *The Orthodox intellectual crank centers his work on a religious problematic defined in rigidly either/or terms.*

In Kurzweil's case, this problematic is the absolute gulf separating the world of pre-modern religious faith from the secular outlook of modernity. For Kurzweil, modern and secular are synonymous, and it is the rise of secularization that has made modernity an age of permanent crisis. The starting point of Kurzweil's thinking is the assumption, as Diamond puts it, that the "only absolute in human life, human history and human culture is faith in the living transcendent God." In the absence of faith — which is what secular modernity has brought about — human existence loses its one sure anchor, opening itself to what Kurzweil variously calls the "void," the "absurd," and the "demonic." (These are key terms in his lexicon.) The meaning of this change, as Kurzweil sees it, is described by Diamond in the following manner:

> In this new setting man is thrust into a cosmos bereft of certainty. He lives now not in the presence of God but of the abyss, of Nothing. The individual ego becomes the center and gradually enlarges to fill the void. Man for the first time conceives of himself as an autonomous being who is self-sufficient. There is no transcendent source for values and morality, nothing to hold in check man's instinctive capacity for self-aggrandizement, *hubris,* domination and destruction. . . . Now man is utterly alone, beyond all values and all relationships with society or his fellow-men — yet he is unsatisfied. He has lost his soul but failed to gain the world, for the demons are insatiable.

A key element in Kurzweil's thinking is the notion of "late return," which occurs when an individual, caught in the web of modernity, seeks to escape his situation by turning back to a life of pristine faith. It is just here, however, that the either/or element comes to the fore, in that Kurzweil takes it for granted that no such return is possible for the vast majority of moderns. Kurzweil is not an evangelist calling for the restoration of religious faith; rather, he is a diagnostician of secular unbelief, describing what he takes to be the permanent condition of modern man. If Kurzweil devoted his career to the study of modern literature, it was because he saw it as offering telling testimony to this very condition. And the chief testifier, of course, was modern Hebrew literature.

Kurzweil's interpretation of modern Hebrew literature is clearly set forth in *Our Modern Literature: Continuity or Revolt?* In this work, now a classic in the field, he argues decisively for the latter position. The emphasis here is on radical discontinuity, on modern Hebrew literature as a product of secularization and the collapse of religious faith. Kurzweil states: "The secularism of modern Hebrew literature is a given in that it is for the most part the outgrowth of a spiritual world divested of the primordial certainty in a sacral foundation that envelops all the events of life and measures their value." Kurzweil mocks those who fail to see the "difference between the sacral world of traditional Judaism, in which the Divine Torah structures the totality of life activities, and a world which has become secularized in its totality but still preserves individual corners of interest in religious elements and subjects." The former — the "sacral world of traditional Judaism" — is the domain of the "vision," while the latter — a "world which has become secularized in its totality" — is the place of the "void." Modern Hebrew writers, in Kurzweil's view, sort themselves out most fundamentally by their varying responses to the confrontation with the "void."

In Leibowitz's case, the religious problematic is the radical disjuncture between theocentric and anthropocentric conceptions of religion; between religion as the service of God for its own sake and religion as an instrument for the satisfaction of human needs. Eliezer Schweid has shrewdly labeled Leibowitz's position "neo-neo-Orthodoxy," in that Leibowitz "frees Judaism of every tie . . . to human culture." Leibowitz's key claim, Warren Harvey indicates, is that "in Judaism, questions of ethics, politics, science, or history have *no value whatsoever* except insofar as they might be means to the service of God in accordance with the

Torah and the commandments, that is in accordance with the Halakhah." Leibowitz himself states the matter as follows:

> Every reason given for the *mitzvot* which bases itself on human needs from any consideration of the concept need, whether intellectual, ethical, social, national — voids the *mitzvot* from every religious meaning. If they are meant to benefit society or if they maintain the Jewish people, then he who performs them does not serve God but himself or society or his people. In any case, he does not serve God but uses the Torah of God for his benefit and as a means to satisfy his needs. The reason for the *mitzvot* is the worship of God.

Amazingly enough, Leibowitz consistently invokes the name of Maimonides in putting forward this radically anti-humanistic conception of religion. A more appropriate model here — although Leibowitz would vehemently deny it — is Søren Kierkegaard, whose influence can be felt on virtually every page of Leibowitz's writings. (Kierkegaard, incidentally, knew a thing or two about being an intellectual crank!) Is it a mere coincidence that Leibowitz points to the *Akedah,* to Abraham on Mount Moriah, as a paradigm of how man must stand before God? He states: "Christianity's highest symbol is the crucifixion, and sacrifice which God brings for man, whereas the highest symbol of faith in Judaism is the *Akedah* where all man's values are canceled and cast aside for reverence and love for God." So powerful is the image of the *Akedah* for Leibowitz that he actually employs it to describe his intellectual hero, calling Maimonides "Abrahamic man." He observes:

> In Maimonides, more than in any other Jewish figure, there appears the image of the first Jew facing the crisis of the *Akedah* where all human thought, human feeling, and values are completely obliterated before the fear and love of God. This Abrahamic sense was alive in Maimonides. . . .
> The God of Maimonides is not . . . [a] functionary for the human group serving as a cosmic minister of health, law, police, and economics. Only for a God who is "true being" and not a provider of man's needs does it befit man to take "the fire and the knife" in hand and go uncomplainingly "to the place of which

God spoke to him" and sacrifice his only son, thereby relinquishing both his human aspirations and all hope for the future. . . .

Proposition 2: *The Orthodox intellectual crank displays radical openness to key aspects of the modern experience.*

In Kurzweil's case, this is the openness he shows to modern literary expression in all its forms. Far from spurning modern writing as the illicit fruit of the secularization process, Kurzweil lavishes endless attention on it, producing a body of literary criticism that is nothing short of massive. More importantly, it is also first-rate. Kurzweil's critics are legion, but even the severest of them would have to admit that he was the very model of the engaged literary scholar. Thus Diamond — who personally is quite sympathetic to Kurzweil — points to the "marvelous coherence and consistency" of Kurzweil's method, to the "passion and the struggle with which he carried out the critical enterprise." Stanley Nash, in a review of Diamond's book, maintains that Kurzweil "brought a rhetorical intensity and intellectual acumen to Hebrew criticism that have rarely been equaled."

Consider, then, the strange phenomenon of an Orthodox intellectual identifying the realm of heresy and then settling in for the lifelong study of it. A study, moreover, carried out in loving detail and with a considerable amount of imaginative sympathy for the heretics. That certainly is what Kurzweil offers us in his literary criticism, which yielded brilliant analyses of the work of, among others, Bialik, Brenner, Tchernichovsky, Greenberg, and, of course, Agnon. All that Kurzweil asks of his writers is that they testify honestly to the confrontation with the "void" and the "demonic" — wherever that takes them. What he could not abide, however, were attempts at evasion, such as he saw in the younger generation of Israeli writers. Kurzweil took it upon himself — as if he needed any prodding! — to expose their "snobby immaturity and inflated nothingness." With a straight face, he declared Amos Oz's *My Michael* to be more dangerous to Israel as a nation than all the Arab armies.

In Leibowitz's case, the openness shows itself in everything associated with the scientific realm — most especially the natural sciences, but social science and history as well. Eliezer Goldman, in an article entitled "Responses to Modernity in Orthodox Jewish Thought," uses the words "radical acceptance" to describe Leibowitz's stance in this regard. Radical it certainly is, in that Leibowitz fully endorses the empiricist descriptions of reality. Goldman summarizes Leibowitz's position as follows:

> Leibowitz's conception of science is thoroughly empirical. However much of our knowledge may be imported into it by our intellectual schemes, the final arbiter in all questions of fact is our experience, and this is forced upon us. . . . The world picture we all really accept when we do not delude ourselves is "secular." . . . This applies not only to nature, but to human history in its factuality.

It is important to note that Leibowitz extends this line of analysis even to the study of the Bible, thus supporting the findings of modern critical scholarship. Leibowitz, David Hartman observes, regards the Bible not "as a source of factual information, but only as a source of normative direction — that is, as Torah and *mitzvah*."

What is remarkable about Leibowitz's embrace of the modern scientific outlook is that it is organically linked to his anti-humanistic conception of Judaism. From the religious standpoint, Leibowitz wishes to divorce the service of God from all other facets of the human endeavor. From the secular standpoint, however, this very divorce frees him to accept the world of science on its own (empiricist) terms. Declaring nature and history to be absolutely irrelevant to the religious quest, Leibowitz can approach them in a thoroughly modern manner. This is of no small importance to an Orthodox Jew who functioned as a serious research scientist long before he emerged publicly as a religious thinker. Leibowitz, quite clearly, has hit upon a marvelous formula for reducing cognitive dissonance. Is that not one important consequence of Leibowitz's position, as outlined by Hartman?

> Leibowitz . . . make[s] the important claim that religious language is totally prescriptive. . . . All of Judaism can be translated into a way-of-life language that does not require any theological metaphysical claims about the nature of God and the way He acts in history. Whereas empirical descriptions have to be confirmed or falsified by the canons of scientific and logical thought, God-

51

talk cannot be made intelligible outside of the normative language of the *mitzvot*. Halakhic Jews, therefore, should not look to nature or history in their religious quest. That quest is fully exhausted in their participation in the framework of the *halakhah*.

Proposition 3: *Despite his receptivity to key aspects of modernity, the Orthodox intellectual crank's ultimate allegiance is to a version of Orthodox Judaism that negates the basic thrust of the modern experience.*

In Kurzweil's case, this is the metahistorical vision of Jewish history advanced by Samson Raphael Hirsch and his grandson Isaac Breuer. Kurzweil first befriended Breuer during his years in Frankfurt, when, in addition to attending the university there, he enrolled in the yeshivah that Hirsch had founded in the nineteenth century. It was Hirsch, of course, who provided Kurzweil the model of an Orthodox Jew who is meticulous in religious observance, but also open to secular culture in its various forms. Breuer affirmed this model as well, but more importantly, he taught Kurzweil to oppose all attempts at the secularization of Jewish life. When Kurzweil argued that "Jewish existence without God is the Absurd with a capital 'A,'" he was directly echoing Breuer. More generally, Kurzweil followed the Hirsch-Breuer school in regarding Judaism and the Jewish people as metahistorical realities. In this view, Diamond explains, the Torah is "God-given, a timeless absolute that transcends the limitations of human history. The Jews, therefore, exist for the sake of Judaism; Judaism does not exist for the sake of the Jews." "Kurzweil's commitment to a metahistorical fideism," Diamond rightly concludes, "is antipodal to the perspective [of] most Hebrew literature in the twentieth century."

It is precisely here that Kurzweil's famous attacks on Ahad Ha'am and Gershom Scholem come into the picture. Kurzweil saw these two "arch culprits" aiming at a secularization of Jewish life, an enterprise he saw as nothing short of "demonic." To struggle within the world of the "void," as did modern Hebrew writers, was one thing; to establish the "void" as the new foundation for a Jewish life, as did Ahad Ha'am and Scholem, quite another. Against this tendency, Kurzweil was unsparing in his criticism, referring to the "palpable absurdities of the Ahad Ha'amist philosophy." This was child's play, however, compared to his polemic against Scholem, whose sins, in Kurzweil's view, were threefold. First, he employed historicism as a tool to relativize the Judaic absolute. Second, he assigned "demonic" mysticism a position of importance in the framework of normative Judaism. Third, and most important, he legitimated secular Zionism as an expression native to Jewish history. "There is no more penetrating proof of the absurdity of our time," Kurzweil railed, "than the fact that Scholem is today the spokesman for Judaism."

Leibowitz, as indicated above, sees himself as a disciple of Maimonides in advancing his anti-humanistic conception of Judaism; indeed, he claims to be doing nothing more than laying bare Maimonides' esoteric teaching in the *Guide* and elsewhere. The key point, however, is that Leibowitz wishes to make this teaching fully exoteric, believing that this is a vital necessity in the modern context. Why is this so? Harvey explains Leibowitz's thinking on the matter as follows:

> Leibowitz is convinced . . . that it is foolish to try to advance religion by pointing to its utility in satisfying human needs when these needs are in fact presently being satisfied quite well *without* religion. To teach religion today as a means . . . is to teach that it is *superfluous.* . . . He consequently insists that today Judaism must be taught unequivocally as the service of God out of love. . . . In every age . . . the true service of God entails rebellion against utilitarianism and anthropocentrism, but today it is additionally a rebellion against the reigning secularist values of society.

In calling for "rebellion" in the modern situation, Leibowitz intends nothing less than the absolute rejection of modernity's key operative assumption: man as the center of value.

Proposition 4: *Crankitude is a coping mechanism that enables the Orthodox intellectual crank to maintain a reasonable equilibrium in a situation of extreme stress.*

From everything that I have said thus far about Kurzweil and Leibowitz it should be evident that theirs is not a placid synthesis of Orthodoxy and modernity *à la* Samson Raphael Hirsch. On the contrary, their encounter with modernity is characterized by sharply conflicted feelings, by powerful attraction on the one side and violent rejection on the other. The crucial factor here is the element of simultaneity — the fact that Kurzweil and Leibowitz feel drawn to and repulsed by modernity at one and the same time. It is no exaggeration at all to state that the measure of their attraction is the measure of their repulsion, and vice versa. It is precisely this tension that makes the work of these two Orthodox intellectuals so fascinating, and, I would contend, that accounts for their crankitude.

Crankitude, in short, is a coping mechanism, a tool for handling the severe pressures that result from a sharply conflicted response to modernity. Given what Kurzweil and Leibowitz wish to affirm and negate in the very same breath, is it any wonder that their writings are characterized by excess — by extreme formulations, by overheated language, and, let us add, by patently absurd claims? If they denounce their intellectual adversaries in the harshest of terms, can we not see in this a desperate attempt to beat back the enemy that lurks within — within, that is, Kurzweil and Leibowitz themselves? And if they insist on confronting modern Jews at every turn with either/or decisions, is it not because they themselves, at the most fundamental level, are forever unable to decide? To be a crank is a relatively simple matter; to be an Orthodox intellectual crank is a much more complicated undertaking.

God and Gender in Judaism

MATTHEW BERKE

In 1996, the Reform movement issued its new High Holy Day prayerbook, for the first time putting between hard covers a major liturgical work incorporating "gender-sensitive" language. Gender sensitivity is the rubric that for two decades has been used to purge Reform worship of masculine imagery and symbolism and to replace it, gradually, with sexually neutral or (in some cases) explicitly feminine language. This process has not been limited to changing phrases like "God of our fathers" to "God of our ancestors" in the English translation, or even to adding the Hebrew *'imoteinu,* "our mothers" (Sarah, Rebecca, Rachel, and Leah), where previously only *'avoteinu,* "our fathers" (Abraham, Isaac, and Jacob), were mentioned. More significantly, Reform liturgists have been altering the God-language of the prayerbook — a course of action with enormous, though largely unexamined, theological implications, not only for the Reform movement but for all of American Judaism.

The new High Holy Day prayerbook, *Gates of Repentance,* is actually a revised version of the 1978 Reform *makhzor* of the same name. As with the various paperbound services produced by the Central Conference of American Rabbis (CCAR) in recent years, most of the changes in God-language are in the English translation — a fact attributable more to caution than religious conviction. (A rabbi prominent in liturgy revisions told me that changes in the Hebrew will be slower in coming, since "Some people seem to think the Hebrew is more sacrosanct.")

Thus, *'Adonai* (Lord) is usually rendered as "Eternal One," occasionally as "God," or sometimes is simply left untranslated in the English section; *Melech* (King) yields most often to "Sovereign"; *'Avinu* (Our Father) gives way in translation to "Source," "Our Maker," "Our Creator," or "Our Parent." Third-person pronouns referring to God are eliminated by translating them into the second person or by recasting sentences into the passive voice. (Even prior to the written changes, many rabbis were "editing" the old prayerbooks, replacing every "He" or "His" with a repetition of "God" — e.g., God saw that God's work was good and so God rested from God's work.)

For the most part *Gates of Repentance* employs gender-neutral rather than feminine language. *'Avinu Malkeinu* (Our Father, Our King), one of the most venerable and beloved formulations of the Jewish liturgy, is left untranslated in the main text — though an alternative prayer is offered to the *Shekhinah,* the divine spirit, which is traditionally regarded as feminine. The use of explicitly feminine imagery is actually carried further in the CCAR's booklet for S'lichot services, *Gates of Forgiveness* (1993). That service alters both the Hebrew and the English of the *'Avinu Malkeinu* prayer to yield *'Avinu Imeinu* (Our Father, Our Mother). Masculine imagery is tolerated, but only (it seems) when it is immediately counterbalanced by feminine language. Later in the same book, balance is abandoned for outright feminization: the *Shekhinah* is invoked as a "Mothering Presence" and "Mother present in all"; a blessing begins, *Barucha 'At . . .* "Blessed are you" (feminine), instead of the traditional *Baruch 'Atah* (masculine).

Gender neutrality is regarded by the CCAR's Liturgy Committee as a transitional style. In five or six years the CCAR plans to revamp *Gates of Prayer* — the Reform *siddur* for Sabbath, weekdays, and festivals — employing a good deal of explicit feminine imagery. It remains to be seen whether this means "Father," "Lord," and "King" — expunged from all the most recent liturgies — will be allowed to come back into prayerbooks for gender balance.

To Jews in other movements, the liturgical changes in Reform must seem just another instance of Reform's ultraliberal heresy and *mishegoss* that imitates trends in the secular world and liberal churches. Yet Reform innovation is often an advance indicator of developments in the other branches of Judaism. The Conservative movement, which followed Reform on the ordination of women and has adopted much of

Reform's liberal political agenda, has already made some concessions to gender sensitivity in its current prayerbook, and Conservative rabbis are now discussing the possibility of using demasculinized God-language. Orthodoxy is relatively immune to liturgical ferment, but not absolutely so. Increasingly, one finds Orthodox women breaking out of traditional religious roles — undertaking intensive Talmudic studies, forming women's prayer groups, and davening publicly on commuter trains and in airports. As some Orthodox women explore a feminized God-language within the limits of tradition, nondenominational women's minyans venture beyond. Whether the new God-language becomes a source of further division within American Judaism or the basis of a new theological consensus, its assumptions and arguments need to be evaluated more carefully — starting with the Reform case.

The idea behind gender sensitivity is that religious teaching and liturgy should reflect the religious equality of women — as full partners in the covenant and as creatures equally made *bĕtselem 'elohim,* "in the image of God." Many women say they feel excluded by a theological and liturgical vocabulary that is overwhelmingly masculine: they can neither relate to nor find any self-reflection in the awesome, patriarchal God-figure who relies so heavily on power, fear, rules, and hierarchy. To include women in the religious life of the Jewish community, they argue, God must be *re-imaged* in a way that incorporates the feminine aspects of the divine nature.

Liturgical reformers contend that such reimaging is easily accommodated within a traditional Jewish framework. After all, it is argued, the sages insisted that God has no body and is beyond the categories of male and female, incorporating both but limited by neither. The ancient rabbis were aware that God is *'eyn sof*— unknowable, unfathomable, indescribable — and they regarded all God-language as approximate and figurative. Even in the Bible itself, as well as in mystical texts and other writings, feminine imagery is occasionally employed to describe God. The dominant imagery is masculine, the revisers claim, only because women have been powerless and marginalized throughout Jewish history; their voices have been silenced by men who have had all the power and who, idolatrously, projected onto God their own male image. This male-centered social construction of God has been a perennial instrument of oppression against women, and serves, even today, to define women as inferior and radically "other" — religiously, culturally, and politically. If Judaism is to survive and flourish, it cannot afford to alienate half of its members with outdated sexist language and conceptualizations.

The question arises, then: Is there any reason, in the face of such potent challenges, to insist on the continued pervasiveness of masculine God imagery? In fact, there is good reason for both women and men to refrain from embracing the new feminized liturgies. God-language is loaded (to borrow Marx's famous phrase about commodities) with "metaphysical subtleties and theological niceties" such that seemingly innocent revisions change the religious substance of Judaism in unexpected and undesired ways.

One may readily concede that all God-language is in some sense figurative, that human language and understanding are unable to grasp the Ultimate. However, it does not follow that all figurative language is therefore equal in approximating the mystery of the divine. Though we never penetrate to the inner reality of God, we do encounter Him in certain relationships that *are* humanly describable, however imperfectly. To address God as Father or Lord or King does not identify the sex or describe the essential being of God so much as it defines certain relationships between Him and us. While the God we pray to is beyond male or female, He has chosen to disclose Himself in distinctly masculine ways that are structured into the meanings of the Torah and the prayerbook, and cannot therefore simply be altered at will.

For God's divine parenthood, neither mother nor father is an entirely satisfactory metaphor. Children have a genetic link to their natural mothers and fathers, whereas God's parenthood involves no genetic connection and no role for sex or procreation. Nevertheless, parenthood is a necessary metaphor for God's relation to humankind: it expresses the sense of personal care and solicitude that the words Creator and Maker fail to capture. Because generic parenthood is a meaningless concept — we have no sense or experience of a generic parent — we are stuck with the alternatives of mother and father.

There can be little doubt that, for Judaism, divine parenthood is better symbolized by fatherhood than motherhood, or at least that fatherhood is far less problematic than motherhood. In Genesis, God — like a father — generates outside of Himself. In the creation myth of feminine deities, however, everything emerges from the womb of the Mother God, conveying a sense that the world is an emanation or extension of the divine, and therefore divinized, as in pantheism. But at the very center of Jewish monotheism is the denial of a divinized nature: Nature is good, because God has made it so, but nature is not divine, and human beings are not made of godstuff.

The moral and theological implications of the Mother God and "birth metaphor" have been cogently described by Rabbi Paula Reimers in her essay "Feminism, Judaism, and God the Mother" (*Conservative Judaism,* Fall 1993). If "the universe and its processes are 'birthed' by the deity," Rabbi Reimers argues, then nature and its cycles are "held to be an expression of the divine will." In such a cosmology, good and evil lose all meaning, everything being good in its proper time. Suffering and death no less than flourishing and life are to be regarded as "necessary stations on the great wheel of existence." In a "birthed" universe, more-over, "human beings are not qualitatively different from anything else that exists. They share in the divine essence, as children of the goddess, but only to the same extent that everything else does. Human life objec-tively is no more or less significant than the life of animals or plants. . . . Human free will is dissolved in the face of the determinism of nature." Human beings need follow no moral standard other than to accept and submit "to the divine rhythm of existence, of which they are a part."

Rabbi Reimers contrasts the "inherent pantheism of goddess reli-gion, rooted in the birth metaphor," with Jewish monotheism, which "is rooted in the creation metaphor of Genesis." In Judaism, nature and hu-manity emerge not as part of an undifferentiated birth of the universe, but through discrete acts of creation in which all things are appointed a place in the hierarchy of the world. Good and evil, right and wrong, are known not by reference to nature's processes, impulses, and vitalities, but through the words and commandments of a transcendent God. Be-cause God is not identified with the cycles of natural recurrence but with unique revelations and mighty acts — especially the Covenant — time is given meaning by progressive development, and history is im-bued with direction and purpose. Human beings are not permitted to view themselves or their impulses as divine; they are to understand themselves, rather, as creatures made "in the image and likeness of God," with a dignity and worth above the rest of nature, and with free will to act according to transcendent laws concerning good and evil.

The Father-God metaphor, then, while revealing certain limits and imperfections of human language and understanding, provides a better symbolization than motherhood of the sense of distance in the divine-human relationship and is less likely therefore to invite a pantheistic cosmology. As Rabbi Reimers explains, "Those who want to use God/She language want to affirm womanhood and the feminine aspect of the deity. They do this by emphasizing that which most clearly distinguishes the female experience from the male. A male or female deity can create through speech or through action, *but the metaphor for creation which is uniquely feminine is birth*. Once God is called female, then, the metaphor of birth and the identification of the deity with nature and its processes become inevitable." Her last point is not a matter of mere conjecture or speculation: in ancient times female deities were in fact seen as having given birth to the world, with nature-worship following almost invariably. Today, too, feminist theology regularly falls back upon the birth metaphor, and, not surprisingly, often lapses into a pantheistic worldview as well (often under the guise of "deep ecology").

In sum, according to Rabbi Reimers, "the composers and compilers of those [biblical and rabbinic] texts knew that the deity *could* be understood as female; many of the peoples among whom they lived worshipped goddesses" (and, she might have added, their societies were male-dominated all the same). "Our ancient teachers" used masculine language for God not so much as an expression of chauvinism as a means to prevent the "introduction of alien theological ideas into the heart of monotheistic religion."

Even beyond the creation story, the divine-human relationship is in crucial respects paternal rather than maternal or generically parental. Maternal care arises more or less naturally, and mother love tends to be unconditional. Fatherhood, by contrast, is largely a socially constructed phenomenon, and it is far more conditional and hierarchical than motherhood — demanding obedience, threatening punishment, and setting standards in return for love and approval. In families without fathers or strong male authority figures, order tends to break down, particularly among the male children, who become wild and predatory.

The God of Israel introduces Himself into history as a kind of adoptive parent, in particular as a father figure who steps in to bring order to a chaotic and violent world. At times He exhibits the gratuitous love and tender care associated with femininity and motherhood — but more often our broken, unredeemed world calls forth from Him a specifically *paternal* form of authority, implemented over and against His human children, especially His sons. While women, in their own fashion, may sin as much as men, it is the pride and willfulness and violence of men that most radically disrupts the world's peace and order. Feminist reformers may have no trouble in recognizing this fact, but they seem not to notice that breaking the arrogance and power of men requires a God who is, among other things, the Judge of Nations, the Lord of Hosts, the "King of glory . . . mighty in battle" (Psalm 24:8).

Feminist critics and modern liturgy revisers often assume that God's awesome patriarchal aspect is merely an idolatrous projection of the male image, which it can be and sometimes is. At the same time, God's lordship is the only plausible check on the predatory tendencies of wicked men and nations, from Pharaoh to Haman to Hitler. The feminist argument that traditional God-language stresses power, fear, rules, and hierarchy is essentially correct; but it misses the point that these things are required for the good of women as well as men. It is precisely His capacity as a warrior-judge that enables Him to be a God of justice who frees the captive and releases the oppressed, who answers the cries of the poor, the widows, the fatherless. "King" and "Lord" are the most convincing symbolizations for this aspect of divine action.

Reimagings that magnify characteristically feminine traits undermine the plausibility of God's ultimate power to overcome evil. Such undermining can be seen, for instance, in the celebrated fantasy of Rabbi Margaret Moers Wenig (*Reform Judaism,* Fall 1992), which depicts God as a graying, late-middle-aged woman.

> She moves more slowly now. She cannot stand erect. Her hair is thinning. Her face is lined. Her smile no longer innocent. Her voice is scratchy. Her eyes tire. Sometimes she has to strain to hear. Yet, she remembers everything. On Rosh Hashanah, the anniversary of the day on which she gave us birth, God sits down at her kitchen table, opens the Book of Memories, and begins turning the pages; and God remembers.

God kvells over the achievements of her children, but laments their waywardness. "They rarely visit me," she sighs. However, if we did visit her, "God would usher us into her kitchen, seat us at her table, pour two cups of tea." Then, after listening to us spill out our troubles for a while, "finally, she touches her finger to her lips and says, 'Sha. Be still. Shhh.'"

Later on, "God holds our face in her two hands and whispers, 'Do not be afraid, . . . I gave birth to you, I carried you. I will hold you still. Grow old with me.'"

Rabbi Wenig's God wonders why her children don't visit her, but she shouldn't be surprised. Though kind and gentle, she is totally ineffectual in the things the world needs most from God. There is scarcely a hint of transcendence about her. She dispenses tea and sympathy but doesn't deliver justice with a mighty hand. She offers to hold hands and grow old together, but not to heal the sick, lift up the fallen, and resurrect the dead (or, as Reform liturgy fatuously puts it, "give life to all").

It might also be said of this God that she is as thoroughly idolatrous a projection of the modern female self as one can imagine. No Jewish man, certainly no modern or liberal Jewish man, could possibly get away with a comparable self-deification. To the extent that Jewish men have too closely identified God's characteristically masculine actions with their own sex, at least they have recognized that God means to judge them, and not, as feminist reimagers propose, simply to succor and adore and vindicate them.

Another famous feminist reimaging — by Rabbi Rebecca Alpert (*Reform Judaism,* Winter 1991) — is more vital than Rabbi Wenig's God, but no less self-deifying.

> The experience of praying with *Siddur Nashim* [a prayerbook coauthored by Naomi Janowitz and Rabbi Wenig] . . . transformed my relationship with God. For the first time, I understood what it meant to be made in God's image. To think of God as a woman like myself, to see Her as both powerful and nurturing, to see Her imaged with a woman's body, with womb, with breasts — this was an experience of ultimate significance. Was this the relationship that men have had with God for all these millennia? How wonderful to gain access to those feelings and perceptions.

The Reform movement is probably not ready for such bold feminist reimagings in its mainstream liturgies. There has been some experimentation with alternating references to God as Father and Mother, and more is planned. This device, however, has certain drawbacks. It implies, perhaps even more dramatically than a lone Mother God, a pantheistic worldview (i.e., the universe as product of divine copulation), or else a sexually protean deity, a hermaphrodite, or dualistic godhead.

For now these bizarre and unseemly images are avoided by emphasizing language that is scrupulously gender-neutral; but this only causes theological distortion of a different kind. The constant repetition of "Eternal One" as a substitute for Lord (*'Adonai*) not only de-genders God, it radically depersonalizes and sedates Him. The Jewish God is, in a certain sense, eternal, in that He is everlasting. But the word "eternity" is problematic in the context of biblical Hebrew; it is really a philosopher's term, implying a kind of timeless essence, unchanging and inactive, frozen in isolated splendor. Such a God is perhaps relevant to a sterile religion of abstract ethics, but It provides little aid or comfort to the sick, the oppressed, and the bereaved. The God of the Bible and traditional prayerbook is personal and active. Moreover, He is caring. For all the severity of His patriarchy and hierarchy, the old biblical God is more caring and approachable than the vapid, comfortless entity now being forced on Reform congregants. Their "Eternal One" represents not so much a *re*-imaging as a *de*-imaging of God.

Can it be that Jewish women really prefer this abstract deity to the venerable "Lord" of their ancestors? Has feminism driven women to such resentment against all things masculine that it is impossible for them to imagine a benevolent Father or King? It is far from obvious that the traditional God is necessarily alien or alienating to most women. There is, however, a strain of feminism that is hostile toward any notion of distinctive masculine traits or social roles, and its influence within the Reform movement has persuaded — or intimidated — the rabbis to blot out all masculine God-language and imagery from the prayerbook. The result at this stage is not a full-fledged Mother God — which, by feminist lights, is the true way to make religion more accessible to women — but a compromise deity that is inaccessible to both women and men.

This genderless God also represents a profound betrayal of the Torah narrative. We can no more make the God of the Bible into a generic parent or sovereign than we can make King Lear into a mother/queen or Hamlet's mother, Gertrude, into a father/king. Father and king are aspects of Lear that are structured into his story (as Gertrude's femininity is structured into *Hamlet*). If we can respect this integrity in works of secular literature, we should want to respect it even more faithfully in the Torah. For to change the sex of a character is no longer to have the same story.

Which brings us, finally, to the most important point of all in understanding what is at stake in the issue of God-language: namely, reverence for the Torah, for its integrity, and for its role as an 'ētz chaim — "a tree of life" (to borrow a phrase from the prayerbook). The most simple and compelling reason to reject gender-reimaging is that God, though not a man or a male, has used masculine terms in making His self-disclosure to humanity. Our words for God are controlled by the word of God.

The notion of "God's word" will of course be understood differently by Reform, Conservative, and Orthodox Jews, but it must be maintained in some sense by any movement that claims to be authentically Jewish. Orthodoxy understands the Bible in relatively fixed ways, and it holds that the received Torah is a perfect transcription of that which was written by God's own finger. Liberal Judaism holds that the Bible cannot always be understood according to the tradition's fixed or literal readings, and that, moreover, it is a document touched in many respects by the limitations and frailties of human nature. But this ability to criticize, while creative up to a point, must have some limits. Even liberal Judaism must maintain that the Torah is still substantially a work of transcendent truth, the inspired word of God. Otherwise the Torah becomes merely a record of all the influences that have conditioned Judaism, and it is no longer an 'ētz chaim. And if it is not a tree of life, why cling to it?

The movement to revise the liturgy along feminist lines — which stresses above all else the Torah as the ideological rationalization of an oppressive patriarchy — is not an expression of liberal Judaism but of radical deconstruction. The Fatherhood, Kingship, and Lordship of God are central and pervasive elements of Jewish tradition. The masculine character of much of God's revelation is not only structured into the story of the Torah, it is repeatedly and unambiguously affirmed. Even in the handful of biblical passages (so eagerly seized on by feminists) where the God-imagery is maternal, the verb forms remain masculine. God's predominantly masculine character may be textured so as to account for the feminine — which is also contained in the divine — but it cannot be repealed. To allow such a radical move is to concede that there is no limit on the relativizing and deconstructing of Jewish texts and teaching. It is to grant, in effect, a license for the repeal of any Torah precept at all — the oneness of God, the Ten Commandments . . . anything. Feminist-inspired liturgy is not the extension but rather the extinction of liberal Judaism. It does not continue the tradition of reforming an old religion so much as set the stage for the creation of a new one.

Many people who support the new gender-sensitive liturgies no doubt believe themselves to be continuing a tradition of critical reflection and religious reform going back to the great rabbinic sages. In fact, though, the current liturgy revision betrays not only traditional rabbinic method but also modern liberal — and especially feminist — emphasis on "process." Classic rabbinic decisions were reached after extensive debates, in which all sides of an issue were given full expression and review. The current Reform rabbinate simply decided to repeal the God-language of several millennia with nothing more in mind than applying a rather wooden understanding of the principle of sexual equality. Having received a mandate from the CCAR's Executive Board, the Liturgy Committee undertook extensive discussions on how to implement the changes, but never deliberated on the wisdom or rightness of such change.

In short, there was no rabbinic debate, no invitation of opposing views, no dialectical give and take, no formal statement or explanation from the Liturgy Committee to the Reform laity, or even to the Reform rabbinate at large. Some form of consultation with the laity and rabbinate is planned for several years down the road, when the next generation of highly feminized liturgies are composed. But by then there will be very little opportunity to make changes; feminine God-language will be a fait accompli.

The Reform conceit, of course, is that liberal Judaism is the most authentic expression of Torah living because, like our father Jacob, we liberals do not slavishly accept tradition but instead wrestle with things human and divine. This view may have had a measure of truth many years ago; today, however, the wrestling match increasingly resembles the "professional" wrestling seen on television: little morality plays between caricatures of good and evil, with the result fixed in advance.

The whole process of liturgy revision may be legally and formally in accord with the institutional requirements and mandates of the CCAR. But it lacks the openness to reason and deliberation normally associated with the word "liberal." Indeed, there is a hierarchical, top-down quality to the process that contradicts the frequently heard feminist demand for open process. And there is a certain irony in having the new liturgies advertise themselves as "sensitive" and "inclusive" when, in their content and method of introduction, they rather rudely exclude those Reform Jews who want greater stability and respect for tradition in the movement. Tradition, according to one nostrum, has a vote but not a veto in Reform decision making; now, it seems, tradition is disenfranchised while feminism has all the votes plus an absolute veto.

The introduction of feminized liturgies also reveals the Reform movement's continuing recklessness toward the principle of *Clal Yisrael* — the larger unity of the Jewish people. That sense of unity is now under heavy, almost unbearable, stress. In fairness, there is probably nothing the Reform movement can do that would soften the Orthodox rabbis' implacable hostility toward all non-Orthodox expressions of Judaism (the Conservatives actually receive most of the Orthodox scorn — Reform being beneath contempt in Orthodox eyes). Yet, if the situation cannot now be improved, the Reform movement should at least be at pains not to make things worse. Though the divisions within Judaism show no sign of healing at present, wholly unexpected possibilities may arise in the future. If Reform continues to move farther and farther from a traditional Jewish theological worldview — if it continues (in effect) to show contempt for Torah and deference to political correctness — it forecloses future possibilities of cooperation and reconciliation. It will probably divide its own house as well.

The Reform movement has made some legitimate prayerbook changes in the past, but that precedent should not be used to rationalize the latest wave of radical innovation. A movement perpetually tempted by secular fashion needs liturgical continuity as a vital link to our ancestors and as well as to *Clal Yisrael*. In his book *Understanding Jewish Prayer* (1972), the late Jakob Petuchowski, one of Reform's greatest teachers, spoke of Jewish practice as "a source of obligation — even in instances where the purely human origin of a given practice is clearly recognized and admitted, and where no claim of a direct divine revelation is being made."

> For community prayer to be *community* prayer, there will have to be certain features which represent a recognizable constant, linking one worship experience to another. . . . That is why Jewish

community prayer would cease to be *Jewish* community prayer if today's worship service were to be something totally and entirely different from yesterday's worship service, or last week's, or last year's, or that of a hundred years or two thousand years ago. Similarly, the Jew who travels from Bombay to Chicago must find some elements, known to him from Bombay, in the Chicago service.

Gender-sensitive prayerbooks may still retain "some elements" in common with traditional Jewish liturgy — but not enough. Their adoption by the Reform movement will lend credence to the frequent charge that Reform is not "real Judaism."

If we can get through this slightly mad period without embracing the new feminine God, perhaps we will be able to give more serious attention to women's legitimate grievances with the tradition. Women *are* different from men in the way they think and feel and understand — a point on which feminism, modern psychology, and traditional religion now seem to agree. Jewish prayer and ritual should address those different faculties and tendencies more than it has in the past. This purpose is not well served, however, by the current liturgical trend, which seeks to eradicate ancient truths and images, thus enshrining female resentment and male guilt and abdication. Women and men, both, have to find ways of dealing with this strange God of the Bible and prayerbook. Though we approach God with our many differences (not least the difference between men and women), we have in common the need for joy and consolation and forgiveness through prayer. In order to find these things, however, we must know that when we open our *siddur*, we are praying not to an idol of our own imagining but to the God of the Torah — that our prayer might be a tree of life to us.

Pluralism v. Multiculturalism

ALAN L. MITTLEMAN

For some decades, American Jews have made sense of the relation between their Americanness and their Jewishness through the concept of cultural pluralism. This concept allowed a flexible but expansive Jewish ethnic and religious identity to coexist with an equally normative American identity. The content of both Jewishness and Americanness may have been somewhat protean, but both mattered. Most Jews did not consider their Americanness to be simply a matter of citizenship, of what sort of passport they carried. Being an American implied a set of identity-shaping commitments. Citizenship in a liberal democracy, such as America, bore with it its own myths, history, and fellowship. Pluralism reconciled this complex American identity with an equally complex Jewishness.

Within the last several decades, however, the concept of cultural pluralism has given way to another concept, which, if only superficially, appears to derive from and improve upon it: multiculturalism. But this concept is fundamentally distinct from the pluralism that has well served American Jews. Multiculturalism, if it were to succeed pluralism altogether, would be inimical to American Jews.

The term pluralism was popularized by a Jewish professor of philosophy, Horace Meyer Kallen (1882-1974), shortly after the First World War. Kallen, like most Jews of his day, was extraordinarily proud to be an American, but was troubled by the idea of the American Melting Pot. He did not believe that it was ethical or wise to insist that different peoples entirely efface their differences. He imagined that the various immigrant groups could hold on to some significant portion of their heritage and, precisely because of that distinctive identity, offer a unique contribution to America.

On the one hand, Kallen envisioned Americanness as a substantive, normative cultural identity. America was more than just a place of opportunity. America and its civil faith (which he called "the American Idea") stood for a distinctive set of moral and political values. Values such as optimism, progress, democracy, individualism, and freedom could and should unite the nation. Yet precisely because America stands or falls on its ideas, we can come to its ideas or articulate its ideas in our own distinctive ways. To be united by the values of America, one did not need to shed one's ethnic identity. Indeed, one ought not to. Kallen's favorite metaphor was the orchestra. Distinctive ethnicities, like different instruments, could contribute harmoniously to the whole.

Kallen's notion of cultural pluralism was an adaptation of the metaphysical philosophy of his Harvard teacher and mentor, the famous American philosopher William James. In 1909, James published his Hibbert Lectures at Oxford under the title *A Pluralistic Universe.* James meant by pluralism a philosophical vision that opposed Hegelian absolute idealism. Pluralism was meant to account for reality as we actually experience it in its individuality, vitality, and empirical concreteness. James hoped to refute the modern forms of idealism and monism, stemming from Spinoza and Hegel and their Anglo-American imitators, and return us to the pre-philosophic world of actuality, a "turbid, muddled, gothic sort of an affair, without a sweeping outline and with little pictorial nobility." James prized the individual, the particular, the personal. He rejected, no less than Kierkegaard or Rosenzweig, philosophy's effort to subsume the part in the whole.

Kallen's contribution was to take the metaphysical mood of Jamesian pragmatism and apply it to culture. And who better than a Jew striving to be an American to do so? America was founded in an environment of religious pluralism. Religious pluralism, which generally implied the considerable variety of Protestant denominations as well as the Catholics and some few Jews, was a fact that most Americans had come to accept as relatively benign. But cultural or ethnic pluralism, aggravated by the great migrations after the Civil War, was far more challenging and difficult for the older American stock to accept. America had two answers. The first was nativism — the view that only the older American stock could properly understand and maintain distinctive American values. The second answer was the melting pot: the cauldron in which out of many cultures would come one. Kallen rejected both.

Like most Jews of his day, Kallen found an uncanny agreement between the core values of Judaism (or "Hebraism," as he preferred to call it) and those of America. This, of course, was not surprising, since America was settled, if not founded, by people who took the Bible rather seriously. Furthermore, the way they took the Bible seriously was significantly similar to the way Jews took the Bible. That is, both Calvinists and Jews read the Bible, with its pervasive theme of covenantalism, as (in part at least) a political text.

Covenant was not just a theological idea for the Puritans; it was an eminently political one. They founded their towns and commonwealths as covenantal republics: voluntary societies bound together by the laws of God and the desire to serve Him in freedom. These covenants were later transformed by political theory and practice into the somewhat more secular compacts and social contracts of eighteenth-century thought.

The basic idea remained the same however: societies are originated by free men in order to enable persons to have a common life directed toward the fulfillment of a noble end. Participation in the society requires consent to the founding principles. Liberty within the society is not absolute or negative. It is liberty to work within and to promote the common good.

It is this basically biblical and rather secular vision that Jews such as Kallen found intrinsic to America. Proud of his Jewish heritage and convinced of its affinity with American ideals, Kallen thought it reasonable that the more Jews cultivated their heritage, the more they would contribute to the American whole. Similiarly, the more they discerned the true values (however imperfectly realized) of America, the better they would refine and live their Judaism. Assuming then that the Jewish difference was real and valuable, Kallen also believed that ethnic differences on the whole were real and valuable. At the same time, however, ethnic differences should be negotiable and malleable. They must be directed to or ordered by a concern for an American common good.

To put it somewhat abstractly, primordial identity and the citizenship identity of the liberal society must condition one another. Civil society is not just a blank page on which the ethnic communities write their own stories for their own readership. Civil society has its own demands and requirements. It will and ought to have a transformative effect on primordial groups. The groups must have their liberty, however, and will, in turn, have a transformative effect on the civil society.

It is easy to see how cultural pluralism served as a useful ideology for generations of American Jews who wanted to retain their Jewishness while uninhibitedly affirming their Americanness. But it is easy to forget that this perspective worked only because Americanness and Judaism were conceived to a significant degree as ideals, indeed, as mutually compatible ideals. If we allow ourselves no coherent formulation of what America means or of what Judaism means, then we can obviously claim no link or essential likeness between them. And this is apparently precisely what has happened. Serious thought about the relationship of Judaism to Americanness no longer occurs. It seems terribly old-fashioned now, a relic of Kallen's time inappropriate to our own. Rabbinic sermons, a good guide to popular Jewish thinking, dealt frequently with the relationship of Judaism to America in the 1950s. But this theme is nonexistent today.

One might explain this absence as caused by a normal coming of age. The theme was crucial for the immigrant and second generations, but taken for granted by the third and subsequent generations. Undoubtedly there is some truth to this. But I think another issue is at stake: the hollowing out of Americanness — the loss of any consensus, however minimal, of what being an American means. Against this background, cultural pluralism is increasingly superseded by the ideology of multiculturalism.

Multiculturalism, I would suggest, is a mode of decoupling ethnic and religious communities from some imagined normative Americanness. Multiculturalism celebrates or affirms difference for its own sake and as its own terminus. The multiculturalist does not see a need to order difference in relation to a common good. If there is a common good, it is a good common only to members of a given group. The common good is a tribal good.

Of the factors that contributed to the rise of this ideology, the most salient one is that America no longer holds any radical or unique meaning for many Americans. After the assassinations and cultural upheavals of the 1960s and 1970s, after the debacles of Vietnam and Watergate, we are left with no innocence and much reticence about ourselves. We no longer believe that we have a monopoly on the export of ideas. We are no longer certain that we have any distinctive ideas. Nor do we any longer believe that belief in ourselves is the panacea for our own ills. Even the Reagan revolution, for all its cheery boosterism, failed to restore the old confidence in America.

Reaganism replaced Americanness, it seems to me, with a stirring, but not a soul-stirring, ideal: the American Dream. We still talk much in America about this American Dream. We argue about whether it is possible to achieve it, and about who can achieve it. We even argue about what, precisely, it is. Of course, almost everyone agrees it has to do with money, with employment, with security. But beyond the basics of economic opportunity, there is no coherent or accepted vision of the American Dream. It is for this reason that the American Dream is not a substitute for the bygone ideals of America. Its vision is too narrow. It is the vision of *homo oeconomicus,* of the consumer, of the private person. It is not really the dream of the citizen, of the defender of a culture, of the aspirant for a good society. It is not a bad dream, but it is not the stuff that great dreams are made of.

Americanness as a civil religion is, to all intents and purposes, dead. There is thus a vacuum where our belief in our own exceptionalism used to be. As the poet Robert Bly once wrote, "The world will break up into small communities of the saved." This eerie eschatological premonition seems to me increasingly to describe our present. A vacuum has sucked all the pieces of stained glass out of the window of American pluralism. Multiculturalism is the attempt to reassemble them without, as it were, a surrounding frame.

Multiculturalism should not be confused with pluralism or the tolerant and empathetic cosmopolitanism that often accompanies pluralism. Critics of multiculturalism are often mistaken for old-fashioned chauvinists, nativists, or know-nothing advocates of a nasty melting pot, as if they were rejecting pluralism or cosmopolitanism per se. Could any serious intellectual really argue that students at a serious university not study Chinese poetry or African art or Jewish literature, for that matter? This is unthinkable. What critics of multiculturalism criticize is not the cosmopolitan breadth to which educated persons have always aspired, but a certain dogmatic dismissiveness toward the Western tradition.

Pluralism v. Multiculturalism

The Western tradition, as conceived by contemporary academic multiculturalists, is little more than the aesthetic and religious false consciousness of various types of oppressors: the racist, the classist, the heterosexist, the misogynist. Far from being a source of moral guidance, the Western tradition seems more and more like a roadmap of destinations to avoid. It shows you what not to emulate, what not to hope for, how not to live, what not to be. It is this attitude of scorn — which is as little justified in the university as an attitude of boosterism — to which the critics of multiculturalism call attention.

While pluralism affirmed cultural difference on account of its service to a common good, multiculturalism, as noted above, denies the integrity of a common good. It cannot or will not see beyond a tribal good. This disposition is born, it seems to me, less of pride or satisfaction in what is one's own than in despair of or rage toward the public world. The ideas of the public world, formerly constitutive of Americanness, were not, multiculturalism tells us, truly public, truly shared. They were actually the intellectual property of the reigning elite. The ideal of an open, pluralistic society was a sham.

Consider a typical case, in which American Jews had a considerable role and investment. American Jews, good pluralists that they were, generally endorsed the policy of racial integration. They certainly believed that blacks had a right to their culture, that they had a right to be proud of their culture, both American and African, and that they had a right to a fuller share of economic and social goods. American Jews worked to dismantle racial barriers, to open up greater educational opportunities, to end discrimination in the work place. They imagined that they were acting out of the deepest convictions of the Jewish tradition and in accordance with the high, if as yet imperfectly realized, ideals of America. This was cultural pluralism at its best.

But as the black civil rights movement turned increasingly toward nationalism and black separatism, Jews found that the values they thought were constitutive of the public world, such as equality of opportunity and merit, were now thought parochial and pernicious. Integration was rejected by black nationalists as a malevolent strategy of assimilation. Nationalists such as Stokely Carmichael called it "the final solution to the Negro problem" and "a subterfuge for white supremacy." Robert Browne, echoing Carmichael's Nazi allusion, called integration "a form of painless genocide."

73

The idea of merit, once considered by liberal pluralists to be a neutral rule for allocating goods, was now assigned a strictly demonic, oppressive character. In fact, an essayist in the leftist Jewish journal *Tikkun* argued, the entire "rhetoric of reason, neutrality, and objectivity actually constitutes the particular discourse of power that white Europeans employed in order to justify their own privileged status." When confidence in a morally substantive public world is lost, there are no ideas that rise above race, above primordial loyalties, above the war of all against all.

When the black nationalists of the sixties and seventies rejected the ameliorative agenda of the Great Society, they spoke from the far edge of a radical fringe. But today the political and theoretical assumptions from which they spoke have become a kind of orthodoxy, at least in much of American academia. Our professors of humanities assure us that reason has no universal form, but is merely a set of social practices that ensure one group's domination over others. Knowledge is not only power, it is nothing but power. This equation of knowledge and power, of truth and politics is deeply entrenched in the academy. But is it not especially malign for a nation constituted by its ideas, such as the United States, and for a people which has lived for its ideas, such as the Jews?

Jews have been able to flourish in the United States because the primary American form of identity is that of citizenship. Jews and others have had the best of both worlds: they have enjoyed a citizenship identity in the national polity and have, without contradiction, enjoyed a more primordial identity conferred by their own historic tradition. Other modern states, of course (or at least the liberal elements in them), tried to base participation in the polity upon citizenship as well. But, in practice, the primordial identity of ethnicity, race, or religion often imposed severe limits on the possibilities of citizenship. In America, by contrast, citizenship has proved more normative than it has in European countries. One obvious reason for this is that America is an immigrant society, without any organic national base. But another reason is that America, the "first new nation," was built on ideas. Citizenship meant subscription or consent to the ideals and principles of the founding national covenant. Primordial loyalties and identities were in some significant way irrelevant to participation in that covenant.

Multiculturalism seeks to attenuate citizenship identity and to substitute primordial identity as a more radically satisfying, self-sufficient

74

framework. But this can only be done at the cost of forfeiting any shared moral language, any meaningful public discourse, any thick concept of what it means to be an American. The erosion of cultural pluralism and the drift toward the new ideal of multiculturalism pose real hazards for American Jews, because they weaken the citizenship on which Jewish participation in modern society is based.

Multiculturalism also seems to offer some attractions, however, and it has its defenders, both on the right and on the left. As a consciously formulated ideology, it appeals to Jews on the left because it offers a new rationale for solidarity with oppressed and colonialized people around the world. In this version of multiculturalism, what I have called primordial identity must not be thought of as a fixed or stable property. Jewish identity becomes a matter of millennial otherness, of historical marginalization. Devoid of essentialistic or substantive criteria of identity, "Jewishness" becomes another "otherized" (and "otherizing") social construct, a product of the exclusionary practices by which dominant groups define themselves.

Jewishness is what is left to the losers after the dominant groups distribute the spoils of social conflict. Jewishness is not fundamentally different from blackness, femaleness, gayness, etc. These have no essence, no inner life. They are but names we assign to complex, shifting indices of the power dynamics of social life. The multiculturalist Jews of the left would link the Jew to every marginal and disempowered "other" at the cost of letting nothing but some elusive "otherness" remain.

But multiculturalism also describes an attitude found among those who would normally not speak its name, the Jews on the right. Sociologists of American Jewry have long noted both the resurgence of Orthodoxy and the enfeeblement of that same Orthodoxy's moderate center. Orthodoxy survived in the modern world in two forms: a sectarian, separatist hard core that resisted modernization and a modernist wing that accommodated itself to secular society. The latter group gave Orthodoxy its public face in America. Associated with Yeshiva University and the teaching of the late Rabbi Joseph Soloveitchik, "modern Orthodoxy" prized both traditional piety and practice and the values and cognitive norms of modern culture. This modernist Orthodoxy has been severely eroded. The more insular sectarian Orthodoxy, far less concerned with accommodation to the contemporary world, is today far more confident than centrist Orthodoxy. The children of Orthodox

Ph.D.s, raised in American suburbia, now spurn their parents' universities and hope to spend their lives in right-wing Jerusalem yeshivot. Where Orthodox congregants once followed the Torah reading in the Hertz Pentateuch, with its vigorous polemic against the documentary hypothesis, they now read the Art Scroll edition, a volume that has not the slightest interest in establishing any links between Torah and secular consciousness.

To a certain extent, the motivation here is the same as that of the left. The Enlightenment and the values of modernity are thought a kind of sham, an idol. They seduce Jews away from their own primordiality, from their overwhelming intimacy with God. The hyper-Orthodox want to live in an integral, sacred cosmos. The political realm, if it cannot be assimilated to that cosmos (which of course it cannot in the Diaspora), is of marginal significance. The national polity is not an object of care or concern for its own sake. It must simply be dealt with in terms of the crassest interest politics as the need arises. There is no distinctive or normative significance in an American identity.

These Jewish variations on the multicultural theme are born, like their gentile counterparts, out of the conviction that citizenship no longer constitutes a significant or distinctive identity. The balance between the public and the primordial has tilted. Without a renewal of our conviction that being an American implies meaning and confers a distinctive worth, the consensus, however minimal, upon which a free society rests can only weaken. If people revert to more primordial forms of belonging, civil society will dissolve and American Jews might find themselves in what the prophet Ezekiel called a *midbar ha-'ammim,* a wilderness of the peoples. This would be a nightmarish denouement to Kallen's once admired American Idea.

Blacks and Jews Entangled

EDWARD S. SHAPIRO

In her 1991 autobiography, *Deborah, Golda, and Me,* Letty Cottin Pogrebin argued that black-Jewish relationships rested on a common history of oppression. "Both blacks and Jews have known Egypt," she wrote. "Jews have known it as certain death (the killing of the firstborn, then the ovens and gas chambers). Blacks have known it as death and terror by bondage." Paul Berman agreed. "It was the past that made the blacks and the Jews almost the same," he wrote in the February 28, 1994 issue of the *New Yorker,* "and the past has the singular inconvenience of never going away." Jewish attitudes toward blacks have developed within the context of this faith in a common history and destiny. Of the many pieties of American Jewry, few have been accepted so readily and widely at face value or have been so influential as the easy assumption that blacks and Jews share vital interests arising out of what the rabbi-historian Arthur Hertzberg termed the "comradeship of excluded peoples."

The dismay of American Jews regarding the current status of black-Jewish relations arises from the presumption that blacks and Jews should stand side by side through thick and thin. "The truth is that Jews do feel different vis-à-vis the black community," Abraham Foxman, national director of the Anti-Defamation League of B'nai Brith, recently stated. "There is a history, there is a kinship, and it goes beyond the rhetoric. Look, there's never going to be a crisis in Irish-black relations or Italian-black relations, because they have no relations. But we do."

Jews have supposed that they, more than any other group, could and did empathize with the plight of blacks, and that blacks recognized this. Jewish newspapers early in the twentieth century compared the black movement out of the South to the exodus from Egypt, noted that both blacks and Jews lived in ghettos, and described anti-black riots in the South as pogroms. Even European Jews voiced compassion for the American black. *Uncle Tom's Cabin* was translated into both Yiddish and Hebrew. In his 1902 book *Old New Land,* Theodore Herzl wrote:

> There is still one other question arising out of the disaster of the nations which remains unsolved to this day, and whose profound tragedy only a Jew can comprehend. This is the African question. . . . I am not ashamed to say, though I may expose myself to ridicule in saying so, that once I have witnessed the redemption of the Jews, my people, I wish also to assist in the redemption of the Africans.

Among Jewish leaders, if not the Jewish man-in-the-street, it became an article of faith that the fates of blacks and Jews were intertwined. Jews were propelled into the civil rights movement by the belief that Jews and blacks shared the same agenda. Joel and Arthur Spingarn helped found the National Association for the Advancement of Colored People, Jack Greenberg succeeded Thurgood Marshall as head of the NAACP Legal Defense Fund, and Jewish organizations such as the American Jewish Committee, the American Jewish Congress, and the ADL were in the forefront in the campaign against racial prejudice. The financial contributions of Jews were crucial in the work of the NAACP, the Urban League, the Congress of Racial Equality, the Student Non-Violent Coordinating Committee, and other civil rights organizations. More than half of the whites who went to Mississippi in 1964 to challenge Jim Crow were Jews, and about half of the civil rights attorneys in the South during the 1960s were Jews. No white ethnic group voted more readily for blacks than did Jews. This was true in Philadelphia and Los Angeles, in Chicago and New York. Tom Bradley, Harold Washington, and David Dinkins would not have been elected the mayors of Los Angeles, Chicago, and New York City had Jews voted the same as Italians, Poles, and the Irish.

Jews have been far more interested in blacks than blacks have been interested in Jews. George Gershwin wrote *Porgy and Bess,* while Eddie Cantor and Al Jolson spent much of their stage careers in blackface. In academia there is not one black scholar, apart from Julius Lester, a convert to Judaism, whose major field of interest is Jewish studies. By contrast, many of the most prominent authorities on black history and black sociology have been Jews. One thinks immediately of Melville J. Herskovits *(The Myth of the Negro Past),* Frank Tannenbaum *(Slave and Citizen),* and Charles Silberman *(Crisis in Black and White),* among others. The field of black history in America is studded with such names as Herbert Aptheker, Ira Berlin, Philip Foner, Herbert Gutman, Lawrence W. Levine, Leon F. Litwack, Gilbert Osofsky, George Rawick, and Seth M. Scheiner. Robert W. Fogel, the cowinner of the 1993 Nobel Prize in Economics, coauthored the most controversial economic analysis of slavery, *Time on the Cross,* and Stanley Elkins wrote *Slavery: A Problem in American Institutional and Intellectual Life,* the most debated study of the impact of slavery on blacks.

The historian Peter Novick in his 1988 volume, *That Noble Dream: The "Objectivity Question" and the American Historical Profession,* noted a difference in the way that gentile and Jewish historians have approached black history. While white historians who wrote of white attitudes and behavior toward blacks — George Frederickson, Winthrop Jordan, C. Vann Woodward — were usually gentiles, those white historians who wrote of blacks as subjects were generally Jews. Jews seemingly were better able to write about blacks from the black point of view. Thus Herbert Gutman wrote a mammoth history of the black family and Lawrence Levine wrote an outstanding book on Afro-American folk culture. Nell Painter, a contemporary black historian, claimed that while most white historians wrote from a white perspective, historians such as Levine and Gutman "are able to think about history in what I'd call 'black' ways."

Jewish spokesmen emphasized that this affinity of Jews toward blacks stemmed not only from idealism but also from self-interest. Jews would benefit the more America moved toward a society of merit in which religious, ethnic, and racial barriers were unimportant. One year before the Supreme Court outlawed school segregation in the 1954 Brown decision, the Jewish Community Relations Advisory Council declared, "In a still imperfect society, Jews, together with many other groups, suffer from inequalities of opportunity and other forms of discrimination." Jewish leaders stressed the similarities rather than the differences between the Jewish and black experience in America. Both groups, they asserted, were powerless and victims of persecution. Both included in their ranks martyrs to American intolerance, Leo Frank in the case of Jews and Emmett Till in the case of blacks. The murder of James Chaney, Andrew Goodman, and Michael Schwerner in Mississippi in 1964 strengthened the presumption that the fates of blacks and Jews were intertwined.

This presumption has continued to resonate among American Jews. One curious manifestation of this was the Public Broadcasting System documentary film *Liberators: Fighting on Two Fronts in World War II.* This film and an accompanying book that appeared simultaneously described the role of black soldiers in liberating Jews from the Buchenwald and Dachau concentration camps in April 1945. The film opened on November 9, 1992, the fifty-fourth anniversary of *Kristallnacht,* at Alice Tully Hall in Lincoln Center with Jesse Jackson and other luminaries in attendance. One month later it was screened at the Apollo Theater in Harlem under the sponsorship of a group calling itself the Liberators Commemoration Committee. The screening was followed by a reception attended by black leaders, black veterans of World War II, and Holocaust survivors.

Liberators could not have appeared at a more fortuitous time for New York City politicians and black and Jewish leaders. Mayor Dinkins hoped that it would lessen tensions between blacks and Jews that had been exacerbated by the 1991 riot in Crown Heights and the refusal in October 1992 of a Brooklyn jury to convict Lemrick Nelson of the murder of Yankel Rosenbaum. Dinkins had been elected in 1989 as the city's first black mayor, and he had emphasized during the election campaign that he could best heal the city's ethnic and racial divisions. Dinkins' hope for reelection depended on support among Jewish voters, and *Liberators,* with its premise that Jews and blacks shared a common agenda, was grist for his political mill. The New York City Board of Education planned to distribute copies of the documentary to all of the city's public junior and senior high schools, and Jewish philanthropists competed for the privilege of funding the operation. They hoped that the film could help stem the tide of increasing black anti-Semitism and repair the badly frayed black-Jewish liberal coalition.

Liberators received an Academy Award nomination for best documentary even after doubts had been raised by black World War II veterans, Holocaust survivors, and Holocaust historians regarding the film's veracity. It soon became clear that black soldiers had never liberated Dachau and Buchenwald, although they had been in the vicinity. Jeffrey Goldberg, the New York bureau chief for the *Forward,* a Jewish English language weekly, blew the whistle on *Liberators.* In an essay titled "The Exaggerators," which appeared in the February 8, 1993 issue of the *New Republic,* Goldberg quoted the denials of both black soldiers and survivors that blacks had liberated Dachau and Buchenwald. The American Jewish Committee issued a fifteen-page report which concluded that *Liberators* contained "serious factual flaws well beyond what can be written off as 'artistic license.'"

The black veterans were particularly angry regarding the liberties that had been taken with the truth. "I first went to Buchenwald in 1991 with PBS," one black soldier who appeared in the film told Goldberg. The black soldiers had had an enviable record of service in Europe in 1944 and 1945, and they did not want this record sullied by fantasies which, once discredited, could bring into question their wartime performance. E. G. McConnell, one of these soldiers, said, "We had been stripped of our history in our slavery, and I didn't want to come up with anything that could tarnish our record. But apparently some other people didn't mind a few lies."

Perhaps the most interesting aspect of the controversy surrounding *Liberators* was not the deceit practiced by Nina Rosenblum, the film's Jewish cocreator, but her continuing refusal to recant even after the movie's misrepresentations had been exposed and the film and videotape had been withdrawn from circulation. She described as racists those whites who would deprive the black units of credit for liberating Dachau and Buchenwald. This she argued even though the black veterans themselves had been the first to raise doubts about the film. Rosenblum in fact described McConnell as "severely brain-damaged" due to being hit in the head with shrapnel during the war. The black veterans were not the only blacks who objected to the film. Blacks who had been involved in making the film soon realized that their artistic integrity had been compromised for the sake of Rosenblum's political and social agenda.

Rosenblum was not the only Jew unwilling to allow the minor point of historical accuracy to detract from the laudable effort to cement black-Jewish relations. If the film was not factually true, they seemed to be saying, so much the worse for truth. Peggy Tishman, one of the cohosts for the Apollo showing, asked rhetorically, "Why would anybody want to exploit the idea that this is a fraud? What we're trying to do is make New York a better place for you and me to live." The truth of the film was subsidiary to its role in reviving the black-Jewish alliance. For Jews on the left, *Liberators* was a disaster not because it was a fraud but because it encouraged those elements within the Jewish community who were skeptical of the black-Jewish alliance.

Letty Pogrebin, writing in the radical Jewish magazine *Tikkun*, feared that the controversy engendered by the film played into the hands of those political forces who sought to capitalize on black-Jewish hostility. For her, the dispute mandated a search for truth "at a level deeper than facts." "The film presents us with a problem of ethical slippage and well-intentioned embellishment," she wrote, but "not a hoax." "Truth must be defended, yes; but so must the liberal vision of Black advancement and the struggle for Black-Jewish harmony."

It is precisely because Jews have presumed that blacks and Jews have common interests that they are so disappointed by the reluctance of Jesse Jackson and other black leaders to strongly condemn the anti-Semitic rantings of Louis Farrakhan and his ilk. This disappointment stems not only from the belief that blacks have not shown the proper gratitude for all that Jews have done for them. More important is the fact that black anti-Semitism throws doubt on an important element of the identity of American Jewish liberals and radicals — the presumption that blacks and Jews comprise a community of the oppressed and that Jews are never acting more true to their religious and ethnic heritage than when they are working side by side with blacks to create a society free of racial and religious prejudice. If anything, this belief of Jews in their special relationship with blacks encourages anti-Semitism. As Arch Puddington has argued ("Black Anti-Semitism and How It Grows," *Commentary*, April 1994), anti-Semites such as Farrakhan are encouraged in their anti-Semitism "in the knowledge that Jews, unlike other whites, will react not simply with anger, but with wounded innocence and appeals for 'dialogue' and 'healing.' Abandoning the fiction of the special relationship might thus have the paradoxical effect of contributing to a reduction of racial tensions."

Black anti-Semitism, however, is simply incomprehensible to Jews who would like to believe that their own history of affliction, culminating in the Holocaust, has made them incapable of racism. This ignores the sociological and historical context within which black-Jewish relations have evolved. A curious effort along these lines was the editorial "Victims and Victimizers" that appeared in the March-April 1994 issue of *Tikkun*. It argued that the color of people's skins was determined not by pigmentation but by political correctness.

> [W]ho gets labeled "white" and who gets labeled "persons of color" derives not from the color of one's skin . . . but from the degree to which one has been a victim of Western colonialist oppression. By that measure, Jews have been the greatest victim of Western societies throughout the past two thousand years and must certainly be understood to be one of the "peoples of color." Our literature was systematically excluded from the academic canon and so deserves to be part of the multicultural corpus. And our history ought to be studied as a prime example of oppression.

For Jews on the left an entente with blacks was necessary in order to define their sense of self. This entente vindicated Jewish liberalism and encouraged a Jewish identity free of religious obscurantism. "We are all forced to confront . . . the question of what is a Jew and what does this all mean," Ellen Willis, a Jewish radical, said in 1982. "And to me the status of Jews as outsiders and as persecuted outsiders is the core of what Judaism and Jewishness is all about." It is this Jewish need for close cooperation between blacks and Jews that accounts for their strong response to the bluster of Khallid Abdul Muhammad. Catholics have every right to feel equally aggrieved, since Muhammad called the Pope a "cracker." But most Catholics have taken his comments with a pound of salt, perhaps because they don't expect much better.

Jews have continued to call for the maintenance of the black-Jewish alliance despite the socioeconomic differences between the two groups. Leonard Fein, the founder of *Moment* magazine, has been among the most eloquent spokesman for this position. In his 1988 book *Where Are We? The Inner Life of America's Jews,* Fein admitted that American Jews were no longer among the oppressed. Nevertheless, Jews should continue to identify with blacks because of "our continuing need to see ourselves among the miserable — or, at least, the still-threatened." The involvement of Jews in the civil rights movement, Fein concluded, "has helped preserve our sense of ourselves as still, and in spite of all the successes we've known, among the oppressed, hence also among the decent, the just, the virtuous." Those familiar with the history of anti-Semitism in Europe, the Middle East, and even the United States would hesitate before conflating, as does Fein, being oppressed with being decent, just, and virtuous.

Even a cursory examination of the history of black-Jewish relations in the United States reveals that they were never as warm as Pogrebin and Fein would have us believe, nor are they today as frigid as alarmists claim. If support for blacks is an ineluctable result of Jewish values, then one would expect that the most Jewish of American Jews — the Orthodox of Brooklyn — would be the most sympathetic toward blacks. The exact opposite, however, is true. Secure in their Jewish identity, they do not require close relations with blacks to define their Jewish identity. Their Jewishness rests on more substantial grounds.

One does not have to be Orthodox, however, to be wary of blacks. Norman Podhoretz's 1963 essay in *Commentary,* "My Negro Problem — and Ours," reveals how wide was the cultural gulf between immigrant Jews and their children who resided in the solidly Jewish neighborhood of Brownsville in Brooklyn and the blacks in adjacent neighborhoods. Podhoretz and his friends were simultaneously repulsed by and attracted to the superior athleticism and sexuality of the blacks, an attitude also reflected in Norman Mailer's famous essay "The White Negro."

If the most Jewish of Jews are the least receptive to blacks, Jews most alienated from Jewish culture and religion have been the most supportive of black demands. It is difficult to draw any connection between the fact that the parents of Andrew Goodman and Michael Schwerner were Jews and the fact that their children risked and ultimately lost their lives working in behalf of blacks in Mississippi. Goodman and Schwerner evidenced little attachment in their daily lives to things Jewish. Goodman's parents were radicals, and his father was president of the board of directors of the radical New York City radio station WBAI. Schwerner professed to be an atheist. It was fitting that, just as they had lived their lives remote from Jewish concerns, so neither Goodman nor Schwerner had Jewish funerals. What was true of Goodman and Schwerner was also true of many prominent Jews in the civil rights movement. The Spingarns were hardly ardent Jews. William Chafe's recent biography of Allard Lowenstein shows the extent to which Lowenstein was embarrassed by his Jewish background, as evidenced by his decision to attend the University of North Carolina rather than a northern university where there would be a sizable Jewish enrollment. Jack Greenberg did not participate in Jewish political or social affairs, and he seldom set foot in a synagogue. Indeed, it would seem that for Greenberg and Lowenstein, as well as for Howard Zinn, William Kuntsler, and others, an involvement in black causes was a surrogate identity that helped fill the vacuum in their lives stemming from their estrangement from things Jewish.

The myth of black-Jewish identity also mistook the nature of black-Jewish relations and the attitude of blacks toward Jews. It is true that in a variety of ways blacks ever since the time of slavery have modeled their lives on the Jewish experience. As indicated by black spirituals such as "Go Down, Moses," blacks drew parallels between their own situation in the South and that of the Jews in Egypt. Just as Jews escaped from slavery and, in the process, inflicted punishment on their taskmasters, so blacks anticipated flight from slavery and the chastisement of the South. The popularity of "Zion" in the names of black churches shows the extent to which the experience of the exodus resonated among blacks. Black nationalists used the Zionist movement as a model for their own back-to-Africa movement. Finally, blacks used the example of the upward social and economic mobility and bourgeois values of Jews as a model for their own people. For groups such as the Black Jews of Harlem this admiration for Jews led to syncretic religious cults containing Jewish elements.

Despite, however, what affinity they might have felt to Jews, blacks believed that there was still a vast racial gulf separating the two groups. No matter how much Jews did for blacks, in black eyes Jews were whites with all the privileges accruing to those with white skins. For blacks, the great fault line in America was not between the oppressors and the oppressed, including Jews, but between those with white skins and those with black skins. The rapid decline of American anti-Semitism after 1945 combined with the nation's continuing pervasive racism was proof to blacks, if they needed any such proof, that the condition of American Jews bore little resemblance to that of blacks.

Even during the first two decades after World War II — the supposed "golden age" of black-Jewish relations — James Baldwin, Kenneth Clark, and other blacks warned liberal Jews that their image of a close black-Jewish affinity was a fiction of their imagination, and that candor and realism were now required. As Baldwin noted in a famous statement, "Georgia has the Negro and Harlem has the Jew." Whenever the black had to pay rent to a Jewish apartment house owner, or shopped at a Jewish-owned store, or was taught by a Jewish school teacher, or was supervised by a Jewish social worker, or was paid by a Jewish employer, the fact of black subservience to Jews was driven home. The title of one of Baldwin's essays was revealing: "Blacks Are Anti-Semitic Because They're Anti-white."

The constant advice to blacks to look to the Jewish experience as a model exacerbated the problem. That advice assumed that if Jews could make it in American society then presumably so could blacks; but this assumption ignored the crucial fact that Jews were white. Furthermore, the fact of Jewish social and economic advance was painful to blacks in the face of their own less rapid progress. It was as if Jewish success was a constant insult, drawing continual attention to their own inadequacies and failures. One could hardly think of a more effective way to increase anti-Semitism among blacks than to encourage blacks to emulate Jews and to harp continually on the disparity between black and Jewish economic and social development. If Jews and blacks were really oppressed brothers, how could one account for the disparity in their social and economic conditions?

One can only imagine the impact on blacks of Eric Hoffer's comparison of blacks and Jews. The example of Jews, Hoffer wrote,

> shows what persistent striving and a passion for education can do . . . even in the teeth of discrimination. This is a fact which the Negro vehemently rejects. It sticks in his gullet. . . . The Jew impairs the authenticity of the Negro's grievances and alibis. He threatens the Negro's most precious possession: the freedom to fail.

From this perspective, the success of the Jew was a continual contradiction of the cult of victimization fostered by black spokesmen.

Blacks had a far more realistic attitude of the black-Jewish connection than did Jews, and they were not as concerned as Jews by the unraveling of the black-Jewish alliance in the 1960s and 1970s. Jews needed blacks to authenticate their image of themselves as liberals, but blacks did not need Jews to authenticate their image of themselves as blacks. They merely had to look in the mirror. "Jews interested in rebuilding coalitions," Julius Lester said, "had to get to know blacks better, had to get to know them as people instead of as liberal icons."

Blacks also realized that they were hardly the equal of Jews, and that relations between the two groups reflected this disparity in economic and social status. As much as Jews might have done for blacks, the relationship was essentially one of paternalism. A paradigm of this association was the one between Jack Benny and Rochester on the popular radio and television show of the 1940s and 1950s. As close and warm as the dealings between the two men might be portrayed, there was never any mistaking the fact that Benny was the boss and Rochester the servant.

Letty Pogrebin's dismay concerning the debate over *Liberators* derived from her fear that it could prevent a refashioning of the traditional relationship between the two groups. The furor over the film's historical accuracy, she claimed, had obscured the "deeper" truth of the film, namely, that in the past blacks had helped Jews just as Jews had helped blacks. The opponents of the film, in her view, hoped to obliterate the memory of this reciprocity. "Any such reshuffling of the power balance between our two peoples," she said, "disturbs the well-burnished narrative that for decades has reflected the Jewish self-image in warm, flattering tones."

Blacks had resented Jews not because they did not do enough for them but because they did too much. This gave rise to the joke about the man who was shocked to find himself attacked by blacks. "I haven't done anything *for* them," he responded. Harold Cruse's 1967 book, *The Crisis of the Black Intellectual,* was a revelation for its Jewish readers, indicating as it did the extent to which blacks resented Jewish involvement in black affairs. The pervasive anti-Semitism of *The Crisis of the Black Intellectual* stemmed from Cruse's bitterness over the fact that the black drive for self-determination had been deflected by Jewish radicals into causes, such as communism, that were of little relevance to black nationalism.

For decades sensitive observers warned Jews that black-Jewish relations were not what they presumed. In 1964, Rabbi Richard C. Hertz discussed the "Rising Tide of Negro-Jewish Tensions" in the black magazine *Ebony*, and two years later the sociologist Dennis Wrong prophesied that "Negro anti-Semitism is not a passing phenomenon." This prediction seemingly has come to pass. Recent polls have revealed that 63 percent of New York City's blacks believe Jews to have too much influence in the city and that blacks are twice as likely to hold anti-Semitic views as other Americans. Gary E. Rubin of the American Jewish Committee has raised serious doubts about the methodology of these polls, and he insists that they overestimate the extent of overall American anti-Semitism. Still, there seems little question that anti-Semitism is more widespread among blacks than whites. American blacks are the only major American ethnic group that has leaders who are clearly anti-Semitic.

Black anti-Semitism seems to have repealed the traditional sociological laws of anti-Semitism. Whereas for whites anti-Semitism is more prevalent among those older, less affluent, less educated, and more religious, among blacks the exact opposite is true. Within the black community there is a positive correlation between youth, schooling, income, and lack of religiosity on the one hand and anti-Semitism on the other. Yet are these results so surprising? Is it really so strange that upwardly mobile blacks would see Jews as part of an undifferentiated mass of whites bent on limiting their advancement? Is it so odd that blacks, after contrasting their economic and social status with that of Jews (or Asians), would hold ambivalent, frustrated, and resentful attitudes toward them? Nevertheless, Jews continue to assume that black anti-Semitism is irrational and transitory. Since blacks and Jews have supposedly been close in times past, black anti-Semitism appears incongruous. Hence Gary Marx's 1967 book, *Protest and Prejudice*, which discounted the presence of black anti-Semitism.

Some Jews on the left would prefer to explain away black anti-Semitism because its existence casts doubt on the myth of black-Jewish comradeship. Thus one participant in a roundtable on "Beyond Crown Heights," published in the January-February 1993 issue of *Tikkun*, asserted, "It's no surprise that we might expect a problem with anti-Semitism after twelve years of Reagan and Bush in which social inequalities have grown." Jews were forced to resort to such bizarre arguments because they consistently misunderstood the history of black-Jewish relations and the relative status of the two communities. Hillel Levine and

Lawrence Harmon's *The Death of an American Jewish Community: A Tragedy of Good Intentions* (1992) exemplifies another attempt to hold on to the black-Jewish alliance. This study of the transformation of the Jewish neighborhood of Roxbury-Dorchester-Mattapan in Boston into a black slum blamed the hostility of blacks and Jews on unscrupulous bankers, realtors, and politicians, who presumably were only too happy to pit the two groups against each other.

The problems between Jews and blacks, however, go much deeper. American Jews, whatever their problems with prejudice, never experienced anything remotely resembling the enslavement, discrimination, and racism encountered by blacks, while blacks, whatever their gains in status, never experienced the economic and social prosperity of Jews. Blacks and Jews derived different lessons from American history. "The Jewish travail occurred across the sea and America rescued him from the house of bondage," Baldwin wrote in 1967. "But America *is* the house of bondage for the Negro, and no country can rescue him." Their own experience convinced Jews that America was an open society in which education and merit would eventually win out. Hence their firm opposition to affirmative action. History, however, suggested to blacks that American society was irredeemably stacked against them and that something more than the merit principle was necessary if the legacy of three and a half centuries of racism was to be overcome.

On every possible social and economic index — and for whatever reasons — blacks have lagged far behind Jews. Jews, who comprise less than 3 percent of the American population, made up over 25 percent of the names on the most recent *Forbes* magazine list of the four hundred richest Americans. By contrast, there was only one black on the list, the entertainer Bill Cosby, even though 12 percent of Americans are black. Blacks were still waiting for one of their number to be selected to head an elite American university, while Jews had already served as presidents of Princeton, Dartmouth, Columbia, Harvard, Yale, the University of Chicago, and the University of Pennsylvania. Blacks have also lagged behind Jews in national politics. There are ten Jewish United States Senators and thirty-three members of the House of Representatives. Jews are overrepresented in the Senate by a factor of four and in the House by a factor of three. Although blacks comprise roughly 10 percent of the House of Representatives, there was in 1994 only one black Senator — Carol Mosely Braun of Illinois.

While Jews constitute an economic and social elite group within contemporary America, a significant minority of blacks comprise what sociologists call the "underclass." The disparities between Jews and blacks regarding crime, family breakdown, drug addiction, alcoholism, and educational achievements are well known. There is nothing in the American Jewish experience similar to what exists today in the inner city and what the sociologist Oscar Lewis called "the culture of poverty." Jewish criminality, such as that found on the Lower East Side of New York and in Brownsville, Brooklyn back in the 1920s and 1930s, was largely a one-generation phenomenon, as was the Jewish working class. Jewish membership in the American labor union movement is concentrated in the white collar unions of teachers, government employees, and social workers. While the major problem facing America's Jews today is maintaining Jewish identity in the midst of affluence, acculturation, and declining anti-Semitism, the major problems facing most blacks are the more immediate ones of economic survival, family breakdown, and continuing racial prejudice. If the comradeship of Jews and blacks as victims was not a mirage in times past, it certainly is one today.

Black-Jewish relations can never be on a sound footing as long as Jewish leaders remain wedded to romantic notions regarding the links between the two groups. The fact is that on a whole host of issues the interests of Jews and blacks diverge, and there is nothing unusual or surprising about this. It is demeaning to both blacks and Jews to argue that each must reflexively support the other's agenda in order to avoid antagonisms. As Michael Meyers, a black leader in New York City, recently asserted, Jews should face "the tough realities":

> It's true that Jews and Blacks have been allies, but we've also been rivals. To many Jews racial quotas are anathema, for many non-whites affirmative action must be distinguished from exclusionary quotas. We have rivalry about housing. . . . We have disagreements about how and where there are double standards in the criminal justice system.

Meyers could also have added that Jews and blacks have disagreed as well over Jesse Jackson, Israel, and multiculturalism.

Two centuries ago George Washington in his Farewell Address laid down the standards by which the United States should conduct itself with other nations. Here he warned American citizens not to take sides in European conflicts engendered by the French Revolution.

> In the execution of such a plan nothing is more essential than that permanent, inveterate antipathies against particular nations and passionate attachments for others should be excluded, and that in place of them just and amicable feelings toward all should be cultivated. The nation which indulges toward another an habitual hatred or an habitual fondness is in some degree a slave. It is a slave to its animosity or to its affection, either of which is sufficient to lead it astray from its duty and its interest. . . . Sympathy for the favorite nation, facilitating the illusion of an imaginary common interest in cases where no real common interest exists, . . . gives to ambitious, corrupted, or deluded citizens (who devote themselves to the favorite nation) facility to betray or sacrifice the interests of their own country without odium, sometimes even with popularity. . . . I hold the maxim no less applicable to public than to private affairs that honesty is always the best policy.

Washington's advice — above all that honesty is the best policy — is equally applicable to relations between blacks and Jews.

When Jews Are Christians

DAVID NOVAK

By now it is obvious that in the past twenty-five years or so there has been considerable progress in the Jewish-Christian relationship. Overcoming centuries of mutual hostility and indifference, some Jews and Christians are now able to engage in honest and fruitful dialogue and, as religious communities struggling in a larger secular society and culture, they are now able to recognize a number of overlapping interests. For Christians, this progress has required overcoming triumphalist attempts to delegitimize postbiblical Judaism. For Jews, this progress has required overcoming the assumption that Christianity is incorrigibly anti-Jewish and that all Christians are ultimately, if not immediately, anti-Semites. Progress has grown out of a healthy balance between otherness and commonality. Some Jews and Christians are now able to recognize the otherness of the other community as something to be respected rather than feared. And they are now able to recognize enough commonality in terms of common past origins, common present concerns, and common hopes for the future to enable a genuinely mutual relationship to take root and grow.

Despite this progress, a problem lies just beneath the surface. It is a problem that must be discussed if the progress we have experienced in the Jewish-Christian relationship is not to regress. The problem concerns a new type of Jewish convert to Christianity, who has of late become more visible and more vocal.

It has always been inevitable that, living as a small minority among a

Christian majority, some Jews would convert to Christianity. At certain times of great persecution, like the Inquisition, some feigned conversion, becoming "secret Jews" (e.g., the so-called "Maranos"). Faced with the alternative of death or exile, they would adopt some kind of pseudo-Christianity, which might be abandoned at the first opportunity. By a grisly irony, the Inquisition correctly assumed that such Jewish converts were not really Christians and never had been. Other Jews converted to Christianity and remained in the Church because they saw it as socially or economically advantageous. Finally, still others converted to Christianity because they sincerely believed that Christianity is the true faith. Although by Christian standards Jews who convert to Christianity for opportunistic reasons are clearly "bad" Christians, and Jews who convert to Christianity for religious reasons are clearly "good" Christians, the one thing they had in common was that they both believed themselves to be Christians and no longer Jews. Both kinds of converts believed that they had made a decisive leap from one community to another.

As far as Christianity was concerned, they had, like any other converts, indeed become members of the Church. Following Paul's assertion that "there is no such thing as Jew and Greek . . . in Christ Jesus" (Galatians 3:28), the Church refused to recognize any special status for Christians of Jewish origin in its ranks. For their part, the Jewish authorities considered converts to Christianity to be apostates *(meshumadim)* whose return to Judaism was a hope never to be abandoned, however unlikely that return might in fact be. And the Jewish converts to Christianity themselves almost always accepted the Church's definition of their new status. They no longer regarded themselves as Jews and were often quite vehement in repudiating their former identity.

Now, however, there is a new kind of Jewish Christian, one who poses an altogether new problem for both the Jewish and the Christian communities. These Jewish converts to Christianity not only claim to be Jews, they also claim still to be practicing Judaism. Some of them insist that they are indeed practicing *the* true Judaism, implying that all other Jews are practicing a false Judaism. Others merely insist that they are practicing *a* true Judaism, thus implying if not actually demanding that their practice be accepted as a legitimate form of Judaism. The vast majority of Jews refuse to accept either what might be termed the maximalist claim or even the minimalist claim of the Jewish Christians.

In relation to the Christians, the new Jewish Christians claim a special role for themselves within the Church, offering themselves as a kind of personal link between the now gentile Church and its Jewish origins. This claim often includes a demand for recognition of their right, or even obligation, to perform the ritual commandments of the Torah, from which all other Christians have been exempted by Christ (see Matthew 12:8). Some of them go so far as to refuse the name "Christian" altogether, preferring to call themselves "Messianic Jews." For even though the Greek *Christos* is no more than a translation of the Hebrew *Mashiah,* the connotation of the word has come during the course of history to mean something quite different.

The various branches of the Church have reacted variously to this new type of Jewish Christian. Yet it would seem that any formal conferral of a unique status upon them would mark the acceptance of a permanent division of Christians *de jure* into a Jewish and a gentile branch. This would, theologically speaking, pose a far greater threat to Christian ecumenism than the present *de facto* divisions within the Church — divisions, after all, that can be seen as merely temporary obstacles for Christians to overcome.

Beyond posing a special kind of problem to both the Jewish community and the Christian community, these Jewish Christians also constitute a problem to the new Jewish-Christian relationship. For the acceptance of their unique status by some Christians strongly suggests to many Jews — very much including those most favorably disposed to the new Jewish-Christian relationship — that the Jewish Christians are being held up to the rest of the Jews as exemplars. In other words, Christian recognition of their unique status strongly suggests a new form of proselytizing, specifically directed at Jews, that is quite different from a general Christian proclamation of the Gospel to the entire world. Inasmuch as the Gospel is in essence similar to the Jewish proclamation that "it shall come to pass in the end of days . . . from Zion shall the Torah go forth and the word of the Lord from Jerusalem" (Micah 4:1-2), most Jews can live with it. But proselytizing efforts that are specifically directed at Jews must be abandoned by Christians who wish to engage in any dialogical relationship with Jews. For we Jews cannot be expected to allow ourselves to be the objects of efforts designed specifically to lure us eventually, if not immediately, away from what we believe is our own true covenantal identity. In fact, those of us in the Jewish community who favor dialogue and cooperation with Christians have had to contend against certain of our fellow Jews who see the new Jewish-Christian relationship as a clever ruse designed by sophisticated Christians to take in gullible Jews. Thus Christian acceptance of the self-proclaimed Judaism of the new Jewish Christians, as opposed to accepting them simply as *any* converts are accepted, can only undermine the position of the pro-dialogue and cooperation party within the Jewish community.

Jewish rejection of the claim of the Jewish Christians that they remain part of the life and faith of the people of Israel has taken legal form in several important decisions of the State of Israel's Supreme Court. The most recent decision of the Court on that issue, in 1989, involved two Jewish Christians, Jerry and Shirley Beresford, who petitioned for Israeli citizenship as Jews under the Law of Return *(hog ha-shevut),* which guarantees immediate Israeli citizenship to every Jew. The Court rejected their petition on the grounds that the Law of Return specifically precludes from the right it confers any Jew who has affiliated with another, non-Jewish, religious community. In this decision, the Court essentially followed the precedent of the 1962 rejection of a similar petition by Oswald Rufeisen, a Jew who had become a Roman Catholic monk under the name of Brother Daniel. (The only basic difference between these two cases is that Rufeisen was clearly a member of a discernible non-Jewish community, the Roman Catholic Church, whereas it was somewhat unclear just what Christian community the Beresfords were members of.)

The Court's rejection of this petition, which is wholly consistent with the attitude of virtually all of world Jewry, has angered a number of Christians, even some who are otherwise favorably disposed to the new Jewish-Christian relationship. For does it not seem to single out Jewish Christians for rejection? Why, some of them have asked me and other Jewish friends, are Jewish Christians any less Jewish than Jewish atheists? These questions are quite understandable, and they must be addressed by thoughtful Jews, especially Jewish theologians who have been able to communicate with Christians theologically.

Being, on the whole, biblical literalists, the Jewish Christians assume that they can simply pick up where the Jewish Christians in the earliest Church left off. The Jewish Christians, especially when they designate themselves as "messianic," assume that they are that branch of the Jewish people who have accepted Jesus of Nazareth as the Messiah. In their opinion, it is merely that the rest of the Jewish people have not yet done so. Thus they see the messiahhood of Jesus as the sole point of difference between themselves and their fellow Jews. Like most biblical literalists, they choose to ignore the testimony of intervening history. But that intervening history also counts as an indispensable factor for the normative judgments of both Judaism and Christianity.

And it is intervening history that has made any simple division between messianic and non-messianic Jews inappropriate. The question of which Jews accept Jesus as the Messiah and which do not is no longer applicable. The fact is that neither Jews nor gentiles relate to Jesus as the Messiah now. Messiahhood is a political designation for a divinely restored (or, at least, divinely sanctioned) Jewish king in Jerusalem, who will gather in the exiles, establish a state governed by the Torah, and rebuild the Temple. For Christians, Jesus is different from, and a good deal more than, that; he is also believed to be divine. He is mainly acknowledged as the incarnate Son of God, the second person of the Trinity. His messiahhood, for Christians, has now been postponed to the Second Coming, when Christians believe he will rule on earth as Christ the King (see John 18:36). In Jewish belief, on the other hand, Jesus was not the Messiah precisely because he did not bring about the full restoration of the Jewish people to the Land of Israel and God's universal reign of peace.

The real issue that now separates Jews and Christians is not messiahhood but the incarnation and the Trinity. Unlike the issue of messiahhood, which arose when Jews and Christians were members of the same religio-political community and spoke the same conceptual language, the issues of the incarnation and the Trinity divide people who are no longer members of the same community and who no longer speak the same language. There is no longer any common criterion of truth available for debating, much less resolving, the fundamental differences between Judaism and Christianity.

Once the Church decided that gentile converts no longer had to undergo halakhic conversion to Judaism first (see Acts 15:8-11), it was inevitable that Jews and Christians would separate into two distinct communities. Eventually the Church condemned as "judaizing" any suggestion that Christians could practice Jewish rites in good faith, and contemporary Jewish authorities were equally disapproving of this type of syncretism. Although Christians, in their rejection of the Marcionite heresy (which attempted to sever Christianity from its roots in Judaism), still consider themselves part of the Jewish story *(aggadah)*, they do not consider themselves to be subject to Jewish law *(halakhah)*. In place of the Jewish commandments *(mitsvot)* came the sacraments, which are like the Jewish commandments in that they are structured by their own law (what became the canon law of the Church). This legal separation enabled the Church to evolve from a Jewish sect into a fully independent religious community. Gradually, many Jewish authorities came to look upon the now independent Christian Church as an essentially gentile community, but one uniquely related to Judaism because of its acceptance of Jewish Scripture as authoritative in some basic matters of faith and morals.

Today's Jewish Christians, then, are not a simple throwback to the first Jewish Christians. They can, rather, be more closely compared to the Jewish Christian syncretists of the second and third centuries. But neither normative Judaism nor normative Christianity has been willing to tolerate such syncretism. Both communities have seen it as a type of error that is inconsistent with the independence of each of them.

The important thing to remember when dealing with the issue of the Jewish Christians is that according to normative Judaism, they are still Jews. Jewish status is defined by the divine election of Israel and his descendants. One does not become a Jew by one's own volition. Even in the case of converts to Judaism (whose number is increasing today), they are not "Jews by choice," as some would erroneously call them. A gentile's choice to become a Jew is a necessary but not sufficient condition of conversion. No conversion is valid without the express consent of the convert, to be sure, but the convert's choice is not sufficient to make him or her a Jew: it only makes one a *candidate* for conversion. The actual conversion itself is the act of an authoritative Jewish tribunal who, in effect, *elect* the candidate before them, as God elects Israel and his descendants. Like God, the tribunal is under no compulsion to elect, which is to say convert, anyone.

Since Jews are elected by God, there is absolutely nothing any Jew can do to remove himself or herself from the Covenant. The rule concerning individual apostates is based on a Talmudic judgment about the Jewish people as a whole: "Even when it has sinned, Israel is still Israel" (Sanhedrin 44a). No one who accepts the authority of normative Judaism can rule that Jewish Christians are not Jews. What they can and do rule, however, is that the Christhood (incarnation/trinitarian status) of Jesus of Nazareth is not an option within God's everlasting Covenant with the people of Israel. Jewish Christians are still Jews, but they are no longer practicing a religion Jews regard as part of Judaism.

Why is Christianity not a legitimate covenantal option for Jews? There are two ways to answer the question.

One way might be termed exegetical. This had a complex development in ancient and medieval times, and it frequently reappears in modern times in encounters between Jewish fundamentalists and their Christian counterparts. Here Jews invoke Jewish Scripture because it is accepted as authoritative by Christians too as their "Old Testament." Through exegesis of commonly acknowledged Scripture, Jews have tried to show that the messiahhood of Jesus is invalid according to scriptural criteria, and that the Christian doctrines of the incarnation and the Trinity have no true foundation in Scripture at all. Of course, through their own exegesis, Christians have tried to show that the contrary position is validated by Scripture. Frequently, the most intense exegetical disputations between Jews and Christians have involved the very same Scriptural passages. Just think of how much ink has been spilled over the issue whether Isaiah 7:14 should be interpreted "behold the young woman *(ha'almah)* shall conceive and bear a son" (the Jewish version), or "behold the virgin *(he parthenos)* shall conceive and bear a son" (the Christian version). Nevertheless, one can conclude from studying the long history of these Jewish-Christian exegetical disputations that they have largely been exercises in futility, convincing only the already convinced.

The reason for the inconclusiveness of this exegetical method of argumentation is not difficult to find. Modern Jewish and Christian scholars have alike come to the understanding that Scriptural exegesis is much more a process whereby the teachings of the tradition of a religious community (what Jews call *Oral Torah* and Catholics call the *magisterium*) are *connected to* Scripture than it is one in which these teachings are simply *derived from* Scripture in some unproblematic fashion. Thus it is that Jews and Christians can read a common text so differently and therefore cannot resolve their differences by appealing to the authority of Scripture. The commonality between Judaism and Christianity can be affirmed and developed only in those areas where our respective traditions do indeed overlap. But on the whole question of who Jesus is, they do not overlap. All our divergences pale in comparison to this one fundamental difference. Many Jews — I among them — and many Christians now believe that this fundamental difference will remain until God's final redemption of the world at the end of history.

Since Jews and Christians are still *within* history rather than at its end, the best approach to the question as to why Christianity is not a legitimate covenantal option for Jews is historical rather than exegetical.

From the fact that the first generation of Christians were mostly Jewish ("according to the flesh," as Paul put it in Romans 4:1), one could argue that Christianity was *at that time* a form of Judaism, perhaps even a heterodox form of pharisaic Judaism. (There is a voluminous scholarly literature on this subject by both Christian and Jewish scholars.) However, it is clear from the historical record that in the succeeding generations, the Church became a predominantly gentile community. This was because gentile converts to Christianity were no longer required to convert to Judaism by following the halakhic prescriptions of circumcision and acceptance of all the commandments of the Torah *and Jewish tradition.* (The halakhic requirement of immersion was adapted by the Church into the requirement of Baptism.) The descendants of the original Jewish Christians quickly became gentiles themselves through intermarriage with gentile Christians in the Church.

Had the Church decided otherwise, that is, had it chosen what might be called the "halakhic" Christianity of the "pharisaic Christians" mentioned in Acts 15:5, it is conceivable that the whole Jewish-Christian relationship might well have developed altogether differently than it did. However, history cannot be erased (not, at least, by human creatures). The choice of the Church has been to be a gentile community according to the flesh — even though it sincerely claims to be grafted onto Israel according to the spirit (Romans 11:21), a point with which many Jews could basically agree. This historical choice led Jews subsequently to identify the different doctrines and practices of this now gentile community as doctrines and practices prohibited to Jews.

The refusal of the Supreme Court of the State of Israel in 1989 to grant Jerry and Shirley Beresford Israeli citizenship *as Jews,* and its insistence that they could become Israeli citizens only *as Christians* (who are eligible for Israeli citizenship, too), is the decision of a secular court in a secular state. Nevertheless, there were two opinions in the case. In practice, both opinions ruled against the petition of the Beresfords as the

Court had ruled against the petition of Brother Daniel in 1962. But in theory, the two opinions are quite distinct. This distinction has important theological implications.

The minority opinion based its conclusion on what might be called "ordinary language" criteria, that is, the theory that says that the meaning of terms is determined by the way they are currently used in ordinary conversation, not by the way they are defined in learned texts. By this criterion, the minority opinion based itself on the fact that in ordinary language Jews and Christians are considered to be two separate groups, that one cannot simultaneously be a member of both communities. If one were to ask the proverbial "man in the street" if a Christian could also be a Jew, or a Jew also a Christian, the answer would surely be a simple "no."

The Court's majority opinion, on the other hand, did base itself on Jewish tradition, "following the language of the Torah, not the ordinary language of humans," as the Talmud puts it. The exclusion of the Beresfords from Jewish status in the State of Israel is based on the traditional power of the authorities of the Jewish community to exclude those considered apostates from many of the privileges of the community. Thus, for example, apostates are to be excluded from the privilege of being called to the reading of the Torah in the synagogue, or even from being counted in the quorum of ten *(minyan)* required for a full synagogue service to be conducted. The apostate is still a Jew; no human court can change that fact. But the apostate is excluded from communion with the normative Jewish community *(keneset yisrael).*

I purposely use the term "communion" because Christians, especially Catholic Christians, can recognize the same process in "excommunication." Since Catholics regard baptism to be indelible, no one is ever totally removed from the body of the Church. Excommunication means that because of serious mortal sin — such as apostasy — someone is not allowed the privilege of receiving communion, that is, participating in the eucharist. Proper repentance can lead to the removal of the ban of excommunication. No doubt a Catholic who converted to Judaism would be subject to such excommunication. This does not mean that the Church is denying its roots in Judaism. It simply means that it does not regard Judaism to be a legitimate type of Christianity, a point with which very few Jews would disagree. Similarly, regarding the Jewish convert to Christianity as an apostate does not mean that Judaism is denying that Christianity is uniquely connected to it. It simply means that it does not regard Christianity to be a legitimate type of Judaism, but rather regards it as an independent religious community in its own right, a point with which very few Christians would disagree.

The question of why Jewish authorities are harder on Jewish Christians than on Jewish atheists is one that Jewish theologians must answer. Christian anger about what might appear to be a double standard would otherwise be entirely understandable.

In a purely religious context, such as a synagogue service, for example, a professed Jewish atheist has no more right to be a participant than a professed Christian. By "participant" I mean one capable of being counted in the quorum of ten and being called to the reading of the Torah. Anyone, of course, may attend a synagogue service. Anyone may attend a church service, but not everyone may receive communion. Practically speaking, there is little likelihood that a professed Jewish atheist of any moral integrity would want to participate in a *religious* service. Until quite recently, there was equally little likelihood that a professed Christian, of whatever origins, would want to participate in a *Jewish* religious service. At present, however, there are certain Jewish Christians who regard themselves as Jews — even religious Jews — who do want to participate in Jewish religious services. Whereas Jewish atheists do not regard their atheism as a Jewish *religious* option, some Jewish Christians do regard their Christianity as such an option. Since there is a greater possibility for confusion regarding Jewish Christians than Jewish atheists, Jewish authorities have to be harder on Jewish Christians. Considering the claim of many Christians throughout history to be the "true Israel" *(verus Israel)* — a claim made by no other religious community — strong Jewish reaction to Jewish Christians who seem to be repeating that claim, one so offensive to Jews, should come as no real surprise.

Another reason why Jewish Christians are to be treated more severely than Jewish atheists is that, despite all their protestations to the contrary, Jewish Christians have joined *another,* non-Jewish, community, and Jewish atheists have not. (A distinction has to be made here between doctrinaire Jewish atheists and the many secularized Jews who may not act on, but nevertheless have not explicitly renounced, Jewish religious belief and practice.) This basic point was an integral part of the Israeli Supreme Court's decision to deny the Beresfords citizenship as Jews. Here again, historical experience as much as theological-legal definition played a key role. For non-fundamentalists, moreover, history and theology and law are integrally related.

Jewish Christians, then, pose unique problems of one kind for Judaism and unique problems of another for the Church. In addition, they pose problems for the cause of a new, improved Jewish-Christian relationship. I am not asking Christians to reject them, or even to question the sincerity of their belief that their form of Jewish Christianity is not a figment of their imaginations. (For this reason, I did not see it to be my business as a Jew to join some other Jews who protested Pope John Paul II's beatification of the Jewish Christian Edith Stein. When the Church accepted Edith Stein as a convert, she became a member of its religious community. I mourn her death along with the deaths of all the victims of Nazi idolatry, Jewish or gentile.) But as one who has worked long and hard for the progress of this new, improved relationship — especially on the theological level — I do ask Christians to regard the Jewish Christians who claim to be practicing Judaism as an exception rather than the rule. To see them as a unique link between the Jewish people and the Church, and to expect faithful Jews to concur in that judgment, asks too much of us.

In our open society, there are going to be Jews who become Christians for religious reasons just as there are going to be Christians who become Jews for religious reasons. But these great existential decisions are not meant to be cost-free. In any religious conversion, something is gained and something lost (see Yevamot 47a-b; Matthew 10:34-39). I believe at the end of time God will show each one of us whether the gain or the loss is greater in the ways we chose to listen to His voice.

Those Troublesome Messianic Jews

ISAAC C. ROTTENBERG

When it comes to Christian-Jewish relations, particularly Christian-Jewish dialogue, the most sensitive issues of all, of course, are those of mission and conversion. Thus those of us Christians who are seriously engaged in such dialogue need to be particularly sensitive about conduct on our part that could even remotely be interpreted as being missionary in nature.

At the same time, the question as to what constitutes "authentic Christian witness," particularly vis-à-vis our Jewish interlocutors, is as unavoidable as it is unresolved for us. From time to time assemblies of major denominations, in the course of discussing pronouncements about Christian attitudes toward Jews, have come close to concluding that Jews ought to be exempted from any Christian outreach. In the end, however, it would seem that the imperatives of the gospel prohibited them from going so far: the missionary mandate was maintained, albeit — practically speaking — in a state of dormancy.

Dr. Michael Kogan, writing in the *National Dialogue Newsletter* (Winter 1990-91), proposed that we move toward something called "total dialogue," that is, risk the vulnerability of "expos[ing] one's own community's beliefs to influence by the other in a mutual enrichment process." This proposal has inevitably evoked a good deal of debate, raising once again as it does the issues of conversion and mission. Invited by the editor of the newsletter to contribute a few observations on the idea of "total dialogue," I myself decided to up Dr. Kogan's ante

103

by adding a further complication: "To exclude from the dialogue *as a class*," I declared, "all Jews who confess Jesus as Messiah in the Christian sense is wrong, as wrong as any other violation of people's conscience." My comment was accompanied by an editorial stating that such a position would lead to the "overnight destruction of dialogue," because people like Jews for Jesus insist on engaging in proselytizing activities toward their own people.

By coincidence, just around the same time, David Novak's article "When Jews Are Christians" appeared. In it, Novak warned that the progress made in Jewish-Christian relationships could be jeopardized because of a "new type of Jewish convert to Christianity," namely, one who claims to remain a Jew while accepting Jesus as the Messiah of Israel and the Savior of the world. Arguing that the views of Messianic Jews are a problem to both the Jewish and the Christian communities, the author pointed out that a sympathetic hearing for these views on the part of church leaders could well cause difficulties for those Jews who have precisely been the strongest supporters of Christian-Jewish dialogue.

The complexities involved in this situation — theological, historical, and psychological — are clearly immense and may not be possible to overcome. In addition, there is often no common language in which to discuss the problem. Take, for instance, the terms "a follower of Jesus" and "a convert to Christianity." Some Jewish Christians accept the former designation, but assiduously avoid the latter because to them it seems to imply that they embrace all of historic "Christendom." By focusing on Jesus, they can retain a critical stance toward much that goes by the name of "Christianity."

There is also the question as to whether a Messianic Jew is by definition someone who confesses Jesus as Messiah. Some Jewish Christians do not wish to define themselves in those terms; they are content to be known as Christians, period. But what if those same people still claim to remain Jews? Such is clearly the position of Aaron Jean-Marie Lustiger, archbishop of Paris. In his book *Dare to Believe* (1986), he is reluctant to discuss his decision to be baptized in the Catholic Church — out of a desire to avoid provocation. However, when pushed by reporters, he is most emphatic about his conviction that he has not ceased to be a Jew. "I am discovering another way of being Jewish," he reports having told his parents, because to him Christianity is "a natural extension of Judaism."

If the status of Cardinal Lustiger presents a problem to Jews, even more problematic, not only to Jews but to many Christians as well, is what could be called "the organized Messianic Jewish community" — Jewish Christians who form separate Messianic congregations, observe the Jewish Sabbath, continue many Jewish practices and celebrate certain Jewish festivals. Such congregations have also organized themselves into national and international networks, such as the Messianic Jewish Alliance of America (MJAA), the Union of Messianic Jewish Congregations (UMJC), the Messianic Jewish Movement International, etc. Then there is Jews for Jesus, a separate organization with its own agenda and constituency. The same is true of various Hebrew-Christian mission societies. A monthly, *The Messianic Times,* reports on items of interest to all these groups. As an increasingly organized community with a strong missionary thrust, such groups are sometimes viewed as a major threat to Jewish-Christian rapprochement.

There have been periods in history when the problem of Christianity for Jews was very much focused on Jesus. He, as the central figure of the Christian faith, became the great symbol of all the evil that had been perpetrated against Jews in his name. It was not uncommon for pious Jews to spit in disgust at the mere mention of that name.

Much has changed in this respect. Jesus, as a Jew who was faithful to Torah, has become a figure with whom many Jews have become quite comfortable. He is seen as "one of ours." As a matter of fact, many students today are gaining profound insights into Jesus through the large and rich body of literature on the subject by Jewish authors. The line, to be sure, is drawn at the Christian belief in Jesus as Son of God.

As it is on the question of conversion. It is always difficult for faith communities to see one of their own convert to another religion. But a Jew converting to Christianity has often been experienced by Jews as particularly painful. Not only has the Jewish community historically had a profound sense of peoplehood, but it has also been a minority community regularly subjected to persecutions in which, one way or another, Christians have played a part. So in the case of a conversion there has not only been a painful sense of loss to the community, but a bitter sense of betrayal as well. Moreover, the fact that expediency sometimes played a role in a Jew's decision to convert didn't make things any easier. Assimilated Jews were usually despised because they tried so desperately to be just like gentiles.

Today, the Jewish community is confronted with a very different kind of conversion problem, namely that of converts who, having embraced Christianity, seem to feel a greater need than before to accentuate their Jewishness, sometimes even to the point of Judaizing their names. In many cases these people are well-educated members of the yuppie generation, determined to raise their children as Christians with a strong sense of Jewish identity. They appear to want to flaunt what assimilated Jews of previous generations often sought to hide.

Ironically, it is precisely their desire to retain a Jewish identity and to maintain certain aspects of the tradition of their forebears that often is turned against them, leading to accusations that all this is a ploy, part of a covert and deceptive missionary strategy whereby they seek to seduce other Jews to forsake their faith as well. For centuries the Jewish community has had to struggle to maintain its faith in the midst of an often hostile gentile world or in the face of the Church's missionary efforts. But the movement of Messianic Jews must look to many like a fifth-column assault.

Permit me here to introduce my own experience, which has offered me a very special vantage point from which to view some of the perplexities of this most perplexing issue. My wife and I both grew up in Dutch Reformed homes. Our fathers were not only committed church members, but professional workers. Our youthful experiences in life were by and large typical of Dutch Reformed children in the Netherlands, even though my grandfather was a Hasidic rabbi in Poland and my father a convert to Christianity, while her father had been a socialist activist in that same country who had also converted. We were never really part of the Jewish experience, until the Nazis made us so.

Hitler and his cohorts reminded us constantly about "the blood in our veins." They made us part of one of the most traumatic experiences in all of Jewish history. My father was arrested as a Jew who had written books critical of Nazism and, after spending some time in Buchenwald, was murdered in Mauthausen. When Jewish children put on a show for International Red Cross executives who came to inspect Adolf Eichmann's "Paradeise ghetto" Terezin (Theresienstadt), my wife was there and her younger sisters were part of the group that so famously performed "The Tales of the Vienna Woods." So you might say some experience of "Jewishness" had come into both our lives, almost in spite of our upbringing — and along with it, a sense of ambiguity about being at the same time part of a people's history but basically still "outsiders."

We have never talked much about these experiences, certainly not among the wide circle of our Jewish friends and acquaintances. Not only would it somehow seem an intrusion, but we have no desire, either, to join the ever growing band of Christian Holocaust specialists. Thus it has been granted us to live and work at the borderline of the Jewish experience and the Christian encounter with that experience.

This will explain the impulse behind my comment to the *National Dialogue Newsletter.* I have come to feel increasingly uneasy about a certain current tendency to characterize converts from Judaism as people of questionable integrity.

None will deny that the greater the fervor to convert others, the stronger may be the temptation to engage in questionable missionary tactics. Nor can serious Christians oppose the idea that there should be a constant critical evaluation of Christian evangelistic methods and practices. Converts (to almost any kind of movement) tend to be highly aggressive in their attempts to persuade others. The prophetic-apostolic witness too knows of an inner imperative to speak, a mandate to proclaim. "If I say, 'I will not mention him, or speak anymore in his name,' there is in my heart as it were a burning fire shut up in my bones, and I am weary with holding it in, and I cannot" (Jeremiah 20:9). "Necessity is laid upon me. Woe to me if I do not preach the gospel" (I Corinthians 9:16). Sometimes it can be a bit uncomfortable to be confronted by a zealous convert.

Certainly all of us must be prepared to listen to the critiques of other faith communities, and especially those of our Jewish brothers and sisters. But critical analysis also requires that we avoid quick and easy answers, particularly if they are motivated more by feelings of guilt about past sins than by faith commitments.

In this connection, the word "proselytizing" ought to be used with some care. It tends to be applied in an indiscriminate fashion, and not seldom with an implied negative connotation, so that by simply stating that someone engages in proselytism, one can implicitly be making a moral judgment.

Historically, the word "proselytism" did not necessarily carry such baggage. Highly respected Jewish scholars like Dr. Bernard Bamberger (*Proselytism in the Talmudic Period,* 1939) and Dr. William C. Braude

(*Jewish Proselytizing in the First Five Centuries of the Common Era,* 1940) have used the term quite unapologetically. Building on their research, Rabbi Ely E. Pilchik felt that he was in the spirit of ancient Jewish tradition when he wrote the following — to many, no doubt controversial — sentences: "We need numbers. We need more Jews lest we wither and disappear. We need proselytes. We need to win over Christians, Moslems, Hindus, Shintos, and other 'goyim' to Judaism" (*The Jewish Week,* December 24, 1981). This was not meant as a Christmas Eve threat; it was meant as a call to righteousness and concern about the future of the Jewish people in the post-Holocaust era.

Still, in the minds of many, proselytizing has become a code word for unethical missionary practices, implying coercion, deceit, and even bribery. The Catholic scholar Tommaso Federici, in an important 1978 address, defined rather carefully what he meant by the word, namely "attitudes and activities engaged in outside Christian witness . . . anything which infringes or violates the right of every person or community not to be subjected to external or internal constraints in religious matter. . . ." Judged by such a standard, it becomes a bit more difficult to object to any kind of evangelization as unethical.

David Novak, in the aforementioned article, does not confine himself to quick brush-offs with terms like "proselytism" or "deception" as he presents his case for why Messianic Jews could pose a threat to the future of Jewish-Christian dialogue. Rather, he offers a theological analysis in order to explain why these people, although according to normative Judaism still to be considered Jews, are not justified in making their claims. Today's Messianic Jews, says Professor Novak, should be compared to the (heretical) "syncretists of the second and third centuries," not to the first Jewish Christians (with whom they often compare themselves). At one time it may have been plausible to view Christianity as a form of Judaism, runs this argument, but a long and eventful history, including the history of Christian doctrinal formulations (e.g., "Jesus as the incarnate Son of God, the second person of the Trinity"), makes that now impossible.

Novak is concerned that churches might come to accept the self-definition of Messianic Jews, which in turn would arouse the suspicion among the Jewish partners in dialogue that their Christian counterparts silently condone a new form of proselytizing aimed specifically at Jews. Thus the mission/witness issue which, at least in the "mainline" churches, had been largely but not entirely dormant, is once again moved to the forefront of Christian-Jewish relations.

One statement in Novak's article is particularly striking. He points out that, according to the Pauline principle "in Christ there is no Jew or Greek," the Church has expected Jews to become what could be called "regular members," just like all the other members. As a matter of fact, he then adds, Jewish converts to Christianity themselves almost always "accepted the Church's definition of their new status. They no longer regarded themselves as Jews and were often quite vehement in repudiating their former identity."

Here we remind ourselves that in the Middle Ages it was quite common for church authorities to force Jews to publicly renounce their heritage before accepting them into the Church. We know the formula: "I do here and now renounce every rite and observance of the Jewish religion, detesting all its solemn ceremonies and tenets that in former days I kept and held." In short, a "good convert" was one who had totally abandoned his/her Jewish identity.

But in more recent times it has become recognized in Christian circles, missionary circles in particular, that our blindness to the need for contextualization of the gospel has been one of the biggest mistakes the Church has made in its worldwide outreach. The Christian message must be incorporated into the life and culture of the peoples to whom it is addressed, be it in Africa, Asia, or wherever. It has now become clear that the approach followed previously was unfortunately tainted by a certain ecclesiastical imperialism. A "good convert" was often portrayed as a person well acculturated to our Western ways. Missionary success stories were frequently about "native" evangelists who acted, talked, and even dressed like British Methodists or American Southern Baptists. Jews too were usually most welcome if they adjusted to our churchly ways.

Today the situation is quite different. The need for contextualization is widely recognized, and consequently the development of ethnically oriented churches is not only condoned, but actively encouraged. Even in the United States we see a growing number of Korean Presbyterian churches, Reformed Taiwanese churches, and the like. Each of these Christian communities is recognized as being unique in its own way, and yet all are seen as part of the one Body of the Church.

As it happens, discussions about the preservation of Jewish identity within the Church and the pros and cons of establishing separate He-brew-Christian congregations have been going on for many years now. In the rather extensive body of literature produced by Jewish converts to Christianity one finds all sorts of questions raised, including questions about the early formulations of Christian doctrine. As the U.S. Catholic bishops pointed out in one of their pronouncements, a process of de-Judaization of the Christian faith started very early in its history. Ele-ments of the Hellenistic thought world were introduced, and in many cases Christian theological expression became quite dependent on Greek metaphysical categories.

We know why this happened and how it helped communicate the gospel to the Greco-Roman world. But we also know that the process of de-Judaization eventually became a handy tool in the hands of those who advocated an anti-Judaic theology. After all, the biblical revelation came to humanity in Hebrew context; in order to learn to "spell the Name," it is important that one be able to enter into Hebrew thought. Yet for many Jewish converts the Christian theological climate never seemed very hospitable, nor have they always felt "at home" in our local congregations.

The Church for its part has its own difficulties with trying to deter-mine what constitutes an "authentic witness" vis-à-vis Jewish neigh-bors. Jews as Jews are not outside the orbit of revelation. Quite the con-trary, they are the people of the covenant in whose midst the God of Abraham, Isaac, and Jacob made himself known and revealed his Name. A growing number of denominations have confessed that they were wrong when, over a long history, they taught a replacement form of the-ology and contributed to the sufferings of the Jewish people. In light of that history, it is no wonder that many church leaders are inclined to pause before proposing ambitious missionary schemes. In the words of Professor Krister Stendahl, they tend to hold "the missionary urge to convert Israel . . . in check." For most of them, however, this whole situa-tion is experienced as a dilemma, because, with few exceptions, these church leaders also agree with someone like Professor Gabriel Fackre who, in a commentary on the 1987 United Church of Christ document on the Church and the Jewish people, declared quite unequivocally: "Antisupersessionism does not forbid sharing the Gospel with Jewish people." The question is, how do we do that, while honoring the contin-uing covenant of God with Israel?

The apostle Paul was not yet burdened by the history that so heavily weighs upon the churches. But in his missionary outreach he faced some of the same questions that we must confront today. For instance, he never lost sight of the distinction between those who know Torah and those who do not, even when he argued their equal status before God . . . as people in need of forgiveness. Jews and gentiles live in a different thought-world; they raise different questions, because they do not share the same expectations. Take, for instance, a passage like I Corinthians 1:18-31: "Jews demand signs and Greeks seek wisdom, but we preach Christ crucified. . . ." Jews know Torah. Their expectations about future redemption have always been closely related to historical reality. They want to know where the empirical evidence is to be found that the Messianic age has been inaugurated. How can the message of Christ crucified reveal the power of the Kingdom? Hence the challenge to preach the gospel in such a way that it does not preclude a theology of history and culture. The New Testament does that by emphasizing the cosmic dimensions of a biblical Christology.

The Greeks, on the other hand, seek wisdom. Their fundamental vision is one of world harmony. Hence, the message of the cross seemed, from the perspective of their philosophical presuppositions, a rather foolish idea.

But in terms of guilt before God, Paul sees both Jews and gentiles in need of the same grace. Similar ideas can be found in other passages. Romans 1:18–2:29 is an example. Those who are outside the orbit of revelation of the God of Israel, who do not know Torah, are tempted to deify the cosmos. Instead of glorifying God, who has revealed himself as Creator, they tend to worship their own images (1:23). Jews know better. But, as Paul sees it, they too are without excuse (2:1), because their actions do not conform to the demands of the law, and hence they stand guilty before God and are in need of redemption. So, in the end Paul finds the answer for the predicament of both Jew and gentile in Christ's fulfillment of the law, an obedience he interprets as an act of redemption.

Still, he is deeply aware of the dangers that loom on the horizon as soon as the Church loses sight of the mystery of the calling of Israel, a theme he develops in the much discussed chapters Romans 9–11. Triumphalism takes over; the branches that have become ingrafted into the tree of God's covenant with the people of Israel forget that they do not support the root; the root supports them (11:18).

Paul could hardly have imagined how his fears would play out on the stage of subsequent history. Now, almost 2,000 years later we know what that kind of triumphalism has led to. To the inherent offense of the cross were added offenses that were rooted in the sins of the churches. And so for many Jews the thought of any Christian witness directed at them is scandalous. The late Rabbi Pinchas Peli raised a protest against missionary activities that was both sharp and direct: "What they are doing is something that cannot be pardoned, cannot be forgiven, especially in Israel, especially after the Holocaust. We have not yet settled our account with Christianity as it is. One doesn't need to add insult to injury, and try to take us away from our religion." And so we live in the tension field between our own *peccavi* and the gospel imperative to witness to all humankind. The missionary mandate is not denied, but in practice the issue is often surrounded by an embarrassed silence.

Enter the Messianic Jews, filled with the missionary elan of new converts, more than vocal in spreading the word about their new-found faith in Jesus, sometimes even taking out full-page advertisements in major newspapers. No closet Christians they. They do not see themselves as "targeting" a special group "out there" for their witness, because for them the confrontation normally starts among their immediate family, relatives, and friends, and then spreads through the broader community of which they still feel themselves a part, albeit perhaps in a state of estrangement.

How to respond to these realities? David Novak undoubtedly speaks for the great majority of Jews when he writes that Christians cannot expect them to accept any notion that Messianic Jews might serve as "a unique link between the Jewish people and the Church." However, from the Christian point of view it could well be argued that the idea of such a link ought to be explored. If Hebrew-Christians were to introduce a more Hebraic mode of thinking into our often Hellenized ways of doing theology, the Church could benefit greatly. For decades we have been struggling to develop a prophetic-messianic vision, an eschatology that includes both expectancy and social responsibility, that would help us break out of our sterile either-or theological constructions and ideological preoccupations.

In our search for a vision of the future, we have traveled from fad to fad; from ahistorical existentialist theologies to theologies of revolution; from post-Christian celebrations of the secular city to the establishment of peace, justice, and liberation bureaucracies that are ever itching to be prophetic if denominations will provide secure financial support, even in some cases to the point of assessing (i.e., taxing) their membership for the "service." The churches desperately need a theology of the Kingdom of God that incorporates the broad historical and cosmic themes of the Hebrew Scriptures and apostolic writings.

Can Messianic Jews serve as a link in such matters? Potentially, I would say, "yes." Still, as of now there seems to be little reason to be optimistic on that point. In many instances their thinking seems to be permeated by Christian other-worldliness. Much of their piety is imbued with a "precious Jesus" Messianism that lacks a broad historical vision. The type of fundamentalism that many Messianic Jews have embraced has much to say about the soul (often in very Hellenistic terms), spiritualizing the gospel message so as to virtually empty it of its social-political implications. In short, to me all this sounds too much like more of the un-Hebraic dualistic mode of thinking which the Church needs to overcome. Furthermore, when a historical perspective is presented, it is often so charged with the hype found among some of the television prophecy preachers that a calm discussion of biblical theology becomes almost impossible.

Still, isolation without conversation cannot be the answer. Messianic Jews are part of the Church, a fellowship in which many differences co-exist within a community of common faith. Potentially they have something important to contribute to the whole Church. Nobody's interest is served by pushing them to become an increasingly sectarian movement. True, some of their present isolation may well be self-imposed. Perhaps there is an element of clannishness involved. Honesty, however, demands that we look deeper than that. The fact that these people often see themselves as "twice exiled," rejected by their old home and not entirely welcome in their new one, requires our serious consideration.

Among evangelicals, who by and large do not experience mission, including mission to Jews, as much of a dilemma, one finds a measure of openness toward Messianic Jews. Since the evangelicals' dialogue with the Jewish community is less developed than that of the Christian "mainstream," they also feel less pressure to protect contacts that have been cultivated over a long period of time.

Still, evangelicals who are strong supporters of the State of Israel, even though they may have positive personal feelings toward Messianic

Jews, are often inclined to tone down on their churches' mission theology and to keep cautiously quiet about any contacts they may have with them. The reason is quite simple: they are eager to maintain their close ties with Jewish leaders, both here and in Israel. Consequently, they are caught between conflicting loves and loyalties.

All in all one senses a good deal of ambivalence in the evangelical community at large about the Messianic Jewish movement. Theologically there may be a feeling of kinship, but on the level of community life, there often is a hesitation about the otherness of the other. If dialogue is based on I-thou relationships rather than the absorption of one party into the other, if dialogue means expectant openness to mutual transformation, then it would seem that the evangelical and Messianic Jewish movements have a long way to go.

The "mainline" Christian-Jewish dialogue movement is quite another story. Some of the leading theologians in those circles tend to see a closer link between their faith and traditional Judaism than between them and Messianic Jews. Of course, they also have made a greater effort to develop contacts and exchange views with the Jewish community. Messianic Jews usually are seen as a disturbing, even threatening, element in the mix of Christian-Jewish relations, and hence they frequently evoke feelings of hostility.

Participants in the "mainstream" dialogue have reached a virtual consensus that no true dialogue is possible with anyone who may give even the slightest indication of believing that the answer to life's mysteries in the final analysis is to be found in his/her religious tradition. That, they say, is the true mark of triumphalism and means the death of dialogue. Nevertheless, these same people express a desire to reach out to Islam, even though there is no reason to believe that Jewish-Christian-Muslim conversations presently can be conducted on the basis of a "theology of equality."

No doubt, truth claims can complicate dialogue, but do they necessarily lead to the death of dialogue? All forms of ecumenical and interfaith dialogue were born when, in a general atmosphere of polemics and antithetical positions, some pioneers persisted in listening to each other even though their differences seemed insuperable. On the other hand, the death of dialogue may well be caused by indifference about fundamental beliefs that historically have been seen as touching on people's eternal destiny.

At the moment we are facing a stand-off. Some of our Jewish partners want the issue of Messianic Jews on the agenda under the category of a "threat to dialogue." Some Christian advocates of improved relations with the Jewish community, for a variety of reasons, find avoidance (if not rejection) of Messianic Jews an acceptable position, at least until the latter tone down their enthusiasm to share their new-found faith with others. Messianic Jews themselves, while often eager to portray themselves as potentially a creative link between Judaism and the Christian faith, may — also for a variety of reasons — prefer to make those claims "from a distance," i.e., without making a real effort to contribute to a climate in which such issues can be explored. So, we end up with the worst of all possible dialogical worlds. All the parties seem stuck in their own peculiar fundamentalism.

Where will new incentives come from? The history of religious bodies shows that new initiatives usually come from pioneers who are prepared to probe the boundaries of establishment positions and establishment politics (including the politics of dialogue), people who are ready to take the risk of utilizing all the valuable lessons that have been learned during the past decades of interfaith encounters.

Issues raised by Messianic Jews today have deep roots in church history, going back to apostolic times. They deserve to be discussed, rather than summarily dismissed as mere repetitions of ancient heresies. Christians engaged in conversations with Messianic Jews ought not to be considered a threat to the ongoing Christian-Jewish dialogue, unless they say and/or do things that clearly are inimical to the integrity of interfaith relationships. Whether or not this is the case ought not be determined exclusively in terms of the politics of dialogue, but also, or perhaps, even more so in terms of the moral-spiritual values embedded in our faith.

Religious communities recognize a variety of callings. This is also the case within the context of interfaith dialogue. What we do not need are adversarial postures between people who feel called to explore different areas of dialogue. Maintaining links to both the Jewish and the Messianic communities will require a considerable dose of graceful sensitivity as well as a bit of political savvy. Only Christians who have honestly and humbly confronted the history of the Christian-Jewish experience should apply.

Dialogue, by its very nature, is an open process, always prepared to respond to new challenges. All new venture in ecumenical and interfaith endeavors tend to start out as impossible dreams. The status quo never is good enough, least of all to those who have had long practice in the often painful process of dialogue and have tasted its fruits.

Jews and Catholics: Beyond Apologies

DAVID NOVAK

Something very significant has happened to Jewish-Christian relations, especially Jewish-Catholic relations. In March 1998, the Vatican issued the statement "We Remember: A Reflection on the Shoah," which was prepared under the direction of Edward Idris Cardinal Cassidy, president of the Church's Commission for Religious Relations with the Jews, and introduced by Pope John Paul II himself (see *First Things,* May 1998). The document received wide publicity and stirred up a good deal of controversy. My purpose here is to provide a Jewish reaction to the overall argument of this important document, to express agreement with most of it, but also to point out what I take to be some problems within it.

I first came to Jewish-Catholic relations in 1963, while studying for the rabbinate at the Jewish Theological Seminary in New York. I became a student — indeed, a close disciple — of the man who to the mind of many was the most important Jewish theologian to work in America, Abraham Joshua Heschel. At that time, Professor Heschel was engaged in serious discussions with the leadership of the Catholic Church, especially with the late Augustin Cardinal Bea, in preparation for the Second Vatican Council. In 1965, the Council issued the landmark declaration *Nostra Aetate* ("In Our Time"), which outlined the Church's view of Judaism and the Jewish people, undoubtedly the most significant such statement in modern times. I remember how hopeful my teacher was for this new attitude that was emerging in the Church, and the tremendous chance he was taking in becoming the chief Jewish advisor to the Church in this enterprise. Cardinal Bea and Pope Paul VI were also taking a chance, and for similar reasons. Professor Heschel was subjected to harsh criticism — public and private — by a number of Jewish scholars for assuming that a new relationship was even possible with the Catholic Church. And the leaders of the Church received criticism from those who wondered, since the Jewish people had rejected Jesus as the Messiah, what kind of positive relationship there could be with them.

We are all the beneficiaries of those chances taken more than thirty years ago. Anyone who has watched what has happened from then until now cannot help but marvel at how far we have moved from suspicion to a level much deeper, beyond just good will and tolerance. But the whole Western world and the Jewish people in particular still live very much in the shadow of the Holocaust, the systematic program of mass extermination that resulted in the murder of six million Jews. The question must thus be raised on both sides: Just what role in that tragedy did the Catholic Church play? Until we engage in the most searching discussion of this question, we may very well be at an impasse in this new relationship. The recent statement of the Vatican is certainly a major step in that direction.

With few exceptions, the reaction of the Jewish leaders who have access to the media was negative. The *New York Times* (which although not an "official" Jewish publication certainly reflects and indeed influences a certain type of American Jewish opinion) editorially branded the Vatican statement a whitewash, a rationalization of the conduct of the Church during the Holocaust. The Anti-Defamation League of B'nai B'rith expressed much the same disappointment. This view is not unanimous in the Jewish community. Rabbi James Rudin, who heads the department of the American Jewish Committee that deals with Jewish-Christian relations, issued a much more positive and hopeful response. However, Rudin's reaction seems to be a minority voice, at least so far.

What is the reason for this Jewish criticism? After all, the statement did condemn the Holocaust, it did condemn anti-Semitism, and it even spoke of "the sinful behavior" of certain members of the Church. Shouldn't Jews be happy to hear all this from the Vatican? Isn't this an important way of putting the Holocaust in the kind of perspective that enables us to get on with our lives, not by forgetting but by remembering? My own view is that the Jewish response is largely mistaken, and that it reflects a misunderstanding not only of Catholic theology but of Jewish theology as well. The Jewish leaders' reactions were not just uncharitable, they were also unjust.

The part of the Vatican statement that elicited the most negative Jewish response was a quotation from a speech first made by John Paul II in Rome on October 31, 1997. "In the Christian world — I do not say on the part of the Church as such — erroneous and unjust interpretations of the New Testament regarding the Jewish people and their alleged culpability have circulated for too long, engendering feelings of hostility toward this people." It is ironic that the Pope should be the focus of criticism, inasmuch as there has been no other pontiff in modern times, perhaps in all history, who has done more to develop rapprochement with the Jewish people and Judaism. Karol Wojtyla as a philosopher and a theologian has been deeply interested in the connection between Judaism and the teaching of the Catholic Church for most of his life. Furthermore, Karol Wojtyla has been intimately related to Jews all of his life, beginning with his childhood in Poland, where Jews were among his closest associates. Indeed, the Pope speaks Yiddish. (I know that for a fact because in 1985, when twelve of us had a private audience with him during a conference to celebrate the twentieth anniversary of *Nostra Aetate,* I briefly spoke with him in Yiddish.) And in the face of much opposition, it is during this papacy that the Vatican has established formal diplomatic relations with the State of Israel. So, it would seem that Jews have had nothing but good from this Pope. Why, then, has there been such consternation over this one sentence quoting John Paul II in the Vatican statement?

The criticism seems to be about the fact that the Pope did not apologize for "the Church as such." Those who criticized the Church — and the Pope — have for years placed great hope on the utterance of an official apology by the Church "as such." But in the Pope's statement the Church seems to have separated herself as an institution from her condemnation of the behavior of those of her sons and daughters who cooperated with and endorsed the Nazi program of persecution and murder of the Jews. We must understand just what the Pope meant by "the Church as such." If we do that, we can arrive at a different perspective on this statement, and it can be a *Jewish* perspective properly informed by an understanding of the Jewish tradition. Jewish statements that are not informed by our own tradition are not really "Jewish" in any essential sense, but simply express the views of a group of people who happen to be Jews. None of the negative reactions I have seen to date has been informed by the Jewish tradition — though I do not rule out the possibility that an authentically Jewish negative response could be so formulated.

When a Catholic speaks of "the Church," let alone when the occupant of the Chair of Peter speaks of "the Church," he can mean one of two things. On the one hand, the Church is undoubtedly a collection of fallible human beings. The Church is made up of her members, the parts of her body, so to speak. At this level, it is certainly recognized that these fallible members of the Church can do either good or evil as is their free human choice. On the other hand, when the Pope speaks of the Church "as such," he is not speaking about a fallible collection of human beings; instead he is speaking about what the Church understands as her *magisterium,* her teaching authority, which Catholics see as expressing God's will beginning with Scripture and extending into the ongoing development of Church doctrine. At one level the Church is a human association in the world, but at another level the Church is *mater et magistra* — "mother and teacher" of her members. Understanding the Church at either of these levels, however, one can see why an "apology" is inappropriate. Later, we will examine the word the document did use, a word of far more theological significance than "apology" ever was or will be.

Let us first take the Church as a group of human beings, which is certainly the easier thing for a non-Catholic like myself to do. Now just *who* would apologize to *whom?* If one takes a Catholic who actually participated in the Nazi atrocities against the Jews, how could such a person possibly apologize? How do you apologize to someone in whose murder you were a participant? In order to apologize, you have to make your apology to someone who is capable of accepting your apology. But those who were murdered are hardly in a position to absolve anyone. And who am I as a Jew, who was only a potential victim of Nazi murder, to forgive someone who asks my forgiveness for what he or she did to Jews now dead? How can I exonerate somebody for what he or she did to somebody else? Wouldn't that be what Christians call "cheap grace"?

There is a parallel to this in the Jewish tradition. When the Sanhedrin functioned in ancient Israel and had the power of capital punishment, a criminal about to be executed for murder had the right to confess his or her crime and assert that the death to be undergone was to be "atonement for all my sins." This was seen as one's reconciliation with God in the world-to-come, but it did not release the criminal from the punishment he or she deserved in this world. I am reminded of the report that Hans Frank, the Nazi governor of Poland, when he was about to be executed after having been sentenced to death at Nuremberg in 1946, said that a thousand deaths would not atone for the crimes he committed. But that is between Hans Frank and God. We who have survived have no right to forgive him for what he did; we have no right to accept any apologies from him or anyone like him. On the other hand, if an apology is made by people who did not commit any such crimes, directly or even indirectly, and who do not even sympathize with the murderers, then what would they be apologizing for?

The Jewish tradition on this point is quite clear: We do not believe in inherited guilt. Indeed, when the Church declared in *Nostra Aetate* in 1965 that she no longer regarded the Jews as collectively guilty of "deicide," that is the murder of Jesus as the son of God, she was making a point she now holds in common with the Jewish moral tradition. Each person is responsible only for his or her own sins. Even the Christian doctrine of "original sin" does not mean that humans are punished for the sin of the first human pair but, rather, that humans seem inevitably to copy the sin of the first human pair. Thus the Talmud asks about how God can in all justice "visit the sins of the fathers on the sons" (Exodus 20:5). It answers that children are punished for their parents' sins only when they themselves willingly identify with them and repeat them by their own free choice. Justice, whether human or divine, must recognize with the prophet Ezekiel that only "the person who sins shall die" (Ezekiel 18:20). Thus at either of these levels of humanly applicable justice, an apology makes no sense. At either level, an apology could only be empty rhetoric.

But what about the second notion of the Church, namely, "the Church as such"? This refers to the magisterium, the teaching authority of the Church. Now the teaching authority of the Church does not refer to what we usually mean by "teaching," that is, imparting information. Magisterium means teaching that calls upon the one taught to do something or believe something that is essential for the very existence of that person within the community for whom that teaching is authoritative. When the Church is understood "as such," then she cannot possibly apologize on the basis of her own theological assumptions. For if the Church at this level were to apologize, that would presuppose a criterion of truth and right higher than the revelation upon which the Church bases its authority, the revelation that the Church claims as her own. In other words, the Church cannot criticize herself on the basis of criteria external to her own revelation and tradition because the Church not only claims what she teaches is true, she claims that what she teaches is the truth per se, the ultimate criterion whereby everything else is either true or false, right or wrong. So, for example, the great encyclical of Pope John Paul II is called *Veritatis Splendor,* "the splendor of truth." That is the way the Church presents herself in and to the world.

Now, of course, presentation of oneself as *the* truth is highly offensive to people of a largely secular mentality. That is much of the modern charge against all religion. Religions, in this view, seem to arrogate to themselves divine authority. They seem to hold themselves above judgment by "impartial" criteria. This lies at the heart of much of the criticism of the "authoritarian" character of the Catholic Church. But on this score, Judaism is no different. Even though Judaism and Catholicism make some very different — and in some cases mutually exclusive — claims, the logic of the way the Jewish tradition makes its claims and the way the magisterium of the Church makes its claims is virtually identical. When Jews thank God for giving us the Torah (by which we mean not only the Five Books of Moses but the whole authoritative tradition of the Jewish people throughout history), we speak of *torat 'emet,* which means not just "true teaching" but that "the Torah is *the* truth." The Jewish tradition presents itself as the greatest revelation of God's truth that can be known in the world. That is why we call ourselves "the chosen people." It is not that we choose ourselves. It means that we have been elected by God and given the Torah. The law of heaven has now come down to earth to a singular community entrusted with its teaching. This does not mean we should not share that truth with other people, nor does it mean this truth has nothing in common with other sources of truth. We do not reject science; we do not reject the proper findings of human reason. But a Jew who is committed to the Torah as the word of God cannot in good faith criticize anything taught within the Jewish tradition from a standpoint external to that tradition. Traditionalists like myself have criticized liberal versions of Judaism for in one way or another judging Judaism on the basis of criteria outside Ju-

daism itself, for that is simply contrary to the way the tradition has always defined itself in the past.

That does not mean that religious traditions like Judaism and Catholicism are incapable of any critical development or cannot ever
change their minds. Religious traditions are in a constant state of development and renewed self-understanding. But the criteria of development, the standards for change, are internal. If we discover that something we taught in the past now appears not to be God's will, or is even
contrary to God's will, then we must discover again the fundamental
principles of our revelation and tradition and reinterpret our teaching
so that we do not again lead our people astray. Thus the rabbinic principle that "the Sages be careful in their words" means that even correct
teaching, when not properly formulated, can lead people to conclusions
that are really unwarranted by the tradition. They can lead to "erroneous and unjust interpretations"; in fact, these are the very words the
Pope used when speaking in a self-critical mode about Catholic teaching, words repeated in the document on the Holocaust.

So the charge that the Pope could not criticize "the Church as such"
is true yet mistaken. Of course, the Pope cannot criticize the Church the
way an uncommitted outsider might criticize her. The Church, like the
Jewish tradition upon which she is largely patterned, can only look inward for guidance. The only criticism, then, that could be made either
by an insider or a sympathetic outsider is that either the Jewish tradition
or the Church as such refused to engage in any self-criticism at all. But,
clearly, if that were the stance of the Church, a document like "We Remember" or *Nostra Aetate* could never have been written. That is how
the Pope, when he spoke in the synagogue in Rome (by his own unprecedented initiative), condemned anti-Semitism: "at any time from any
source," which means that when anti-Semitism has come out of Church
teaching, those who so taught it are to be considered in error by the internal criteria of the teaching authority of the Church itself.

Much the same is the case with reappraisals of morally charged issues within the Jewish tradition, which enables Jews who know that tradition and the way it operates to appreciate something quite analogous
in another tradition. A good example of this type of reappraisal is the
way Jews have been dealing with the question of the role of women in Judaism. Such reappraisal would be false to the internal integrity of the
Jewish tradition if it simply assumed that because the role of women had

changed so radically in the surrounding culture, therefore it ought to change within Judaism. One must look into the tradition itself for sources for a process of careful and responsible reinterpretation. That is not to deny that religious traditions are, to a certain extent, influenced by what is happening in the surrounding culture, even when the culture is largely indifferent or even hostile to these traditions. Nevertheless, those external influences can only stimulate thinkers within a tradition to be sensitive to some issues more than others, issues for which there are already sources within the tradition itself.

To make this analogy between Jewish and Catholic moral logic is not to say that the issue of the Holocaust for the Church and the issue of women for Judaism have the same moral gravity. The analogy simply illustrates how much of the logic employed in the criticism of the Church on this issue could be similarly employed against Judaism. Of course, it might well be true that many of the Jewish critics of the Vatican statement on the Holocaust think Judaism can and should be subjected to the same type of criticism they have leveled against the Church. But if that is so, I find it rather disingenuous that such critics would label their criticism in any way "Jewish," unless, that is, they regard the Jews as nothing but a contemporary political interest group, having no tradition from which to draw authority to make any kind of authentic Jewish critique.

When one sees how moral logic within religious traditions like Judaism and Catholicism operates, then it is possible to understand why it is not an apology that is called for. Apologies are cheap. It seems that everyone is apologizing for just about everything in the past these days. No, this is not an apology nor should it be. Instead, it is a process of profound introspection. As such, Jews can appreciate the way the Church, and especially the Pope, are grappling with this issue in the way Jews grapple with this and similar issues. Indeed, as regards the Holocaust, as current scholarship is showing, we Jews have great moral questions of our own to confront and judge.

If, then, the Church, either as an association of fallible human beings or as a community claiming authority from the revelation of God, could not and should not utter an "apology," what should it be doing? Well, the statement says it is "an act of repentance." And then, mirabile dictu, in parenthesis we see the Hebrew word for repentance: *teshuvah.* Here the Church has quite consciously and deliberately chosen a central term straight out of the Jewish theological tradition. Why an act of *teshuvah?* It is because, as the statement goes on to say, "as members of the Church, we are linked to the sins as well the merits of all her children." This means a certain kind of collective responsibility. Of course, in a literal moral sense, I am not responsible for somebody else's sins, and so a Catholic today who is horrified by Nazism and all it stood for and wrought in the world is certainly not responsible for what Hitler did, simply because Hitler was baptized a Catholic. It is not that person's responsibility according to any moral logic I know.

However, both Judaism and Catholicism are "covenantal"; for each, the relationship with God is primarily a communal affair, not merely a relationship between an individual person and God. Human beings are essentially communal creatures. If we are to be related to God in the fullness of our humanity, it has to be in the context of a community. In the covenant, God chooses a particular community for a unique relationship. Traditional Jews can recognize this point quite readily. For example, virtually all Jewish prayer is uttered by plural subjects, "we" not "I." And that is the case even when a Jew is unable to pray with a congregation. He or she is always part of the congregation, even when unable to be physically part of it.

In a covenantal religion, the ties are not only between the community and God. For these very ties with God undergird the ties between the members of the community itself. These ties within the community are much more intense and long lasting than the ties among those in our largely secular society and culture. In a covenanted community, even though one is not *morally* responsible for the sins of fellow members of the community, there still is an *existential* sense of collective sorrow and shame when other members of the community — even those as estranged from the community as the Nazis were — commit sins, especially sins having great public consequences.

In talmudic teaching, "every Jew is responsible for every other Jew"; that is what it means to be part of a covenanted community. I remember how my grandmother would occasionally read in the newspaper that some Jew or other had committed a crime — someone she didn't even know — and she would express her sense of sorrow and shame at what that person had done. She felt that what had been done personally affected her, even if by standards of ordinary morality her reaction would have to be judged irrational. And in the same way, by contrast, she would take pride when some Jew or other — also someone she didn't know — did something that had benefited others. Although my grandmother was not a learned woman, her attitude reflected, in the form of folk wisdom, what the Rabbis called *qiddush ha-shem* ("the sanctification of God") or *hillul ha-shem* ("the profanation of God"). When Jews do good in the world, it reflects well on God who elects them for the covenant; and when Jews do evil in the world, it reflects badly on God. With this in mind, we Jews can see how the Church, which after all learned about covenant from us, is engaged in the covenantal act of repentance, of *teshuvah*.

As regards the Holocaust, the Church feels sorrow and shame about those of her faithful who did not respond properly to Nazism, or who did nothing more than sympathize with the victims of Nazi persecution. That sorrow and shame is not because of a mere association of baptized Catholics with Nazis and Nazi sympathizers; it seems to be sorrow and shame that the teaching authority of the Church did not do enough to encourage such persons to resist the evil to which they succumbed. In other words, perhaps the Church did not do a good enough job of teaching the principles of Christianity to many of her sons and daughters. This failure has led the Church to reiterate its condemnations of racism and anti-Semitism.

The Church learns from her mistakes, and she seems to be doing this by an ongoing process of introspection more prolonged and more painful than any mere apology. An apology under these circumstances would either be a way of getting the Holocaust "out of the way," or it would be an act of moral suicide. That is, again, because no religious community can judge itself by someone else's standards and still exercise its existential claims upon its own faithful. A covenanted community engages in *teshuvah*, literally a "return." Those responsible for teaching the tradition must constantly be returning to its true, revealed sources, always discovering how to interpret them better and make their principles more intelligible and more effective.

To expect an apology rather than *teshuvah* is to call for something quite cheap when there is the possibility of something much more precious. An apology is an event; *teshuvah* is a process. An apology gets us "over" the past, putting it permanently behind us; returning is always on the horizon. Jews pray three times daily for God to enable us to return to Him and for Him to forgive us the sins that have placed a barrier between God and us. To be a member of a covenanted community means to acknowledge the sins of all one's fellow members. This is an awesome covenantal responsibility, beyond the demands of ordinary morality. Indeed, one can bear such responsibility only when one believes that the community has been elected by God and is the object of God's special, supernatural concern. What all of this shows, I hope, is that only Jews who are theologically sensitive can appreciate what the Church is trying to do in this statement. Of course, Jews have a different view than do Catholics about *how* God makes contact with us and *what* that contact consists of. By properly understanding what we hold in common with Catholics, we are better able to understand what makes us different from them. To assume we have nothing in common is as erroneous and spiritually dangerous as to assume that there is nothing that separates us.

The Vatican statement is very significant, not only because it is immediately beneficial to Jews, but even more importantly because it is part of a larger process of the Church's coming to grips with her Jewish origins and her coexistence with the Jewish people until the end of history. I must state, though, in a spirit of friendly response, what I find lacking in the statement. This criticism is neither moral nor theological, but rather rhetorical. On one point in particular, I think the statement tries to say too much and thus does not say it well.

The statement raises the issue of the behavior of Christians who did resist Nazi policies, especially Nazi policies against the Jews. Thus it cites the 1937 encyclical of Pope Pius XI, *Mit brennender Sorge* ("with burning concern"), which condemned Nazi racism quite explicitly. And this was an encyclical, an official statement of Church teaching — written in German rather than the usual Latin — making its point directly to the Nazi powers in Germany. It seems quite likely that the actual author of this encyclical was Eugenio Cardinal Pacelli, the Vatican Secretary of State, who was to become Pope Pius XII two years later in 1939. The Vatican statement goes on, especially in a long footnote, to note and defend the record of Pius XII with respect to the Holocaust.

There is a tremendous historical debate about Pius XII. On the one hand, it is well known that the Pope saved a number of Jewish lives and encouraged others who were doing likewise. On the other hand, Rolf Hochhuth's 1963 play *The Deputy,* which builds on the plausible assumption that the Pope did know about the mass extermination of the Jews from 1942 on, raised the question of why the Pope didn't publicly condemn what the Nazis were doing to the Jews. On that question, the jury is still out. If we assume that the Pope knew what was happening, then the question is whether his public silence was an act of moral cowardice or an act of moral prudence.

Those who make the case for moral cowardice argue that the Pope feared to upset the Nazis under whose control he was living during the German occupation of Italy. Furthermore, he had always seemed more concerned with the danger of communism, with its explicit anti-Christian and anti-Catholic bias, than he had been concerned with Nazism. After all, wasn't it the future Pope who, as Cardinal Pacelli the Vatican Secretary of State, had negotiated the concordat of 1933 with the new Nazi regime in Germany, an act that gave this questionable new regime much international respectability? And wasn't the Pope a good deal less reticent in condemning the evil of communism than he was in condemning the evil of Nazism, as evidenced by the fact that after the war he excommunicated any Catholic who voted for Communist candidates, something he never did to Catholic supporters of Nazism?

Those who make the case for moral prudence note that the Pope reasonably feared that many other Catholics, especially the clergy (who would be taken as his agents), would be killed if he spoke out. There is also, of course, the question of whether public criticism by the Pope of Nazi policies would have had any positive effect. It might well even have been counterproductive.

Because moral judgment in this case requires much more historical inquiry, one can hardly be conclusive about either judgment. The case is further complicated by the fact that we are dealing with a moral judgment that if unfavorable would be for a sin of omission rather than a sin of commission. No one could say that the Pope actually spoke or acted positively on behalf of the Nazi regime (as did some bishops), and certainly not on behalf of the crimes of the Nazis.

It is far more difficult to fix blame on somebody for what he or she could have done but did not do than it is to affix blame on somebody for what he or she should not have done but did do. Of course, that does not mean we cannot condemn sins of omission. We would morally condemn somebody who would, as Scripture puts it, "stand idly by the blood of [his] neighbor" (Leviticus 19:16). But it is not clear that that judgment can legitimately be made in this case.

We can hope that in time historians will be able to allow us to decide whether Pius XII was blameworthy, praiseworthy, or somewhere in-between. That cannot be done now. For that reason, and for the sake of presenting an undiluted theological-moral statement, the Vatican document would have been stronger and less open to the wrong kind of criticism from those hostile to anything Catholic if it had simply not raised an issue it could not possibly have treated adequately.

Finally, the document asserts, "The Nazi regime was determined to exterminate the very existence of the Jewish people, a people called to witness to the one God and the law of the covenant." No Jewish statement could have enunciated more precisely why Jewish people exist in the world. Jews are committed to survival. Much of our language, uttered both to ourselves and to others, is the language of survival. Surely, that is quite understandable considering what the Jewish people have suffered, especially in the twentieth century. But survival for Jews is not enough. Jews always have to understand *for what* — better, *for whom* — we are surviving. Perhaps the true source of the Nazi venom against the Jewish people is that for which or for Whom the Jews are to survive.

This statement of the Catholic Church recognizes the chosenness of the Jewish people, the vocation of the Jewish people, a fact nothing short of *qiddush ha-shem*, "the sanctification of the name of God." If the Church, from the top down, recognizes this as the reason for the survival and continuing strength of the Jewish people, then, despite any reservations, Jews have to see this document as making a positive contribution to the always complex relationship between the Jewish people and the Catholic Church. It is a document Jews can and should embrace because its theological argument and conclusions have a resonance in our own theology and law. It is by no means the last word — nothing is in this world — but its integrity and wisdom should not be missed because of moral and political antagonism stemming from those having less integrity and less wisdom.

Confessions of a Rootless Cosmopolitan Jew

STEPHEN MILLER

I, the grandson of devout Orthodox Jews, am watching my younger daughter being confirmed in the Lutheran Church. The minister, an affable, athletic-looking man, has his hands on my daughter's head as he says a prayer. Afterwards, my wife takes a group picture of the smiling minister with the confirmed kids. I stand in the background — an outsider, mildly uncomfortable, looking forward to leaving this alien realm and returning to my usual Sunday morning activity: reading the *New York Times*. I am what so many Jewish leaders worry about — a non-Jewish Jew whose children, by virtue of my marriage to a gentile, are being raised as Christians.

Many Jewish-gentile families retain some Jewish traditions. My family is thoroughly Christian; we celebrate Christmas and Easter, not Hanukkah or Passover. No doubt, if all Jews followed in my footsteps, the Jewish people would no longer exist. My response to that highly unlikely possibility is: "So what?" I don't feel any obligation as a Jew to preserve the Jewish people, and I find truly offensive the argument of those who speak of a "Silent Holocaust," who argue that assimilation is a posthumous victory for Hitler. How can the slaughter of innocent people on the basis of some absurd racist theories be equated with assimilation — the latter a choice freely made?

Some people would argue that my choice is not "really" a free one — that the demon of Jewish self-hatred has compelled me to move far away from my origins. There is no arguing with those who read my character in such fashion, since whatever I say will be grist for their mill, but I should note that I have never tried to hide the fact that I was born and raised a Jew. And I don't think I'm protesting too much when I say that I have many Jewish friends, including some who practice the rites of Judaism.

Even if self-hatred — a notoriously open-ended notion — is ruled out, there remains the question of duty. I don't think the Holocaust confers a special obligation on me, but I do wonder if I have *some* obligation to the religion I was born into. The notion of obligation is very strong among Jewish intellectuals. Daniel Bell has said that obligation is at the core of Judaism; obligation, he says, "is a redemption of debt to those who have nurtured us, institutions which have fostered us, and so on." In *Commentary* recently, Neal Kozodoy said of a famous Jewish writer's lack of connection with organized Jewish life, "He had conspicuously declined to educate himself about its culture, its traditions, or its modes of self-perpetuation." Do these strictures apply to me as well? I remember my devout grandmother — a generous, amusing, and tough-minded woman who emigrated from Romania when she was seventeen so that, among other things, she would not be persecuted for being an Orthodox Jew — or indeed a Jew, period. Did I casually relinquish what she struggled so hard to preserve? Did I walk away from Judaism too quickly?

Certainly, as a child I walked away from Judaism — even ran sometimes, disliking the Hebrew school I attended three times a week after public school. Though my grandparents on my mother's side were devout Jews (my father's parents died when he was a child), my parents were not devout. In fact, I don't recall that they ever attended a holiday service, although we celebrated Hanukkah and Passover. Nevertheless, perhaps because I was the first male grandchild, my mother — in an effort to appease her Orthodox mother — enrolled me in an Orthodox Hebrew school. I was also supposed to attend synagogue on Saturday morning.

The school was depressing; the air was dank and the lighting poor. Sitting in those classrooms, I thought of all the things I could be doing at the time — playing softball, basketball, stickball, stoopball, handball, boxball, all of which I immensely enjoyed. Instead, I hunched over a desk, deciphering Hebrew letters and memorizing passages from the Pentateuch. The teacher I remember most was a gruff Israeli woman who hit her pupils on the wrists with a pointer if they screwed up. What did I learn in those five years? Not much: the basics of Hebrew, though very little in the way of solid grammar, and a rough knowledge of the first five books of the Old Testament. On Saturdays I heard a lot of prayers and some Hebrew songs, but I had no idea what this religious ceremony was about save to endlessly extol God. The only thing I knew Judaism stood for was the new state of Israel, which I was supposed to help by asking family, friends, and neighbors to drop coins into a blue and white tin can.

To say I hated Hebrew School would be an exaggeration. I liked the Hebrew script, and in college I often doodled by writing out my name in that script, but I certainly was a lot happier when, after my Bar Mitzvah, I no longer had to attend Hebrew School and could spend afternoons playing ball on the Bronx street where I lived. After my Bar Mitzvah, in fact, my connection with Judaism was minimal. My mother expected me to go to synagogue on High Holy Days, but she didn't go herself so she didn't know that I never attended a service — preferring to stand outside and talk to friends. Even before I was Bar Mitzvahed, I rarely sat through a complete Saturday morning service. I would usually sneak out early, heading for the movies or a nearby playground.

I don't know if it was my five years in Hebrew School or my three years in the Cub Scouts, but something in my childhood left me with a strong distaste for any communal activity except sporting events. My connections with organizations have been few and far between — one year as a fraternity member in college, four years as a member of the Republican Party in the early 1980s. I am not a joiner, which doesn't mean that I disapprove of voluntary associations.

In any case, the minor ordeal of Hebrew School left me not only with a distaste for Judaism but also with a strong lack of interest in religion. Yet I never became an atheist — never hated religion the way some friends did who had been raised as strict Catholics. In college, I avoided late-night metaphysical bull sessions. Talking about God, to my mind, was a waste of time, since one couldn't prove (or disprove) his existence.

Yet in college something happened to me that eventually caused me to reassess my attitude toward religion. I had never been much of a reader in high school, but in college I became so devoted to reading that after my sophomore year I quit all my extracurricular activities and read as much as I could. It soon became obvious to me that some of the writers who meant the most to me — Donne, Herbert, Samuel Johnson, T. S. Eliot, Dostoevsky, and Flannery O'Connor come to mind — were devout Christians. Soon afterwards I discovered the sublimities of Christian music and soon after that the power of Christian art.

Nevertheless, I still remained uninterested in religious questions — and still thought that believers were generally stupider than nonbelievers. Although some of the writers, musicians, and painters I admired were devout Christians, I considered the artist's beliefs irrelevant. Nourished on New Criticism, I thought only critical dolts paid attention to the artist's opinions. Were not Wagner and Pound anti-Semitic? Were not Celine and Emile Nolde Nazis? The only thing that counted was the thing in itself — the work of art. Moreover, there were many writers I admired who were not Christian — or only marginally so.

But it was not always easy to tiptoe around a writer's beliefs. There were some writers, Pascal and Samuel Johnson, whose beliefs one could not ignore because they are central to their work. And though one can certainly appreciate Dante, Bach, Giotto, or George Herbert without being a Christian, one cannot deny the centrality of Christian ideas and images to their work. If so many great musicians, painters, and writers were devout Christians, then who was I to smugly dismiss religious belief as something for lesser intellects?

A growing respect for Christian thought — or at least the thought of some Christian thinkers — stimulated my curiosity about the many currents of Christianity. What was Pascal's Jansenism about? Or Johnson's Protestantism? Pure theology didn't interest me, but the history of Christianity did. Fascinated by the seemingly endless struggle between orthodoxy and heterodoxy, I began to read books that centered on periods of crisis in Christianity — especially Late Roman times and the Protestant Reformation. I remember being so struck by Peter Brown's brilliant biography of Augustine that I reread it a year after I finished it.

Reading about these controversies and rereading some of my favorite Christian writers, I came to another conclusion: the views of some Christian thinkers were more profound than the views of some highly touted anti-Christian modern thinkers. It was not that I was persuaded by these writers to become a Christian. Rather, I was persuaded that these writers had a more profound understanding of the springs of human conduct than did the four intellectual gods it was fashionable to worship when I was in college and graduate school: Rousseau, Nietzsche, Marx, and Freud.

In all these years of reading while holding a variety of jobs in journalism and the academy, I did not give a moment's thought to the Judaism of my childhood. My connections with Judaism were marginal — attending a Passover seder once a year — and it never occurred to me that Judaism might also offer some profound insights into the human condition. After all, I was nourished on English literature and had read widely in French and Russian literature. Where were the Jewish writers who might influence me? The Jewish-American writers I read had a lot to say about the trials and tribulations of American Jews, but very little to say about Judaism.

It was not until the birth of my first child that I gave any thought to my Jewish heritage — and it was only a passing thought. My wife, raised in a relatively unreligious family as a Hungarian Protestant (Hungarian Reformed Church), wanted to raise my daughter as a Christian. Why should I object, since I had no quarrel with Christianity? The idea of dusting off my childhood Judaism and becoming a practicing Jew for the sake of my daughter seemed absurd. Children see through such ruses easily. The only other option was raising her ecumenically — that is, exposing her to Judaism and Christianity — but that also made no sense to me. The two religions should respect each other, but at bottom they are profoundly different. To serve up both religions in order to "give my kid a choice" is to trivialize their differences.

So my first daughter, and of course my second daughter, who came along five years later, were baptized and confirmed in the Lutheran Church — not, by the way, because my wife was profoundly attracted to Lutheran doctrine; she liked the fact that music — for the most part very good music — was central to Lutheran worship. Both my daughters, who consider themselves Christians, have asked me why I don't go to a synagogue on Saturday. My answer is always the same: "I'm not a believer." Which doesn't mean that the subject of Judaism is not discussed in my house. My kids have occasionally attended a Jewish ceremony — a Passover seder at the Jewish nursing home where my mother lives — and they have asked me about aspects of Judaism, which I've tried to answer to the best of my ability.

So here I stand, unapologetically, one of these Jews who, as one writer put it, is "fading into the landscape through assimilation and sheer indifference." I have no second thoughts about becoming assimilated — whatever that means — but I'm not indifferent about the path I have taken. In fact, my rootless cosmopolitanism disturbs me for two reasons.

One is the problem of Christian anti-Semitism. If it were true that anti-Semitism was central to Christian thought, then letting my children be raised as Christians — for it was not something I would have chosen by myself — would imply that I've enabled them to embrace a doctrine that is inimical to Jews and Judaism. I have read widely on this question and strongly believe that anti-Semitism is not at the heart of Christianity, though there is no gainsaying the fact that anti-Semitism has been preached by many Christian thinkers, including the founder of the church my wife and children attend. Cynics may say that if I want to keep my self-respect I have no choice but to come to such a conclusion, but others with no personal stake in the matter have come to the same conclusion.

In any case, the problem of Christian anti-Semitism has to do with how I fit into a Christian household; it has nothing to do with my continuing lack of connection with Judaism. After all, I could go to synagogue even if my wife and two children attend church. In my mid-thirties I decided that I should know more about Judaism, so I read a few books on the subject. They changed my life not a whit. Though I gained a greater appreciation of the evolution of Judaic thought, and though I was horrified by the way Jews have been treated in the last 2,000 years, I did not feel any desire to become an observant Jew. In fact, something else happened: I was tempted to become a Roman Catholic, having come to regard the Roman Catholic Church as one that strove to be "above" ethnic differences. I fantasized that if the whole world became Roman Catholic, ethnic and religious strife would end.

I didn't really believe in this fantasy, so I'm not sure why I was so drawn to the Roman Catholic Church that one day I walked into a Catholic reading center and marched up to a priest and said, my heart pounding, "I'm interested in converting to Catholicism."

"Would you like to attend Mass?" the priest asked. "There's a noon Mass that begins in five minutes."

The idea of actually attending a religious ceremony caused me to panic: "No, not right now."

He gave me a pamphlet to read: "Take a look at this," he said.

"Thanks," I said, and rushed out.

I never did read the pamphlet, and gradually the thought of converting dimmed in my mind.

The second reason I feel uneasy about my rootless cosmopolitanism is that it doesn't square with my political outlook. Most non-Jewish Jews, as one observer has said, do have a religion: liberalism. Many liberals subscribe to a number of notions that I disagree with — especially a belief in human perfectibility. Many liberals also tend to regard deeply religious people as neurotic or crooked — a Jimmy Swaggart rather than a Dietrich Bonhoeffer or Alexander Solzhenitsyn. Fearing the flowering of religious belief in American life, liberals often favor a strict separation of church and state. I don't. I think religious belief is for the most part a positive force in American life, one that enables people to withstand some of the destructive and repulsive aspects of mass culture.

If religion is a good thing, then why don't I stop temporizing and hook up with one? After all, I'm not an atheist; I am a believer — or at least a believer to such an extent that I find myself praying at times. "Even in the life of a Christian," Flannery O'Connor says, "faith rises and falls like the tides of an invisible sea." O'Connor, like Pascal, suggests that developing the habit of worship — going through the external motions of faith — fosters belief.

But perhaps because my belief is weak, I have never had the desire to go through the external motions of faith. My intellect recognizes the need for religion, but my heart rebels against being a member of a religious community. Even if I overcome that aversion, there is another problem: which religion to practice. I'm strongly attracted to Christianity, but piety — i.e., loyalty or devotion to one's family — makes it unlikely that I ever will convert.

Constrained by familial piety, why don't I attempt to rediscover Judaism? David Tracy has said that "you can often best rediscover your own religion . . . by discovering other religions, their differences and their truths." Couldn't my knowledge of Christianity lead me to a new appreciation of Judaism? Perhaps, but the will to make this rediscovery is very feeble. Though I am uneasy about having deserted the religion of my Romanian-born grandmother, I don't see myself returning to Judaism. If I had married a Jew, I probably would have remained marginally Jewish, but I have lived in a Christian household for twenty-five years; the gulf between me and Judaism is too great.

So I do nothing. Does that mean that I have failed in my obligation to Judaism? Of course it does. I have not taken Judaism seriously enough because I have never been interested in taking Judaism seriously enough. I prefer to think about belief rather than to practice a religion. On the Sunday mornings when my wife and daughters go to church (they are not regular churchgoers, and my older daughter recently switched to a Unitarian church), I read the *New York Times* — happy to be alone in a silent house yet also frustrated by the Sisyphean task of trying to be reasonably well-informed about political affairs.

On some Sunday mornings, my spirit rebels. I'm uninterested in being well-informed; I want something else — something that marks off Sunday from the other days of the week. Transcendence? I am not sure what that means, but I associate it with music. I only know that some Sunday mornings I feel compelled to listen to music, which is something I rarely do during the week. Silent meditation is beyond me. I cannot do what Bonhoeffer suggested: find ten minutes "to be still and let the silence gather round . . . to stand in the presence of eternity and to let it speak. . . ."

While the music plays — usually classical but sometimes Gospel or even Indian — I sometimes daydream of a "perfect" religious experience, where custom and ceremony work their beauty: a mass held in a majestic Gothic cathedral, the service consisting of prayers in Latin, Hebrew, and the Book of Common Prayer interspersed with selections of great sacred music, from Gregorian chants to Stravinsky's *Requiem Canticles* — the service ending with a reading of several poems by George Herbert, especially "The Windows," whose last stanza implies that Herbert dislikes sermonizing.

> Doctrine and life, colors and light, in one
> When they combine and mingle, bring
> A strong regard and awe; but speech alone
> Doth vanish like a flaring thing,
> And in the ear, not conscience ring.

How nice — a church of my own devising, one without sermons, one that conforms to my own aesthetic preferences.

Flannery O'Connor said that "it is much harder to believe than not to believe." I would say it is much harder to practice a religion than to believe in God. The former requires time, effort, and — usually — money; the latter doesn't require anything.

In *The Heretical Imperative,* Peter Berger says that "the modern individual is faced not just with the opportunity but with the necessity to make choices as to his beliefs." I feel no such necessity, perhaps because the question of which religion to choose does not burn strongly in me. Sometimes I am troubled by my free-floating aesthetic religiosity — but not troubled enough to do anything about it. For reasons only my heart knows I am likely to remain a rootless cosmopolitan Jew, facing toward faith but at ease in neither the temple of my ancestors nor the church of my wife and children.

The Demon in the Jewish Soul

MARC GELLMAN

Demons surface. For most people, demons surface in nightmares, but for us, for Jews, demons seem to surface in history. Pharaoh, Amalek, Nebuchadnezzar, Titus, Torquemada, Chmielnitsky, and Hitler were real demons. They killed real Jews. The night demons can be forgotten, but not the demons that remain when the morning breaks.

These demons have changed something in the Jewish soul. I cannot say what the change is precisely, but it amounts to this at least: we Jews cannot fully trust the world again.

An op-ed piece in the *New York Times* by Seymour Martin Lipset shows it. He tells of a successful, urbane, cosmopolitan New York Jewish publisher who confessed to harboring the deep belief that Gentiles go home at night and dream of killing Jews. Lipset believes that the wild paranoia of this man is present in some greater or lesser degree in the mind of most Jews. When set against the fact of Jewish power and prestige, Jewish wealth and status, this paranoia about the world's Jew-hating might seem incomprehensible. But this is the demon in our soul, and no simple ceremony will exorcise it.

There are things for the world to learn and things for us to learn about our demon. There are reasons for our paranoia, good reasons (if one can speak of a collective neurosis in this positive way), reasons which perdure despite our power. To begin with, the only meaningful Jewish statistic: we are a people who are today three million fewer than we were fifty years ago. And this despite fifty years of Jewish babies and good medicine. We were at least eighteen million in 1940 and we are perhaps fifteen million today, and in that time the population of the world has risen from three to five billion people, so our relative percentage of the world's population is smaller still.

The world must understand what happens to a people who cannot return to the land of their forebears and find distant relatives who will welcome them back home. Irish-Americans can go to Ireland and visit family and friends in their ancestral home, Italian-Americans can renew and freshen their roots in the soil of their native Italy, African-Americans can return as free people to a mostly free Africa and sort out the meaning of slavery in the context of a living and enduring African culture. But where can an Eastern European Jew go to taste the old food and sing the old songs and pray in the old synagogues? The great Jewish centers of Europe are dead, and the synagogues burned down or almost empty. We are cut off from our past and so we must leapfrog back to the past of King David and try to replace our roots in Europe with roots in the state of Israel. But Jerusalem is not Vilna, Beer Sheba is not Krakov, and every time we try to reminisce, the demon in our soul wounds us with the searing knowledge that our European past is, like us, turned to dust. All that and more is what the world must learn about the demon in the Jewish soul.

The world must understand what happens to the psyche of a people who must find a way to cope with an event within the memory of living Jews in which one out of every three Jews in the world was murdered while essentially nothing was done to stop the carnage. These are more than statistics, more than numbers. They are the arithmetic of devastation, and they must be understood, as Judith Miller has pointed out in her new book on the Holocaust, "one by one by one."

Arthur Hertzberg astutely points to these numbers as the explanation for the stridency and excesses of Jewish defense organizations in response to even peripheral threats (to wit: the excessive fuss over Louis Farrakhan and Jesse Jackson, or the instantaneous denunciation of some intemperate remarks by Cardinal O'Connor). The residue of guilt for doing so little to try to stop the Holocaust remains as a part of our demon in every institution we have built after the kingdom of night was destroyed.

The specter of being indolent in the face of catastrophe twice in one generation is simply too terrifying for any Jew or any Jewish organization to bear. On the day of their induction into the army, Israeli soldiers march to the top of Masada and utter the oath, *"Masada lo yipol od"* — "Masada will not fall again." At some time in his or her life, every Jew in the world has taken that oath.

The world must also learn that the demon in our soul is the first warning call to the world whenever freedom is imperiled. Today Europe, east and west, must decide which of the voices freedom has unleashed will be the voice of the new Europe. Perhaps it will be Vaclav Havel's Jeffersonian compassion, or perhaps it will be Jean Marie Le Pen's quasi-fascist and anti-Semitic National Front. Either way, it is the attitude about the Jews, the pitiful remnant still alive in Europe, which will determine everything else about the new world a-borning there. A united Germany may be dominated by the green shirts or by those who dress again in brown shirts. In others' treatment of the Jews lies the barometer of decency, the litmus test of freedom, the yardstick for human rights, the truest measure of decency and democracy in the world, and it is the demon in our soul which makes us cry out. But it is still the world's choice to listen or turn a deaf ear to our warning cries.

How do you tell your child about the demon? My son Max plays first base, goes to camp, does not pick up his socks, and has never once had to fight his way home through groups of bullies shouting, "Dirty Jew!" He is just like most middle-class American kids, and so when he asked me to explain the events at Carpentras, France, and why people would dig up a Jewish body and mutilate it, and why they hate us, I did not know what to say. I told him, of course, that the whole world was not like that, but not so long ago the whole world was just like that.

Now is the time for my son Max to choose what to believe. He must decide whether to trust in his normalcy, or fear the news story which caused his father to cry over the morning coffee. The demon is knocking at my son's door, and I fear he will be different now. But truth to tell, I also hope he will be different, because we are the rememberers and it is the demon who makes us remember.

I want Max to understand that the deal we made with the world was not honored. For two thousand years, from the time of the Roman conquest to our own age, we Jews made a deal to live in the world in a condition of political powerlessness. At the very moment the Jewish defenders of Masada were taking their lives rather than submitting to Roman rule, Rabbi Yochanan ben Zakkai went to the Emperor Titus and asked him for the right to open a rabbinical academy in the city of Yavneh in return for which he would not urge or foment revolt against Rome. The deal was based on the belief that without political power, the Jewish community would not be a target for attack because no prize would be won in attacking a powerless community. But this deal did not comprehend that we would gain economic power, and would need Roman emperors and the emperors of a thousand empires to protect us. By and large, we have learned from history that the emperors were not willing.

Political powerlessness coupled with economic prosperity was, we now understand, a deadly combination. In 1202, Pope Innocent III, realizing that almost 80 percent of church lands were mortgaged to Jews, canceled the debts of the church to Jewish money lenders. He understood that the Jewish community could not protect the wealth it had accumulated because of the flaw in the deal Yochanan ben Zakkai had made with Titus. In 1492, Ferdinand and Isabella explored the new world with confiscated Jewish money and expelled the Jews from Spain because they realized that the Jewish community could not protect the wealth it had accumulated because of the flaw in the deal Yochanan ben Zakkai had made with Titus. After 1933, Hitler armed the Third Reich with confiscated Jewish money because he, too, realized that the Jewish community could not protect the wealth it had accumulated because of the flaw in the deal Yochanan ben Zakkai had made with Titus. Only in America, the land of a democracy born of the dispossessed, could wealth be protected. And now Israel with power and will protects the people and its wealth and future.

Protection from vulnerability is the fetish and foundation point for any informed modern Jewish life. However, it must come to each of us, in the night, or in a moment of uncertainty in the day, that perhaps America and even Israel are just like all the other places; that perhaps we have not built the walls high enough or amassed enough power or might to protect what we have earned. If Russia, a great land of eleven time zones can fear being invaded again from the Balkans, and the world can honor that fear, why can the world not honor the fears of a little people who cannot ever believe they are truly safe?

The curse of the Jewish people is that we must live with the demon, that the world will never let us live in peace. But the world must also live with a demon, the knowledge that it created the demon which torments us so.

There are also lessons for us to learn about our demon. Jews must also grow from the horrid wisdom of the past. There are several lessons we must learn and are trying to learn and with patient friends and peace will surely learn.

We must learn that although we were victims, we are not victims now. We have power now and security now and wealth now and we are part of the elites of the world. Our state of affairs in the diaspora (Russia excepted) has never been better and our state of affairs in our State, though constantly endangered by threats from real enemies, is strong and politically powerful. Tempting though it is to ignore these irrefutable facts, we must face them and alter the way we think about ourselves in the world because of them. We cannot in good faith both pursue power and also cloak ourselves in the moral innocence and righteousness of the victim. Vigilance must continue, particularly in Israel, where the threat is palpable, but we cannot imagine that we do not control our destiny, and we cannot continue to maintain that our behavior even in Israel is solely the result of external hatred.

When FDR met with reporters after Kristallnacht in 1938, he said he had no plan and no commitment to make for the emigration of German Jews. When Bush and Gorbachev met, one of the highest agenda items after arms control was the emigration of Soviet Jews. The world is different today than it was fifty years ago, and in a word, the difference is Jewish power. Lipset points out that there are thirty-one Jewish congressmen and seven Jewish senators and fifty years ago there were none. The world is different today for us and the reason is Jewish power.

Consider two recent New York stories as the telling signs of this change. A grocer in the Flatbush section of Brooklyn was involved in a racial incident as the result of an argument with a customer, while at the same time across town on Wall Street a fabulously wealthy investment banker was convicted of insider trading violations and forced to pay a six hundred million dollar fine. Now, if fifty years ago one had been asked to guess which of these two was the Jew and which the non-Jew, the prudent guess would surely have been that the grocer in Brooklyn was the Jew and the investment banker was not. Of course today, that guess would be wrong, and the difference is Jewish power.

We must accept the reality of Jewish power and we must accept moral responsibility for the uses of power. Whether on the West Bank, or on Wall Street, we are not the victims any more, and we cannot shrink from the accountability power imposes and requires.

Another lesson we must learn from the demon in our soul is that we must learn to trust Christian love.

Elie Wiesel reminds us that only the killers are guilty. We must acknowledge both Christian complicity as well as Christian heroism in the face of death. Rabbi Harold Shulweis from California is now engaged in a project of surpassing moral eloquence. He has formed an organization to help poor elderly Christians who saved Jews during the Holocaust. This is not a repayment for an old debt. Rather it is a statement that only the killers are guilty, and we as Jews can come to acknowledge and believe in, and even trust in Christian love.

I can trust my friend Thomas. Tom is a priest, and I know he would shelter me if the demons should rise up again. I know this because we are dear friends and I have come to trust him. We became friends when I decided to silence my own demon and believe in Christian love. We do a television show together in which a priest and a rabbi who like each other try to explain their traditions to each other on the air. Our show, "The God Squad," seems to have helped lots of folks begin to understand their neighbors and this understanding may lead to trust or something like trust.

In this experience of working together, Tom has begun to understand that the symbols of love for him are often symbols of hatred for me. So Tom came to understand that the cross planted in the ashes of Jewish men and women and children at Auschwitz was not a symbol of love and reconciliation for me, but rather a triumphant return of the crusaders' cross to another field of Jewish blood. And so Tom and I have silenced the demons between us. I do not believe that Tom dreams of killing Jews.

I will say, however, that the demon in me did surface towards the beginning of our relationship. I do remember feeling for more than a moment this dark thought, "If they come to get me and my people, my friendship with Tom will be useful in saving some of us." I am ashamed to have felt that even for a moment, but I am not completely ashamed because I know the demon is in my soul and I know the demon cannot be easily exorcised. However, now I trust Tom with no reservations. We are dear friends and soul mates. I do not believe, I *know* that Tommy dreams of a world where I will not be afraid, and where Max can grow to be just a first baseman and trust the world much more than did my grandparents and a little more than I do.

Truth to be told, we have not only demons but also hopes embedded in our collective Jewish soul. We possess a tradition which, though buffeted by history, has not been morally impoverished by the vicissitudes of history. The same Jewish tradition which contains a song of thanks to God for drowning the Egyptians in the Red Sea also contains a custom of dipping one drop of wine out of the kiddush cup on Passover for each plague, in sorrow for the Egyptian lives that were lost in the Exodus. The same tradition which produced a prayer asking God to pour out His wrath on the Gentiles for what they have done to us, also produced a law which tells us that when we hear a Gentile in prayer who praises God, we must answer, "Amen."

Perhaps it is the amen that will drive away the demon in our soul and help us finally to find each other.

The Fragmented Faith of American Jews

CLIFFORD E. LIBRACH

In August 1966, the journal *Commentary* published "The State of Jewish Belief," a symposium now considered one of the great spiritual and intellectual snapshots of an American religious community. After an introduction by Milton Himmelfarb, thirty-eight leading Jewish thinkers addressed their own and contemporary religious thought with great erudition, intellectual sophistication, and philosophical rigor.

In August 1996, thirty years later, *Commentary* returned to the well with a new symposium — "What Do American Jews Believe?" — including representatives of the three major Jewish branches: Orthodoxy, Conservatism, and Reform, as well as the much-smaller Reconstructionist movement. It is not an entirely representative group. To answer questions about belief in God, the status of Torah as divine revelation, the chosenness of the Jewish people, and the anticipation of a Messiah, *Commentary* had to call upon thinkers all of whom, even the most liberal, take the religiousness of their religion seriously. Missing from the group, as a result, are those who regard Jewish identity primarily as leftist politics (e.g., Arthur Waskow and Michael Lerner) or trans-denominational neo-mysticism (e.g., Zalman Schachter-Shalomi).

The biased sample here may not be a bad thing, however, since religion is precisely the aspect of the American Jewish community that is largely obscure to the public at large, including most Jews. The general perception of modern Jews — confirmed, lamentably, by almost all statistical and anecdotal evidence — is of an adamantly secular people.

Most Jews do not belong to a synagogue or give their children formal training in their own religion. Those who are synagogue members are not usually active, often attending worship services only on the High Holy Days and otherwise using the synagogue as a child-centered bar/ bat mitzvah recital mill, like a dance studio or karate school.

A cynic might declare that the credo of American Jews at the end of the twentieth century can be reduced to two propositions: "Jesus Christ is not the Messiah," and "Because of the Holocaust, the entire world does now and will always owe the Jewish people an ethnic hypersensitivity." (One of the symposium contributors, David Klinghoffer, offers a caustic challenge to such Jewish negativism: "If we have no mission from God, maybe we should all marry Episcopalians, disappear with dignity, and thus quit inflicting ourselves on our Christian neighbors — with our liberalism, our chauvinsim, our self-pity.")

So, while not broadly representative of the Jewish community at large, the concerns and the participants in *Commentary*'s latest symposium do at least attempt to provide a window into the authentic religious dimension of American Judaism. But if the conception of the symposium is worthy, the result is in some ways disappointing. The discussions seem somehow leaner and less significant than the ones presented thirty years ago. This thinness may be attributed, in part, to the editors having severely limited the length of the essays this time around. Still, there is a sense in which theological depth has been replaced by ideological acrimony and quarrelsomeness.

There are interesting differences between the two efforts. In 1966 the respondents were primarily pulpit rabbis, whereas in 1996 the field is dominated by academics; in 1966 all thirty-eight respondents were men, while in 1996 seven women are included. But the most striking difference between the earlier and later symposiums lies in the reversal of ideological momentum between liberal and traditional Judaism. In 1966, the plurality of respondents were Reform rabbis, who, for the most part, wrote with utter self-confidence, barely granting a nod to the struggles of Orthodox Judaism. In 1996, by contrast, the tilt is strongly toward Orthodoxy and the traditional wing of the Conservative movement. That traditionalism, moreover, has become confident and even pugnacious in a way no one could have anticipated in 1966. As David Singer observes, thirty years ago "the Orthodox participants were comfortable in their modernity, but at pains to justify their Orthodoxy. In

1996, for me at least, the situation is exactly the reverse: my Orthodoxy is rock solid, but I am hard-pressed to justify any accommodation with modernity."

Though it still cannot claim more than 10 percent of Jews in the United States, Orthodoxy has, over the last two generations, made significant numerical gains, and its gains in ideological confidence have far exceeded its numerical growth. The 1966 presentations by Orthodox rabbis were notable for the intellectual delicacy with which they defensively justified the strict regimen of Orthodox Judaism in the midst of a dynamic and vibrant American culture. Such thinkers as Eliezer Berkovitz, Marvin Fox, Immanuel Jakobovitz, Emanuel Rackman, Norman Lamm, and Aharon Lichtenstein were obviously quite at home in the world of intellectual modernity but sounded almost quaintly pious in their quiet, passive defense of Orthodox observance.

In 1996, the Orthodox participants answer *Commentary*'s queries positively and aggressively — and proceed to note the vacuity of most everyone else; they are bold in their self-image as representing the only kind of Judaism that can survive in North America. "Reform and Conservative Judaism have failed," asserts David Gelernter, in an intellectual dismissal characteristic of much of *Commentary*'s 1996 tone. "The level of ignorance of classical Jewish sources within" liberal Judaism, observes Suzanne Last Stone, "is, if not unprecedented in Jewish society, certainly unprecedented among those who take it upon themselves to declare the response of Judaism to the complexities of contemporary life." Marshall J. Breger skewers the Reform movement in particular as made up of "those who view Jewish law as some kind of historical archive for spiritual inspiration." Rabbi Barry Freundel rejects Reform's celebration of human autonomy as seductive but ultimately demoralizing: "'Me,' if truly left alone, is nothing but a wretched, infinitesimal dot in the space continuum of the universe.... Is it any wonder that insecurity, meaninglessness, and a painful lack of self-worth and self-confidence are the almost-universal psychic afflictions of the day?"

By contrast, the defensive and, indeed, confused responses of the Reform participants mark an utter reversal of their 1966 confidence. Once upon a time the Reform movement tried to be a fortress of intellectual rigor and ethical integrity. But political correctness and the therapeutic culture have reduced Reform teaching to incoherence. Thus, Eric H. Yoffie, the newly installed president of the Union of American

Hebrew Congregations, says that the "heart of Torah is mitzvah [obligation, or commandment]," but then goes on to declare: "For the great majority of American Jews, there is no leader or institution with the authority to impose commandments; the autonomous individual decides for himself or herself." One might have thought that even a liberal rabbi would allow that God can impose commandments, but even this isn't so clear. "As a mitzvah-inspired Liberal Jew," Yoffie insists, "the only option that I have is to decide for myself what binds me." According to this self-contradiction, then, fulfilling a commandment means doing whatever is right in one's own eyes. Similarly, Sheldon Zimmerman, the newly installed president of Hebrew Union College/Jewish Institute of Religion, prefers evocative phrasing to coherent exposition, as when he defines the Torah so broadly that it can mean anything at all. It is, at once, (a) "the story of our people's encounter with the divine and our story as well," (b) "our starting place," (c) "the prism through which we see and understand the world," (d) "the source of our story," (e) "our ongoing attempt and activity to hear God's voice in our own times as we face issues that challenge us to move to newer understandings," (f) "process," and finally, (g) "our 'lived' response to God and God's gifts."

To be sure, not all the Reform contributions to "What Do American Jews Believe?" are so uninspired. Michael A. Meyer and David Ellenson, for instance, reject postmodernity and radical autonomy as possible foundations for liberal Judaism. Marc Gellman seeks to reappropriate the notion of an afterlife and world to come, a doctrine usually ignored or rejected by modern Jews. (Neil Gillman, a Conservative theologian, develops the idea at even greater length.) Yet, sadly, it is sloppy thinking (and worse) that increasingly characterizes Reform deliberation and action. Reform leadership has begun in earnest to deconstruct Judaism's venerable liturgical metaphors in favor of feminist God-language that is both unpoetic and unintelligible. (Curiously, the only symposium contributor to refer to God as "She" is Saul Berman, an Orthodox rabbi.) Reform has taken unilateral action in redefining Jewish identity, not only embracing "patrilineal descent" as an option but also coming close to eliminating descent as a criterion altogether. Most shocking, perhaps, a resolution in favor of homosexual marriage as a civil right was approved by a voice vote at the Central Conference of American (Reform) Rabbis meeting in the spring of 1996, after some fifteen minutes of largely one-sided debate. (As Dennis Prager observed, it was the specta-

cle of a large organization of rabbis considering one of the most fundamental questions of Western religious and cultural thought — with all
of the profundity and seriousness that might be associated with a resolution on whether to break for lunch.)

Despite being under similar secular and political pressures, the
Conservative movement has been able to preserve far more of the authentic tradition (although recent evidence suggests that the bulk of
Conservative laity may be closer to Reform's intellectual laxity than to
its own rabbinic leadership). David G. Dalin gives a concise articulation
of the problems imbedded in the modern inheritance of a millennial tradition, citing Abraham Joshua Heschel's observation that "Judaism is
based on a minimum of revelation and a maximum of interpretation."
But unlike so much of Reform, in this account it is learned rabbinic interpretation, not antinomian anarchy, that determines how the mitzvot
are understood and performed. Whether this way of thinking — at once
traditional and modern — can ultimately provide a vital center for
American Judaism remains unclear. Few contributors to the symposium
hold out much hope for a center that holds. As David Weiss Halivni puts
it, "The right is moving farther to the right and the left farther to the
left," with little love or tolerance for other Jews.

Some observers cite a small but growing religiosity within liberal
Judaism as a possible source of rapprochement. Pockets of intellectually
and spiritually interested young adults now dot the landscape of Jewish
America, suggesting a yearning for spiritual intensity that is specifically
Jewish. Unfortunately, these efforts sometimes slip into a kind of spiri-
tuality-for-its-own-sake, becoming little more than Jewish-style tours
through psychobabble and pseudo-mystical contentment. The increased use of Hebrew and the greater frequency of yarmulkes in Reform congregations are small, superficial improvements when weighed
against the wholesale capitulation to a secular cosmology. As Jon D.
Levenson, an Orthodox contributor, points out, increased observance is
not necessarily an "indication that one is attempting to overcome the
ethic of self-gratification and to replace it with the ethic of altruism that
is at the heart of authentic Jewish living. The notion that personal autonomy and the quest for self-fulfillment are sacrosanct can also interfere
with acceptance of important elements in Jewish morality such as the
laws governing sexual behavior and the law that a fetus may be killed
only in the rarest and gravest of cases."

If an inescapable theme of *Commentary*'s symposium is the resurgence of Jewish traditionalism at the expense of liberalism, traditionalists should nonetheless be only qualifiedly pleased. The irony is that traditional Judaism, particularly Orthodoxy, owes much of its current success to the past strength of liberal Judaism. The great achievement of the Reform movement was to present a version of Judaism, still grounded in God, for the great mass of educated and culturally assimilating diaspora Jews. Conservative Judaism fulfilled much of the same need while at the same time addressing the desire for ethnic solidarity and greater continuity with tradition. In short, liberal Judaism gave religious inspiration to many whose enthusiasm and intellectual curiosity would cause them later to return to religious traditionalism: Shlomo Riskin, David Novak, David Klinghoffer, Samuel Dresner, Jon Levenson, and Jacob Neusner are prominent Jewish thinkers who made such an odyssey. The current disarray of liberal Judaism, while seeming to some religious traditionalists as pure vindication, should also be an occasion for somber reflection and sorrow.

Why Egalitarianism Is Not Good for the Jews

AARON WILDAVSKY

A pall hangs over the American debate about equality. It is becoming difficult for people to speak their minds. College campuses, of all places, are filled with silences, and the discussions that do occur are often awkward and truncated. Racial minorities and women fear being told they are unworthy; white males fear being dismissed as racist, sexist, or — if they are straight — homophobic.

My concern here is not with that larger issue, but with a more limited (but at least equally controversial) subset of it: Is the egalitarian ideal — one person should count as one and no more than one — good for Jewish political influence?

Polls and election results reveal that Jews are overwhelmingly on the left politically and thus leaders in the fight for equality. Jews constitute a substantial part of the leadership of left-liberal organizations devoted to the reduction of power differentials between rich and poor, black and white, men and women, gay and straight. Is it possible, I ask, in seeking to bring this hitherto subterranean question up for discussion, that this extraordinary political effort is likely to have the effect, whether intended or not, of diminishing Jewish political influence?

Jews have many interests, of course, that stand apart from their Jewishness. That is not in question here. Rather, by "Jewish political influence," I mean the ability of Jews both to defend the specifically Jewish interests they now have — such as support for Israel — and to maintain the politically relevant resources they would need to defend other such interests in the future. It could be argued that Jews no longer have interests that would (or should) set them apart from other Americans. But Jewish history, I think, suggests that such optimism is unwarranted, even in America. The vast majority of Jews believe there are and will continue to be issues of special importance to Jews. Jews also undoubtedly feel more secure knowing they have a reservoir of influence to draw upon should the need arise. This being so, it is worthwhile assessing the resources that have led to political influence for American Jews and asking how these would fare under current egalitarian proposals.

Compared to the general population with whom they both ally themselves and compete for power, Jews may briefly be described as tiny in proportion to the whole, concentrated in big industrial states with large numbers of electoral votes, highly educated, richer than average, far more willing to use money for political purposes, well-organized as a community, and, comparatively speaking again, immensely participatory.

Jews make up roughly 2.5 percent of the total population of the United States. Only two states — New Jersey and New York — are more than 5 percent Jewish, with New York highest at about 10 percent. The Jewish share of the population has been dropping for a long time — it stood as high as an estimated 3.6 percent in 1930. Given current trends, to the extent that Jewish influence depends on population, it can be described as very low and declining.

But population figures, of course, do not tell the whole story of political or cultural influence. A major offsetting factor for Jews has been their very high level of formal education, which has led to statistical overrepresentation in leadership roles in the arts, professions, mass media, and elsewhere. In some of these key areas — most notably, perhaps, the professoriate — Jewish influence may be expected to diminish as egalitarian schemes in the form of affirmative action programs proliferate. (Jewish *male* influence, at least; Jewish women will presumably benefit.)

Jews have also exercised influence beyond what their numbers alone would suggest in various aspects of political life. That influence too threatens to diminish in the wake of a number of egalitarian measures instituted in recent years. The story here begins with developments in the Democratic Party — the overwhelming majority of politically active Jews being Democrats rather than Republicans.

Following the disastrously divisive presidential nominating struggle in 1968, the Democrats accepted the McGovern Commission reforms requiring that specific proportions of delegates to the national convention be women, youth, and people of color. One result was a dramatic drop in the proportion of Jewish male delegates.

The same set of reforms also led to such a proliferation of primaries that they have become the main, indeed the overwhelming, mechanism for selecting presidential candidates. The justification for such heavy reliance on primaries is again egalitarian, the assumption being that "one person, one vote" is the only legitimate principle for nomination as well as election to public office.

Further, the Democratic Party now has rules providing a form of proportional representation in primaries; candidates who receive above a certain minimum of the vote receive a proportional share of the delegates to which a state or district within a state is entitled. The point for Jews is in the consequences of the principle: proportional representation dilutes the value of population groups disproportionately represented in populous competitive states. Why campaign in or pay particular attention to the interests of voters in states like California, New York, and Illinois — where Jews have disproportionate influence — when under proportional representation the gain or loss in delegates is likely to be minuscule?

Again, the point for Jews is clear: Jewish voters are small in number, and any scheme that counts one as one and no more means that Jewish influence will be limited to the 2.5 percent of the population they represent.

Nor does the story end here. In 1988, the primary system for presidential nomination was extended to a regional primary called "Super Tuesday." The logic behind the regional primary has already produced a call (based once more on equality) for a national primary. Why should voters in one region, or several regions, exercise disproportionate influence? Why not combine simplicity with fairness by holding a national primary?

And why should the principle involved be restricted to primaries? What about general elections? What about the inegalitarian electoral college? Surely, among people who will accept no principle other than one person, one vote, the electoral college can only be seen as an unfortunate anomaly. Only direct election of the President can satisfy the criterion of one person, one vote.

And, once again, that would be bad for Jewish political influence. Not for Jews alone, of course: direct election of the President would also be bad for blacks and other strategically placed minorities. But direct election would not be as bad for blacks because they are much larger (11.7 percent compared to 2.5 percent) and, therefore, more worth appealing to if numbers are all that matter. Blacks also have a much higher birth rate than Jews.

The egalitarian principle in politics extends beyond voting to finances. Proponents of campaign finance reform insist that unequal access to financial resources constitutes unfairness. Existing and proposed reforms call variously for mandated floors and ceilings in campaign spending, the principle in all cases being to reduce the influence of private interests in politics and to make election contests more equal. (Opponents of restrictions on spending point out that, given the enormous natural advantages held by incumbents, a limit on spending might well constitute an incumbents' protection act.)

Because Jews have higher incomes than average and contribute more of what they have to political purposes, Jewish influence would decline were campaign finance reforms put into effect. True, Jews could still contribute their labor to candidates, but those who could not or prefer not to spend surplus time on politics would witness a significant decline in influence.

Radical egalitarians insist that equalizing spending on elections is only a first, and rather minor, step toward what should be the true end of the campaign for equality: equalization — or as close to it as practicable — in the distribution of income. And here again, naturally, Jews would be comparative losers. If Jewish income were reduced, support for Jewish community concerns — education, Israel, politics — would necessarily decline.

The pattern of all this is unmistakably clear. Making up for small numbers through education, knowledge, income, effort, location, and unity has been the secret of Jewish political success. Jews are not the all-powerful group that conspiracy-minded zealots imagine, but they have wielded influence beyond their numbers. And the egalitarian impulse currently at work in various segments of society would have the effect of limiting that influence.

To which one response might be, So what? After all, it could be said, Jewish influence should not be seen, or maintained, as a good in itself.

At least a measure of it might be sacrificed for the general good. Being Jewish involves more than religious or ethnic identification. Being Jewish is not simply about means to any end that Jews might decide to embrace, but about the choice of ends themselves. The Jewish ethical tradition, it could be argued, has from scriptural to modern times emphasized support for the weaker elements in society: it has, that is to say, been egalitarian. For not a few Jews, the very meaning of Jewishness involves a striving for egalitarian justice. To be a Jew is to be, in that sense, a person of the left, a seeker after equality of condition.

There is no reason, to be sure, for Jews to view every issue as necessarily imbued with Jewish interests. Or to see the question of Jewish influence as an all-or-nothing affair. Caught between a desire to maintain Jewish influence and egalitarian impulses, Jews might well seek some of each. In most if not all of the areas surveyed here, there is middle ground to be found between pure egalitarianism and maximization of Jewish influence.

The larger philosophical question involves the definition of justice. The desirability or not of maintaining existing Jewish political and cultural influence comes down to differences of political vision. If social justice requires relatively equal possession of resources, then Jews ought to welcome a diminution of their current influence in order to achieve a more egalitarian society. But if one's vision of equality focuses not on equality of results but on an equality of opportunity that might well produce unequal results — and that is, of course, the more venerable and established idea of equality in America — then disproportionate Jewish influence loses its *prima facie* problematic character.

In recent years, Jews have been decertified as a "deprived minority." No doubt this judgment reflects the view that in terms of command over resources, including political influence, Jews have become established. But is it true now, and will it remain true, that Jews, who constitute so tiny a proportion of the American people, will no longer need or want influence beyond their numbers? And should we at least want to consider the possibility that what is good for the Jews might also be good for society as a whole?

I do not argue that Jewish influence must be maintained as a good in itself. I am saying that it ought not to be taken for granted or heedlessly given away without understanding the costs that its sacrifice might involve now and in the future.

A Rabbi's Christmas

JAKOB J. PETUCHOWSKI

In order not to raise false hopes in the hearts of those who still have the expectation that, one day, all Jews will convert to Christianity, it might be best to begin these musings with a few disclaimers. The writer of this article does *not* believe in the Trinity. He does *not* believe that Jesus of Nazareth was either a part of the Godhead or the Messiah expected by the Jews. In other words, the writer of these lines is *not* a Christian.

But the writer of these lines also dissociates himself completely from the annual battle waged each winter by various Jewish organizations against the festival of Christmas, or, at least, against the public observance of Christmas. For one thing, although he does not himself celebrate Christmas in his own home, he rather likes the sights, the sounds, the smells, and the tastes of Christmas. Nor is he beyond relishing such traditional German Christmas delicacies as *Lebkuchen* and *Stollen* — coming, as he does, from a German-Jewish background where those bakery goods figured prominently in the observance of the Jewish winter festival of Hanukkah. Colorfully decorated Christmas trees and crèches, in the homes of Christian friends and in public places, delight his eyes; the sound of Christmas carols is music to his ears; and he avidly follows the rubrics and the pageantry of the Papal Midnight Mass on his TV screen.

Still, all of that is a matter of mere externals. What really intrigues him is the fact that millions of his non-Jewish fellow human beings are celebrating the birthday of a *Jewish* child. And they are doing so by extol-

157

ling the values of peace and good will. All the more misplaced, he thinks, are the efforts by some supposedly Jewish organizations to arouse, through their battles against Christmas symbols in public places, the ill will and resentment of Christians — at the very time when the Christian religion, more than at other times of the year, inspires its followers with irenic and philanthropic sentiments.

Suppose that one day half of the world, including the United States, were to take note of the contributions made to human thought by the seventeenth-century thinker of Jewish origin, Baruch Spinoza, by instituting an annual celebration of his birthday — including the public display of Spinoza's lens-grinding workshop. Would the various Jewish organizations now fighting public Christmas displays also fight the public observance of Spinoza's birthday? Hardly. In fact, they might even enthusiastically welcome it — in spite of the fact that Spinoza had severely criticized the faith of his Jewish ancestors, and had been excommunicated by the rabbinical authorities of Amsterdam.

Or what would happen if there were an annual International Sigmund Freud Day, including public displays of replicas of the couch which once stood in Freud's Vienna consulting room? Would Jewish organizations now fighting public Christmas displays fight that display, too? Hardly. In fact, they might even enthusiastically welcome it — in spite of the fact that Freud had proudly proclaimed his own atheism, and had included the religion of his Jewish ancestors among the rest of the world's religions, all of which he described as illusions.

What, then, is so different about celebrating the birthday of that Palestinian Jew through whose influence, as already noted by the great twelfth-century Jewish thinker, Moses Maimonides, the words of Israel's Torah have been spread to the far corners of the earth? Why does the public celebration of the birthday of Jesus of Nazareth, including the public display of replicas of the Bethlehem crèche, arouse such Jewish animosity?

The reasons are varied and complicated. Traditionally, in spite of its role in spreading major Jewish teachings throughout the world, Christianity, to put it mildly, has not been an unmixed blessing for Jews. Not only the words of the Torah were spread throughout the world in Jesus' name; that same name was also invoked when, throughout the centuries, Christians murdered Jews by the thousands, burned them alive, confiscated their goods, restricted the way in which they could earn their livelihoods, and confined them to overcrowded and unsanitary quarters. The Christian ideals of peace and good will did not extend beyond the entrance of the ghetto. This may no longer be the case today. But Jews have long memories. To many of them, the sign of the Cross is still a reminder of pogroms and persecutions. Their attitude toward Christianity and toward Christianity's founder is, therefore, a highly ambivalent one.

That is particularly true of those Jews — and they tend to be the most Orthodox followers of the faith — whose own personal and family background in Eastern Europe still approximated most closely the conditions of Jewish life in the Christian Middle Ages. Those Jews certainly cannot be expected to "enjoy" Christmas.

Yet, and here we come to an apparent paradox, these East European Orthodox Jews are *not* in the forefront of those who protest most vociferously against the public display of Christmas symbols or the public celebration of that festival. In fact, not only are they not in the forefront; most of them have nothing at all to do with the organizations that lead the battle against the public observance of Christmas in the name of *the* "Jewish Community."

That battle is led by a different type of Jew altogether. He or she is most likely to be a secularist of Jewish origin, who has no use for any kind of religion; and that includes the religion into which he or she was born. And in that battle, the secularist of Jewish origin is liable to be joined by a fellow Jew of the Reform Jewish denomination, which — in its increasingly radical departures from traditional Jewish belief and practice — is itself more and more becoming a wing of American secularism. Such Jews seek alliances with all the other secularist forces in the country that want to denude the "public square" of every last trace of religious influence. They keep insisting upon a strict enforcement of the separation of church and state — enforcement to a degree certainly never anticipated by the founders of the republic.

In other words, what we are really dealing with in this annual battle against public Christian observance is not so much a "Jewish" attack on that observance as it is a *secularist* one — with some of the prominent secularists identifying themselves as Jews. They are the same people who fight *non-denominational* prayers in public schools, the use of public-school facilities for meetings of high school religious-interest groups, and state support of private schools. They fight with equal vigor the attempts by other Jewish groups to have Jewish religious symbols exhibited alongside the Christian ones, such as the efforts of the Chabad (Lubavitch) group of Orthodox Jews to place a Hanukkah candelabrum on the public square when a Christmas tree is put up there, which would be a fitting demonstration of America's religious pluralism. They are, in other words, not singling out Christianity. They are against the public manifestation of religion *per se* — even (or, perhaps, particularly) against the public manifestation of the religion of their own ancestors.

The invocation of the First Amendment as authority for the campaign against the public display of any and all religious symbols seems to involve the demand that the state "establish" the religion of Secularism as the official religion of the United States — which would, to say the least, be a rather curious use of the First Amendment. But even if one were to grant, for argument's sake, that the lawyers employed by the American Jewish Congress, the (Reform) Union of American Hebrew Congregations, and similar organizations have established the "true" meaning of the First Amendment, i.e., that the amendment really and truly rules out the public display of a crèche or a Hanukkah candelabrum, one would still be entitled to wonder what those organizations hope to gain by stirring up animosities every winter.

Traditional Jewish teaching includes the principle of *liphnim mishurat hadin* (cf. Babylonian Talmud *Baba Qamma* 100a and elsewhere), which means that, on occasion, it is preferable not to make use of the full extent to which the law, strictly interpreted, entitles one to go. For there is, after all, a "higher law," which is adumbrated in Deuteronomy 12:28, "You shall do what is good and right in the sight of the Lord your God." Several passages in Jesus' Sermon on the Mount seem to incorporate that principle. It is not a case of "abolishing" the law, but rather, if one so desires — and if one does so to one's own, and not the other person's hurt — of not pressing the full extent of what the law provides. That, admittedly, may not be an everyday occurrence in traditional Jewish life (although the pious will always strive for it), but it is a manifestation of a higher degree of piety. Some of the ancient rabbis even sought to find biblical basis for such transcendence of biblical law.

It would seem to this writer that, even if the strict constructionists of the separation of church and state could demonstrate beyond a shadow of a doubt that the public display of Christmas symbols infringes upon that "separation," Jews might still prefer to abide by the principle of *liphnim mishurat hadin,* of *not* running to the courts in order to get the spontaneous expression of their neighbors' piety interfered with by the Law. After all, what are we to think of a "Judaism" that is so weak that it feels threatened by the display of a crèche at City Hall, or by the sound of a Christmas carol at a public school assembly? Why, then, not show some generosity on the Jewish side at a season of the year when Christians celebrate the birth of the Jew in whose name they proclaim peace and good will to humankind?

And it is, to be quite honest, not *only* a matter of superior generosity. Life in the medieval Christian world — in which, by the way, we no longer happen to live — certainly was no bed of roses for the Jews. But Jews fared infinitely *worse* in those modern societies from which the God of Abraham and of Jesus had been banished. If Jews cannot forget the Middle Ages, they owe it to themselves to remember the most recent past, too. One could argue, therefore, that the very self-interest of the Jews is at stake in preventing the United States from becoming a totally godless society.

Jews may not accept the dogmas and the theology associated with the Christmas story. They would, in fact, cease to be Jews if they did. Nor would they be acting in good taste if, without accepting the Christian belief structure, they were to celebrate Christmas in their own homes. (And it does not help much if they try to justify the Christmas tree in their home by saying that it was originally a pagan, rather than a Christian, custom — as though Judaism approved of paganism!) But they can still recognize in the *Christian* observance of Christmas one of the factors that help maintain the religious character of our society — in which Jews, too, with their own beliefs and practices, and with their very lives, have a considerable stake.

That is why this writer will continue to wish his Christian friends a "Merry Christmas" at Yuletide, and rejoice in the fact that those friends join the angelic choir in proclaiming glory to God in the highest, and peace among humankind on earth. He will most certainly not object at all to the public display of his friends' symbols of religious faith. Indeed, he will continue to be moved by awe and wonder that, through the influence of one of his own remote cousins, some of the words of Judaism's Torah have been spread to the far corners of the earth.

Anti-Semitism and Our Common Future

RICHARD JOHN NEUHAUS

With a somewhat wearied sense of necessity one turns, yet again, to the question of what is and what is not anti-Semitism. One does so knowing full well that it will not be the last time. Jewish-Christian tensions and the attendant charges of anti-Semitism are a staple in American public life, and will be that for as long as some Christians view Jews as alien and many Jews view Christianity as threatening. Of course these perceptions feed one another. At a level deeper than the perennial contretemps over anti-Semitism, and in keeping with St. Paul's reflections in Romans 9 through 11, the continuing tension has nothing less than an eschatological horizon. As weary as we sometimes might be of the subject, Christians must continue to pay attention. Jews, given their demographic marginality joined to their societal influence, have no choice but to pay assiduous attention.

The current round of controversies has everything to do with alarums over the perceived ascendancy of the Religious Right. As a result, some Jews have ratcheted up to an almost painful degree their antennae for the detection of anti-Semitism. A few months ago, one of our local newspapers, the *Times,* went ballistic when the London *Spectator* ran a little article on the self-described dominance of Jews in Hollywood. The somewhat naive *Spectator* author thought he was doing nothing more than reporting an interesting circumstance and, as it turns out, was in large part relying on what Jewish writers had said about Jews and Hollywood. The young man did not understand that, according to the rules of the more extreme members of the anti-Semitism patrol, non-Jews are not supposed to notice when Jews publicly celebrate Jewish influence and success. As Ann Douglas has described in her acclaimed account of New York in the 1920s, *Terrible Honesty* (Farrar, Straus & Giroux), the central role of Jews in American popular entertainment goes back to the nineteenth century and, far from being a secret, has been frequently extolled in film and song. With weeks of letters and commentary in the *Spectator,* our British cousins had great fun with this little squall, chalking it up as yet another instance of American hypocrisy about our professed devotion to free speech.

Another young man, hardly so innocent, has been doing his partisan best to exploit the political potential of Jewish-Christian suspicions. Some years ago Michael Lind fell in with those notorious neoconservatives and for some time was an editor of the *National Interest* before he decided to unleash his arrested outrage and go over to the opposition. Having secured a berth with Lewis Lapham's *Harper's,* Lind's attacks on his erstwhile friends have been popping up with remarkable regularity in publications large and small. He pushed the button for big-time attention when he rabbled the readers of the *New York Review of Books* with a slashing indictment of Pat Robertson, who, according to Lind, runs the Christian Coalition, the Religious Right, the Republican Party, the pro-family movement, and just about everything else that Mr. Lind doesn't like about America. The charge, as best we can understand it, is that Robertson's vast conspiracy is exceedingly dangerous because Robertson believes there are vast conspiracies.

Mr. Lind thought he hit pay dirt with the book *The New World Order,* in which Robertson tells you everything you wanted to know, and more, about how the world got into its present sorry shape. Robertson's eccentric and sometimes bizarre account of modern history gives a prominent role to, among others, "European financiers" who allegedly have been pulling the strings of global politics for a very long time. Lind pounces on the fact that some of the sources cited by Robertson are also cited by anti-Semites who explain modern history by reference to the machinations of "Jewish bankers." That Robertson refers to them as European rather than as Jewish is clear evidence, to Mr. Lind, that Robertson is not only anti-Semitic but is trying to disguise his anti-Semitism. He is the worst kind of anti-Semite, the kind that refuses to criticize Jews. The ever-so-devious Robertson also cultivates Jewish leaders, invites them to speak at his public meetings, and has a Jewish attorney heading his religious freedom organization. Is more evidence of his anti-Semitism needed?

This is not to let Robertson off the hook. True, in justifying his use of notorious sources he invokes the authority of a respectable professor at Georgetown University who uses the same sources, and he notes that President Clinton has on occasion invoked the authority of said professor, who apparently taught him when he was at Georgetown. But none of this gets us anywhere helpful. The fact is that some of the sources employed in *The New World Order* are manifestly anti-Semitic, and Mr. Robertson would have saved himself a lot of sorrow by clearly and explicitly repudiating that anti-Semitism in his book. Even better, he should not have used such sources in the first place. The conclusion remains, however, that while Pat Robertson is guilty of writing bad history, there is no ground whatever for accusing him of anti-Semitism.

Nonetheless, Frank Rich, columnist for the *Times,* picked up on the Lind article to demand that the media dig into the dirt of Robertson's, and the Christian Right's, putative anti-Semitism. Rich has been described as the *Times'* attack dog, which, while not very nice, is apt enough. He comes across as a toy Doberman in perpetual snit. His attack elicited an extended response from Robertson which, to its credit, the *Times* published. Robertson explained that *The New World Order* was written at the height of the Gulf War when he was worried about the compromise of U.S. sovereignty and Israeli safety in a "New World Order" under the aegis of the United Nations. "I do feel," wrote Robertson, "that only someone who is desperately attempting to cause mischief would make the unfounded allegations about me or my book that have recently appeared in the *New York Times.*" He continued: "All who know me, Jewish and Christian, recognize that I have been one of the strongest friends of Israel anywhere in the world. In 1974, when Israel appeared threatened and alone as a result of a worldwide oil crisis, I made a vow that I have kept to this day: I promised to use my influence, and that of the institutions I founded, to vigorously support Israel and the Jewish people. I have kept my vow. My comments on my daily television program have been pro-Israel. In fact, during the Gulf War, I was one of the few voices in America speaking out regularly in support of Israel. I have lobbied for Israel, and donated hundreds of thousands of dollars to Jewish interests and organizations. By every public word and deed, I have kept my promise."

Frank Rich was not impressed. A few days later he came back with a column imaginatively titled "The Jew World Order," in which he notes that Louis Farrakhan accuses "international bankers" of nefarious doings and so does Pat Robertson. So there. "Our two most prominent extremists of the 1990s," wrote Rich, "are both dipping into the same well of pseudo-history that once served Father Coughlin and Henry Ford." This is high hysteria even for Frank Rich. Pat Robertson has as much in common with Farrakhan as Frank Rich has with ordinary decency. The circle of extremists is extended as Rich notes that, at the Christian Coalition convention in 1991, "Phil Gramm, Lamar Alexander, and Elizabeth Dole, standing in for her husband, all kissed Mr. Robertson's ring."

Lest he overlook anyone, Rich concludes with the shocking report that Patrick Buchanan wrote in a publication of the Christian Coalition that Robert Rubin, Secretary of the Treasury, supported the Mexican bailout to enrich his old investment firm of Goldman, Sachs. (Rubin, Goldman, Sachs. They all sound Jewish. Therefore Pat Buchanan is an anti-Semite.) Never mind that many critics of the Mexican bailout, including perhaps a majority of members of Congress, claimed that its chief purpose was to save Wall Street from its own investment follies.

While critics, including some conservatives, believe that Buchanan has in the past toyed with anti-Semitic sentiments, his polemics against the Mexican bailout are solidly within the mainstream of political debate.

As one story triggers another, the *Wall Street Journal* has this big item by Jonathan Kaufman on Jews who see "a rise in bigotry." A Jewish woman in Birmingham, Michigan, reports that parents in her son's sixth-grade class have complained that the children can't sing "Silent Night," and a classmate told her son he didn't like having to learn about Hanukkah. "Mrs. Wagenheim," reports the *Journal,* "watched with growing alarm as Washington politicians proposed reintroducing school prayer." "'I thought I could be like everyone else,' Mrs. Wagenheim says. 'But now we seem to stand out more. I never felt like this before.'" Apparently it has only now occurred to her that 98 percent of Americans are not Jewish, with more than 90 percent claiming to be Christians of one sort or another. If one belongs to a very high profile minority that constitutes little more than 2 percent of the population, standing out should not come as a surprise. It might even be cherished as a distinction.

Rabbi Peter Rubinstein of New York's Central Synagogue says, "To be a Jew is not to be anymore in the mainstream of America. You watch the Republican convention, you read the 'Contract With America,' you listen to talk radio. Before I could have accepted that, as a Jew and as an American, my yearnings were going to be harmonious. Now, I'm not so sure." It would seem that the rabbi's anxieties have nothing to do with being Jewish and everything to do with being politically liberal. For many liberal Jews, however, the two are hardly distinguishable. *The Wall Street Journal* cites other instances of the perceived rise in "bigotry." In Phoenix, Arizona, some Jewish homeowners found advertisements put on their doorknobs promoting a free video on the life of Jesus. A rabbi who represents the American Jewish Committee in Phoenix reports that a woman complained to him that her son was handed a book by a fifth-grade classmate and told, "Read this." The book was about Jesus. Says the rabbi, "People are starting to talk in terms of, 'We are being persecuted.'" A little boy wants to share his faith with his Jewish classmate. Can pogroms be far behind?

The *Journal* suggests there is now a "role reversal" between the Orthodox and what it calls mainstream Jews. Mainstream Jews, it says, never felt anti-Semitism was a part of their lives, while the Orthodox were ever alert to anti-Jewish expressions. This is very dubious history. In the past and at present, it is liberal and secular Jews who chiefly support the hypersensitive institutional alarm systems that flash "Anti-Semitism!" at the suggestion that Jews are not just like everybody else. The Orthodox have always known that being Jewish makes a difference, and should make a difference. There is nothing new in the view of the traditionalist rabbi who, according to the *Journal,* is inclined to "welcoming the religious right and scoffing at suggestions of bigotry." "Moving to the right is a blessing for the country," says Rabbi Joseph Gopin of the Chabad movement. "The government should support religion."

Jews who are astute analysts of the American scene have a similar take on what is happening. William Kristol, the Republican strategist, observes that alarm about anti-Semitism "often does verge into paranoia among Jews." As for his own view, Kristol says, "I prefer the Christian right to the pagan left." Norman Podhoretz, the former editor of

Commentary, observes that conservatives don't hate Jews. "They hate liberals. As it happens, most Jews are liberals." Midge Decter's 1995 Erasmus Lecture is titled, "Being Jewish in Anti-Christian America." If the choice is between a dominantly anti-Christian elite culture and the majority culture of Christians, it is suggested, Jews have compelling prudential and religious reasons to side with the Christians.

Another piece of nastiness that has received almost no attention in this country is a controversy generated over Human Life International, a pro-life organization based in Maryland that in the spring of 1995 held its convention in Montreal. B'nai B'rith of Canada launched an all-out campaign against HLI, charging that it is an extremist organization guilty of anti-Semitism. The campaign received major media attention in Canada, and some went so far as to demand that the government stop HLI delegates from crossing the border to attend the convention. B'nai B'rith also pressured the Archdiocese of Montreal, unsuccessfully, to refuse HLI the use of the cathedral for the convention's opening Mass. The prime exhibit in support of the claim that HLI is anti-Semitic is a chapter in a book by Father Paul Marx, *Confessions of a Pro-life Mission-ary.* Marx is a Benedictine priest and founder of HLI, and in that chapter he deplores the prominent role of Jews in the pro-abortion movement, arguing that Jews, of all people, should recognize the consequences when human life is devalued.

The chapter in question may be injudicious, and some points of fact may be disputed, but it is hardly anti-Semitic. No reasonable person will dispute the fact that Jews are disproportionately represented among the promoters of abortion, and drawing analogies between abortion and the Holocaust is hardly "extremist." Without taking a position on abortion, a number of prominent Canadian Jews courageously challenged the slander perpetrated by B'nai B'rith. In this country, Msgr. George Higgins devoted his column, which has a wide readership in the Catholic diocesan press, to the HLI affair. Msgr. Higgins, usually a more fair-minded commentator, accused HLI of engaging in a "flirtation with anti-Semitism," and says that the fact that bishops are associated with HLI makes it difficult for Jews "to distinguish the preachments of HLI from the official teaching of the Church, which clearly condemns forays into anti-Semitism." The Catholic Church does indeed condemn anti-Semitism in all its forms, but, pace Msgr. Higgins, there is no evidence that HLI is guilty of flirting with anti-Semitism. Promptly upon the appearance of Higgins' column, the interreligious affairs office of the New York-based Anti-Defamation League issued a press release commending him for his bold opposition to anti-Semitism.

The happy fact, documented by every serious study, is that anti-Semitism in America has dramatically declined in the last fifty years, and even more so in the last twenty years. It is kept alive at the margins by fringe groups such as Aryan Nation and by racist skinheads broadcasting their hate messages via Internet. Regrettably, it is also kept alive by institutions such as the Anti-Defamation League. The purpose of ADL is to counter defamation of Jews. If there is no defamation of Jews, ADL has no reason to exist. It is an organization that operates by demand-side economics. It has a built-in institutional need for a dependable supply of anti-Semitism in order to maintain itself. Its fund-raising depends upon sustaining a high level of Jewish anxiety about anti-Semitism. One is reminded of a recent report from the Midwest about a volunteer fireman convicted of arson. The village was going to close down the volunteer fire department, and he wanted to provide a convincing reason for not doing so. We do not suggest that groups such as ADL and B'nai B'rith of Canada are deliberately creating anti-Semitism, but by setting off false alarms they seriously reduce the believability of the anxiety upon which their existence depends.

The above-mentioned account in the *Wall Street Journal* reports the views of Daniel Levitas, described as a liberal Atlanta Jewish activist, who invokes memories of czarist Russia. "The Jews used to have a response when the Cossacks came to town," he says. "You close the doors, you batten down the hatches, and you shutter the windows. Eventually the dust will settle and you can come out again. The Jews used to say 'This too shall pass.' This time it's not going to pass." Such sentiments reflect the paranoia to which William Kristol refers and, not so incidentally, are an outrageous insult against non-Jewish Americans. The United States is not czarist Russia and the American people are not Cossacks bent upon killing Jews. Whatever his own intentions, statements such as those of Mr. Levitas cannot help but exacerbate Jewish-Christian relations, inflaming anti-Christian feelings among Jews and anti-Jewish feelings among non-Jews.

But he got one thing half-right: "This time it's not going to pass." If the "it" in question is the freer expression of religion and religiously grounded moral convictions in public, a major and lasting change does seem to be under way. Given that this is America, such expression will be predominantly Christian in character. This circumstance is understandably worrying to many Jews, but the challenges that it entails can be explored by Jews and Christians in a manner that does not threaten but strengthens our common participation in the American experiment. This was recently demonstrated by a symposium at Harvard marking the fiftieth anniversary of *Commentary* at which Midge Decter and this writer, among others, spoke.

In the last quarter century, it was pointed out at the Harvard meeting, there has been a dramatic change among Christians — from Catholics to evangelical Protestants — in the understanding of Christianity's dependence upon Judaism. Not simply the Judaism of what Christians call the Old Testament but the living Judaism that continues in mysterious relation to God's election and unbreakable promise. References to a "Judeo-Christian" moral tradition, for instance, are not merely a euphemistic trope employed to avoid offending Jews, although that may sometimes be the case. There is a much deeper level at which Christians are coming to understand their providential entanglement with Jews and Judaism, an understanding that has slight precedent in the two millennia of interaction between Jews and Christians. This growing understanding should be carefully nurtured by Jews and Christians alike.

From Birmingham, Michigan, to Atlanta to the Upper West Side of Manhattan, many Jews have assumed that the more secularized America is, the safer it is for Jews. In this view, Jewish security and success has been achieved despite the fact that America is a predominantly Christian society. This view, which is probably shared, at least intuitively, by a majority of Jews, is of relatively recent vintage. An alternative view is that Jews are secure and successful because this is a predominantly Christian society. All too obviously, there have been predominantly Christian societies in which Jews have been anything but secure. But the argument is that Christianity in America really is different, that it has internalized the imperatives of tolerance as a matter of religious duty, and that, more recently, it has come to see Judaism as an integral part of God's purposes in history.

It would be a tragedy of historic proportions were the opportunities of this new circumstance to be wasted in politicized rantings against the public assertiveness of conservative Christians. In a time when we are called to be "sensitive" to every grievance and discontent, a measure of sensitivity is due also those Christians who say that they want to take back their country. With the exception of a few kooks on the margins (who bear close watching), people who talk that way do not mean that the country must be taken back from Jews. They do have opponents in mind — "secular humanists," "the pagan left," "the cultural elites," "the mainstream media." In sum, the people and institutions that have in the past portrayed, and still do portray, millions of Americans as dangerous aliens, as strangers in their own land. These newly activated Americans are fed up with being put on the defensive because of what they see as their adherence to Christian belief and morality. This populist resurgence is undoubtedly driven by a degree of resentment, and it, too, may sometimes "verge into paranoia." For the most part, however, it is a perfectly understandable reaction to being treated with disrespect, even contempt, by the champions of secularism.

Frank Rich and others of fevered imagination to the contrary, the reaction has nothing to do with anti-Semitism. Unless, of course, Jews and Judaism are equated with, inter alia, promoting abortion, eliminating religion from public schools, advocating homosexuality, denigrating marital fidelity, shocking traditional sensibilities, and depicting Christians as potential perpetrators of genocide. Those who slander Jews and Judaism by making such an equation are indeed guilty of anti-Semitism, and it makes little difference whether the slander is peddled by Jews or by Christians.

If our reading is correct, the political culture has been dramatically changed in recent months and years, and more dramatic changes are in the offing. The deepest and probably most long-lasting change is the rediscovery of the free exercise of religion, and the assertion of religiously grounded moral conviction in the public square. This is a change that can be welcomed by both Jews and Christians — as citizens devoted to a free society, and as children of the God of Abraham, Isaac, Jacob, and Jesus. This change is understandably feared by determined secularists, Jewish and other, who are taken by surprise that American history is not turning out the way they had confidently expected. The vibrant resurgence of public religion forces them to reexamine their basic assumptions about America and the course of modernity, which is a difficult and painful undertaking.

There is reason to believe, however, that the next generation of Jews in America will more readily cope with, and even welcome, the free exercise of religion in public. A new study by Seymour Martin Lipset and Earl Raab, *Jews and the New American Scene* (Harvard University Press), examines the ways in which Jewish ethnic identity is fast eroding. Given the rate of intermarriage with non-Jews and other factors, it is quite possible that a few decades from now only half as many Americans will identify themselves as Jewish. Jewish identity that is based upon ethnicity, anxiety about anti-Semitism, and concern for Israel is, say Lipset and Raab, a fragile thing. The Jewish future in America will be secured not by "Jewishness" but by Judaism, and Judaism is, most importantly, religion. "The central core of Jewish identity has been religion, even though an ethnic culture is built into that religion. It is that religious core which provides a special edge of separatist cohesion for Jews."

Those who have constructed Jewish identity on the foundation of political liberalism have, according to Lipset and Raab, built upon sand. "Some want to believe that an intrinsic quality of Jewish life consists of such universally benevolent 'Jewish social values' as equality, social justice, and world peace.... But however strongly held, most of those social values are no longer particular to the Jews, and have clearly not provided the glue which can keep the Jewish community together."

As the Jews of tomorrow are more religiously observant, they will also be more socially and politically conservative. And that is because, as these scholars and many others point out, there is a strong connection between religious commitment and conservatism on a very broad range of questions.

Anti-Semitism is a very serious business. Christians, too, are responsible for seeing to it that it is watched assiduously and countered forcefully. That will not happen, however, if anti-Semitism is equated with opposition to the liberalism that many Jews believe to be the essential core of their "Jewishness." It will not happen if fair criticism of the behavior of some Jews, or many Jews, is recklessly condemned as anti-Semitism. And it will not happen if the dominant voice of Judaism in America is that of secular agencies whose stock in trade is to accuse non-Jews of anti-Semitism. Within American Jewry, there are a growing number of thinkers who point to a more promising way for the flourishing of Jews and Judaism in America. Jews will decide how their message is received, but the rest of us, as Christians and as citizens, have a deep interest in the revival of a Jewish identity that transcends the political partisanships of this historical moment.

Jews who are indifferent to the religious core of Judaism may, as Lipset and Raab suggest, be assimilated into the sector of secular Americans who are equally indifferent to Christianity. There they may maintain for a time an attenuated sense of ethnic identity, much in the way that others are vaguely Italian, Irish, or German "by extraction." But extraction means separation, and identities by extraction are by definition tenuous and short-lived. The interesting and promising future of Jewish-Christian relations rests with Jews and Christians who, in mutual respect and reverence, seek to discern and obey the will of the One who is, through Israel, the light to the nations, and not least to these United States of America.

SHORTER TAKES

Beguiled by the Public Square

MARC D. STERN

There are good reasons for the Jewish community's refusal to adopt equality as the overriding principle for defining religion's public role. Shortly after the Supreme Court upheld the equal access law, fundamentalist and evangelical groups announced campaigns to spread the gospel in the public schools. Describing the decision, one group dedicated to encouraging that effort has written, "God has opened up a huge mission field. Our missionaries to this field must be our high school students. They can reach their generation for Jesus." Equality that encourages such activity is no boon to Jews.

Some Orthodox groups have sought to ensure "equal treatment or encouragement of religion in public life." That is surely true of the Lubavitch's campaign to erect menorahs at government sites, or of its support for moments of silent prayer, or, for the broader Orthodox community, support for aid to parochial schools. These efforts represent the voice of, at most, 10 percent of American Jewry. And the fact is that even within Orthodoxy there are sharp and deep disagreements about the wisdom of these efforts, of which only Lubavitch's really represents a desire to increase government involvement with religion. The

rest of the Orthodox community is motivated by the very different principle of equality, or sheer necessity, not any independent judgment
about the desirability of increased public involvement with religion.

In short, if there is any wholesale shift of Jewish opinion on church-
state issues from a separationist point of view to an equal treatment or
greater involvement point of view, it is not yet visible. It would indeed be
startling if Jews were seeking to inject religion into the public life of the
nation when for American Jewry as a whole religion has less significance than ever.

This is not to say that equality is not *a* religious value for most Jews.
There is a unanimity that synagogues cannot be denied benefits accorded churches. Almost certainly, had the Supreme Court given un-
qualified approval to the display of crèches, Jews would have demanded
equal treatment for menorahs. That demand would have represented
not the view that it was healthy for government to be involved with religion, or that the public square needs greater input from religion, but the
bedrock view of Jews that they should not allow themselves to be treated
as second-class citizens. Equality between religious and nonreligious,
however, is simply not the only, or even the most important, value for
American Jews.

The substantive question posed is what ought to be the role of religion in American public life. That question could mean three different
things: it could refer to the problem of church-state relations — prayer
in the schools, religious holiday observances, and the like. The current
rule has on the whole served the Jewish community well. Beyond such
pragmatic considerations lies an ethical one: it is right that in a society
as diverse as this government should not inject itself into religious matters. And it is hard to see any great benefit to religion from the use of
opening prayers, In God We Trust, or other ceremonial notations of religious influence. Such events only trivialize religion, contributing a pa-
tina of piety, not its reality.

Or the question posed might be whether the government ought to
be especially tolerant of religious practices by exempting them, if at all
practicable, from restrictions imposed by laws of general applicability.
Here, the situation has been unsatisfactory ever since the Supreme
Court's "peyote" decision *(Employment Division v. Smith)* which held
that the Free Exercise Clause did not mandate such accommodation.
The organized Jewish community was for many years not sufficiently

interested in the problems of the religiously observant. If Rabbi Arthur Hertzberg is correct in describing the Jewish community as increasingly divorced from any substantial religious impulse (a description I believe to be correct), this lack of interest is hardly surprising.

But what I suspect the question means is yet a third thing: whether religious leaders ought to inject their religious views into political debates over the secular issues confronting society. Jews of all stripes in fact do just that: Orthodox Jews in the name of *halakha,* Reform Jews under the rubric of the prophetic tradition. Even secular umbrella groups such as the National Jewish Community Relations Advisory Committee invoke the Jewish tradition as justification for involvement in public affairs. Aside from a few early hypocritical denunciations of the religious right (and occasional critiques of anti-abortion activists) the Jewish community as a whole has not challenged such activity, even when it disagrees with the substance of what is said.

It is not all clear that this involvement under the rubric of religion produces very much or has significant impact on the real world. Despite the celebratory claims of Allen Hertzke in *Representing God in Washington: The Role of Religious Lobbies in the American Polity,* I do not believe that American religious groups have any large impact on issues other than legislation directly affecting the religious community as such. At most, religious advocacy gives moral legitimacy to policy urged on other (secular) grounds. On rare occasions that may be significant, but these cases are only a small percentage of the matters in which a religious voice is heard.

There is uncertainty within the Jewish community over how far religious leaders should go in advocating religious positions. May they use religious language? Where are appropriate means of speech? What claim do ministers have on their adherents, whether legislators or government officials? Governor Cuomo, and before him President Kennedy, insisted that the answer was easy — that other than in their private lives, the clergy had no claim to control the action of public officials.

The answer has the advantage of simplicity and of avoiding religious warfare and quasi-theocracies. But it also means that public officials must be religiously schizophrenic. Still, it seems advisable under present conditions for religious leaders as a matter of prudence not to seek to hold office-holders to religious discipline.

The debate over the appropriate role of religion in the public square was the most interesting church-state controversy of the 1980s. That debate led to no clear answers, which is not a particularly troubling situation. The fact is there are conflicting policies and pressures involving a balance among competing interests of religious freedom, pluralism, freedom of speech, and civility. It is instructive that while Richard John Neuhaus made a manful effort in his *Naked Public Square,* he was never quite able to explain — even, if I understand him, to his own satisfaction — what the implementation of his thesis calling for greater religious involvement in the public square would mean for religious minorities. For Jews, that is no minor objection to advocacy of greater political activity by religious groups. Probably the best that we as a society can do is muddle through, giving due regard for the conflicting interests.

In a way, however, the issue is an unfortunate distraction from more pressing realities. There is no lack of religious voice in American society. There is real lack of religious influence. In part, this is because of the give and take of the legislative process, a give and take for which the absolute commands of religious ethics are ill-matched.

But the problem goes beyond that. It is that religion's pronouncements do not produce deep resonance. The question for churches is how to persuade people that their pronouncements are weighty and deserving of implementation. How can religion speak to a society whose organs of communication are secular (and in which religious affairs receive relatively little coverage), a society whose values are pragmatic and short-term, where the commitment to religion is increasingly superficial, where most of the roles that religion once filled — whether setting moral standards, providing social services, or providing community — are now filled by groups and institutions in which religion doesn't play a role. The immediate problem, then, for religion is to persuade internally before turning to the public square. It is ultimately by persuading their adherents that religious groups will have influence, not by getting on the evening news.

I am not calling for a retreat into purely personal piety or a mystical insistence on communing with the Divine to the exclusion of all else, nor do I believe that the secular world is corrupt and beyond redemption. Rather, the question is where struggles for religious influence should be fought — whether the primary forum ought to be the public square. The public square is attractive and beguiling; it offers mass audiences, and the illusion of fame. What it does not offer for religious leaders is a substantial chance of success. That lies in creating communities of believers.

This prescription depends on the existence of religious institutions with the wherewithal to demonstrate the viability of alternatives to the prevailing secular morality, and the legal freedom to implement those lifestyles as much as possible. Both of these preconditions are now in substantial doubt. Here, then, is the future of church-state relations. And on this turns the future of religious influence on the public square.

The Dominating Majority

NICHOLAS WOLFSON

I do not share the assumption that more Jews are having "second thoughts" about the relationship between church and state. In my personal experience in organized Jewish life, there is no major shift. No doubt many in orthodox Jewish groups desire a breakdown in the wall between church and state, but the mainstream liberal Jewish organizations continue to maintain the old position.

They do so with good reason. It is in the self-interest of minority religions to uphold the separation principle embedded in the First Amendment. Breach the constitutional barrier, and dominant religious forces will flood the schools and public life with the majoritarian religious beliefs of the day. There will soon be no breathing space for minority voices.

There is nothing inherently cynical in alluding to Jewish self-interest. It is an interest shared by all the other minority voices in the country. It is, in essence, shorthand for a description of the core purpose of the First Amendment, whether in free speech or in religious expression and the separation principle.

That core is the protection of the minority in fundamental matters from the oppression of the majority, no matter how sincerely or passionately the majority makes its claims. Indeed, in affairs of religion, passionate sincerity is present more often than not. In a democratic society that passion will always lead to excesses, unless checked by the anti-majoritarian principles of the First Amendment.

I believe that some Jewish conservatives, or neo-conservatives, have been influenced by the 1980s rhetoric of Christian conservatives calling for the return to traditional values. I need not remind the readers of this volume of the argument which suggests that morality in private life can be restored only if religion is returned to the public square. It is based on a kind of Aristotelian notion that the state has the opportunity and responsibility to develop a cohesive moral order. This is in conflict with modern libertarian ideas that men and women should be free, as John Stuart Mill put it, to express themselves in word and action so long as they do not harm another.

I do not share the conservative faith in the wisdom of the state. Modern experience with the cruel excesses of state power has taught us the value of government restraint in areas of personal belief and action. Belief in the beneficent role of government, intermixed with religion, embodies a nostalgic longing for an imagined premodern golden age where religious leaders led the common populace in a private (and public) life of piety centered in the happy nuclear family. If ever there was such a world — and I doubt it — it cannot be introduced in modern Western society, without coercive government suppression of heretical (as the government sees them) movements.

There is a passionate diversity in religious belief. For example, Orthodox Jewry, the Catholic leadership, and other religious orthodoxies belittle the role of women in religious leadership. Reform and Orthodox Jewish groups and other religious groups differ deeply over the legitimacy of homosexuality. Reform and Orthodox Jews cannot even agree as to who is a Jew. What religion, then, do we bring into the schools and American public life? The answer, tragically, will be the religious belief that the dominant majority endorses.

Another obvious example of the dangers of religion in public life is the abortion issue. Catholic prelates, driven by fundamental belief, here threatened to excommunicate Catholic politicians who do not toe the line on this great debate. Fortunately, their effort at creating conformity appears to have failed. But their campaign is an indication of the kinds of censorship that will ultimately be brought to bear on minorities if religion is introduced as an instrument of proper belief into the schools and public life.

Unfortunately, Jews have only to look at Israel for a lesson in the dangers that religion in public life will bring. In Israel, Jews are the dominant majority. Religious leaders under a complex set of laws and customs have a powerful grip on the role of religious life in the public square. Marriage, divorce, and family life are largely subject to the dominant religious voices, which in Israel happen to be those of the Orthodox. As a result, although Israel is the only democracy in the region, the freedoms we are accustomed to in the United States as a consequence of the First Amendment are diminished. Indeed, my sense is that American Jews, and many citizens of Israel, are having second thoughts about this problem, which they view as equal in significance to the Israel-Palestinian issue.

Mordecai's Hope

MILTON HIMMELFARB

It has been said before, and needs to be said again: The trouble is not that religion in general has too small a role in American public life or American life simply. The trouble is that a particular religion has too great a role — paganism, the *de facto* established religion. When dissenters pleaded that it is no business of government to endow art like Robert Mapplethorpe's, all they got for their pains was a derisory token victory and the expectable disdain of the *New York Times.*

Let historicists wince at statements that begin, "Judaism is." Judaism is against paganism.

Ha-yehudi, "the Jew," occurs six times in Scripture, only in the book of Esther and always in apposition to "Mordecai," who is also once "a Jewish man" and once "a Jew." In Rabbi Johanan's exegesis (Megillah 13a), Mordecai is so insistently called a Jew "because he abjured paganism ['*avodah zarah*], for everyone who abjures paganism is called a Jew; as is written (Daniel 3:12): '. . . Jews . . . serve not thy gods nor worship the golden image which thou hast set up.'"

For the Rabbis, as for Scripture, the essence of paganism is unchastity. In Leviticus 18 the unchastities forbidden to Israel are not merely the practices of the Egyptian and Canaanite pagans but actually their laws *(huqqot* = Septuagint's *nomima): paganism* does more than tolerate, it demands unchastity. Rabbinically, only paganism's licentiousness explains its appeal. About Israelite paganism in the age of the First Temple, "Rabbi Judah said, citing Rav: Israel knew that *'avodah zarah* has no substance. They adopted *'avodah zarah* only in order to give themselves license for overt sexual transgression" (Sanhedrin 63b).

For the most solemn possible abjuration of paganism/unchastity, therefore, the Rabbis ordained Leviticus 18 to be read in the synagogue toward the close of Yom Kippur. (Was it in Queen Victoria's reign that Reform, fearing that Leviticus 18 might bring a blush to the cheek of the young person, banished it in favor of selected verses from 19? The delayed payoff for a heteroclite rabbinate now is that 18:22 need never be heard by its congregations.)

The honorific subtitle of the historian Peter Gay's *Enlightenment* is *The Rise of Modern Paganism*. The Enlightenment's project was liberal — to liberate us for the pursuit of our happiness — but some of what began as liberal has become libertine, and libertinism has brought enslavement and misery more than it has brought liberation and happiness: AIDS, kids who have kids, the vanishing father. First the French Revolution devoured its children, then the Bolshevik Revolution, and now the sexual revolution.

Drugs, too, are a pagan devourer. In Judaism, you are equally forbidden to injure yourself and your neighbor, but in paganism, you own your body and are free to inflict on it any injury you wish.

With less paganism and less of its bitter fruit, the country would be less diseased, less fear-ridden, less ignorant, less poor. Surely all must agree that American Jewry should try to help bring that about?

As the Duke of Wellington said about something else: If you can believe that, you can believe anything.

A *New York Times* editorial being sacred writ, if the *Times* says so then government must endow exhibits that "documented a sadomasochistic homosexual subculture." We have not yet been instructed about endowing exhibits that documented a sadomasochistic Aryan Nation subculture.

In Cincinnati, a curator was tried for obscenity because his museum defended the cause of Art by showing the Mapplethorpe collection. (He was acquitted, the jury deferring to its betters about "What Is Art?") One expert witness testified for the defense that the photograph of a penis with a finger inserted into it "was a very ordered, classical composition" and that another photograph, of an arm in an anus, was formally similar to the photograph of a flower. In the opinion of the *Times'* photography editor, the curator of a university museum "came closest to the truth when she told the prosecutor . . . , 'It's the tension between the physical beauty of the photograph and the brutal nature of what's going on in it that gives it the particular quality that this work of art has.'" The prosecutor failed to ask her a hypothetical question: What would be her expert opinion of a photograph in which there was tension between its beauty and the brutal nature of what was going on in a Nazi torture chamber?

When the esthetic and the ethical (or moral) conflict, as they do here, paganism sides with the esthetic and Judaism with the ethical. In the nineteenth century, Matthew Arnold's Hellenism/Hebraism and Samuel David Luzzatto's Atticism/Abrahamism drew that distinction. (In the twelfth century, Judah ha-Levi's *Kuzari* drew it.) In Arnold's time he thought that Hebraism pressed too hard on Hellenism. Now the effortless low paganism that ousted his kind of Hellenism presses much harder on Hebraism, but American Jews do not champion Hebraism in its distress. They champion separationism — separation of church and state elevated almost to the rank of *summum bonum* — and separationism favors paganism.

Responding to the backward who say that a Christ-in-urine is not what government should endow, the Establishment shudders at the censorship of not giving an artist the money he applies for. (Besides, it was only a tiny fraction of the Arts budget.) If, implausibly, the tiny fraction had endowed art for a church or synagogue, that would have been an unforgivable breach in the Wall of Separation. Whether the money was much or little would not matter, principle would be at stake. The money must be returned, the guilty exposed, watchdogs posted.

It would be funny if it were not so sad.

I first published my objections to the separationist dogma of the American Jewish community almost twenty-five years ago, and I have since called American Jews diehard conservatives. We have seen the unimaginable become real, the impossible become actual, the obdurate become yielding: Berlin wall down, statues of Lenin toppled, the triumphant religion of Marxism-Leninism in ruins. Can American Jewry, uniquely, hold out against necessary change?

British Jews are always puzzled by what they take to be our fuss about separation. They do not mind at all that their Chief Rabbi is in the House of Lords.

Tiqqûn means "setting right, repairing, correcting, perfecting." For Jews on the left who like to give a Jewish cast to their politics, the tradition's *tiqqûn 'olam,* "setting the world right," means whatever is on the left's agenda, and paganism never is. In the tradition itself the *'Alenu* prayer (which Solomon Schechter called the Jewish "Marseillaise") has this: ". . . in hope we wait, O Lord our God, . . . for Thee to remove the idols from the earth, the no-gods being utterly cut down, to *taqqen 'olam bemalkhut Shaddai* set the world right by the Almighty's kingship. . . ." The prayer ends in two verses from Scripture: "The Lord shall reign for ever and ever" (Exodus 15:18) and "And the Lord shall be king over all the earth: in that day shall there be one Lord, and his name one" (Zechariah 14:9). *Tiqqûn 'olam* is *tiqqûn* from paganism.

When will the Synagogue Council, the National Jewish Community Relations Advisory Council, ADL, and the two AJCs each appoint its Task Force on Combating Paganism? We should live so long.

Are Jews unlikely to bestir themselves soon to seek relief and deliverance from paganism and its bitter fruit? Then let us hope with Mordecai that "relief and deliverance will come to the Jews from another quarter."

On an Equal Footing

JONATHAN D. SARNA

In a petition to the Continental Congress, meeting in Philadelphia in 1787, the German-Jewish immigrant Jonas Phillips enunciated what to my mind should still be the proper approach of American Jews to the question of religion in American life. "The Israeletes," he wrote, "will think them self happy to live under a government where all Relegious societies are on an Eaquel footing."

Two centuries later, we know how difficult even this seemingly simple goal has been to achieve. Equal footing, after all, clashes with basic American notions of majority rule. Why *should* majority faiths have to accommodate themselves to minority ones? Doesn't democracy imply that it is the minority faiths that need to adapt? While the First Amendment would seem to provide the answer to these objections by limiting majority rule in the case of fundamental freedoms, minority faiths in America know all too well that even constitutional guarantees are not iron-clad.

Through the years, zealous legislators have, among other things, forced Catholics to fund Protestant public schools, Jews to conform to sectarian Sunday laws, non-Christians to recognize the national holiday of Christmas, and Mormons and Indians to observe laws of the state rather than the requirements of their faith. Had some political leaders been successful, the Constitution itself would now be Christian, complete with a Christological amendment that would, in effect, have made some Americans more equal than others.

It is on account of this zeal that many American Jews late in the nineteenth century abandoned their longstanding commitment to equal footing and forged a new alliance with advocates of strict church-state separation. Only a complete divorce between government and religion, they came to believe, could prevent the kind of abuses that would otherwise transform America into a bigoted Christian state. The "wall of separation between church and state" that Thomas Jefferson invoked in his famous 1802 letter to the Danbury Baptists became Jews' new rallying cry. In the twentieth century, led by lawyers like Leo Pfeffer, Jews and like-minded Americans fought through the courts to translate this ill-defined wall into a hardy bulwark of constitutional law.

Like many young American Jews, I too grew up believing in this "Wall of Separation" — so much so that I was convinced it had been written into the Constitution itself. The Justices of the Supreme Court in those days were our heroes. We cheered as they decided one case after another in "our favor," further separating religion from the state. Indeed, we fervently looked forward to the day when religion would be totally confined to home and house of worship, and the state would be divorced from religion altogether — better that, we believed, than state-sponsored Christianity.

What we did not know (how could we, it was not taught in our schools), and what I myself came to appreciate only much later, was how valuable and vital a force religion has been in American life. Antislavery, Progressive-era reforms, the civil rights movement, the anti-Vietnam movement, the movement to aid Soviet Jews — all depended, in significant part, on religious activism within the public square. In addition, religious leaders have played a critical role (although, alas, not recently) in promoting high standards of ethics and morality. Historically, they have served as behavioral role models, speaking out fearlessly on behalf of "good government" and against social corruption. Were these, I asked myself, the kinds of activities that I wanted now to curtail by restricting religion to home and to church?

More recently, it has struck me that the separationist ideal, essentially a theory of separate spheres, reflects an ideology that I and most of my friends have long since rejected. At one time, a large number of American Jews fervently believed that one should be a Jew at home and a person like everybody else on the outside. My generation, however, vigorously dissented from this view; we wore our Judaism on the outside too. Since we no longer confined our Judaism to home and house of worship (any more than we confined our wives to "women's sphere"), had we any right to expect others to do differently? Clearly, the whole basis of "strict separation," with its assumption that religion and state should occupy completely different spheres of life, needed to be rethought.

Nevertheless, I today still worry about state-sponsored Christianity. I continue to fear that some of those who pay lip service to "religion in American life" really have in mind one religion — and not mine. I know that even in this, the bicentennial of the First Amendment, numbers of Americans would, given the chance, write *their* religion into American law.

But I also know that religions of every sort need to be nurtured in America. They strengthen the fabric of American life and promote social betterment. Strict separation is neither possible nor desirable. Religion is much too valuable and all-encompassing to be restricted to a "separate sphere" of its own. My own vision resembles instead the hope expressed by Jonas Phillips back in 1787: to live in an America where people of all faiths stand on an equal footing.

Shabbat Candles for Life

MARC GELLMAN

My thinking about the role of religion in public life has been influenced by wildly different forces.

First there was the Vietnam war and the *Kulturkampf* it unleashed in America, which released me from an undifferentiated Milwaukee childhood into the late 1960s stampede of many Americans to find an alternative identity that was not primarily American, with all the ugly imperialistic resonances and responsibilities the name implied. With America seen as a global oppressor, I sought refuge in my Jewish identity. The comforting and conveniently guilt-free identity of the Jew as victim was, in my mind at least, immune to the facts of Jewish power and acceptance in America. In that guilt-ridden time I needed to cloak myself in the moral innocence of a victim. I became a Jewish-Radical, one of the many hyphenated rebels of that tumultuous time.

The one virtue of this charade was that I came to consciousness believing that my religious identity and my sense of political activism were utterly intertwined. My socialism at the time included more quotations from Isaiah than Marx, which was fair enough because my Judaism included more quotations from Marx than from Isaiah. However infantile my theology and my political theories may have been, I believed then, and I believe now, that God commands us to speak the truth of our faith both in our home and on our way, both when we lie down and when we rise up. A religion that does not matter in the streets cannot matter in the pews. I had no real idea at the time how all this played out. I was satisfied simply to trail the Movement providing biblical and talmudic quotes to justify what the left was going to do anyway.

I left the left when I perceived it as turning against Israel. What I felt among my comrades was the strong and frankly anti-Semitic impulse to blame Jews once we were no longer victims. Oppressive Arab dictatorships received nothing like the calumny which the left heaped on democratic Israel, and I resented it deeply. I retain my sympathy for the Palestinian people, but from my vantage point I remain unconvinced that a true Palestinian moderate leader can survive and be followed. Clearly it was my Jewish identity that compelled me to alter my political identity. In other times the opposite would no doubt have occurred.

The second blow from the left came when the black power movement in America turned its back on whites and, with special vitriol, Jews. This was a bitter time for me. My first rabbinic mentor had been fired from his pulpit because he decided to march with Rev. King in the South. I felt deeply proud of the Jewish contributions to the civil rights movement. I considered Schwerner and Goodman to be martyrs, not just political victims. My hero, Rabbi Abraham Joshua Heschel, marched with King in Selma not as a token Jew but as a trusted partner in the struggle.

The civil rights movement was for me redolent with religious meaning and metaphor. For me King was primarily a Reverend, not a Doctor. I felt then and I feel now that it was the power of his faith more than the power of his political ideology that accounted for both his political successes and certainly his oratorical passion. When the civil rights movement was taken over by secular black radicals, that religious vision faded and the movement collapsed. It left me with the lesson that a religious vision is essential to overcoming the social ills of America. I believed then and I believe now that the forces of goodness and understanding, of toleration and justice, must find their authentic religious roots again before the tree of social justice will again bear fruit.

Then I began to think about fetuses. I thought about them first in the context of my doctoral dissertation in Philosophy, and later as a Jew and as a recovering American. To my shock and amazement, the more I thought about it the more I realized that my liberal and radical friends had gotten the abortion thing all wrong.

This struggle for a woman's right to have an abortion when the pregnancy does not threaten her life or her health does not feel like the struggle to get Rosa Parks a place on the Montgomery bus or James Meredith a place in the University of Mississippi. Those struggles were full of the aroma of justice overcoming bigotry. This struggle smells like a fight to keep women and men from accepting the consequences of sexual promiscuity. How narrow and selfish that seems to me now.

I was bewildered why so many of my Movement friends could not translate their compassion and peacefulness, their regard for life and health, into compassion for fetuses who, despite their disputed moral status before birth, would *eventually* and surely become persons with the right to find a life for themselves too.

I suspected that the primary reason for the blindness of the left on abortion was the instinctive cultural disdain felt for prolife advocates. They listened to Lawrence Welk, not the Grateful Dead, they had purple hair and white sequined glasses, not long hair and wire-rimmed glasses. They were the ones we had seen across the picket lines in Selma. But on this issue they somehow got it right and we got it wrong. It did not escape my notice that many of the prolife people were moved by their faith to take this position. I could not say that about the prochoice people I knew. The prolife people spoke of rights and wrongs, while the prochoice people spoke of rights and laws. The former language was far more congenial to me personally, and far closer to my sense of how God wants us to make religion real in the world.

Absent a clear danger or palpable threat to the life of the mother, I found that I could no longer condone the morality of killing fetuses. In consulting my faith and its rich legal traditions, I found that my thinking was much in line with orthodox Jewish law on the morality of abortion. Though Jewish law is relatively clear in not considering the fetus a bearer of moral rights, it is equally clear that save to protect the life or basic health of the mother, abortion is absolutely prohibited.

Never did it occur to me that Judaism's opposition to elective abortions should be considered an inappropriate reason to be prolife. Never did I think that the separation doctrine of the Constitution prohibited my Judaism from informing my moral choices and from motivating me to work to see those choices made real in the marketplace of ideas and politics that shapes public policy. I had never apologized for being pro–civil rights on the basis of the Bible. Why should I apologize for being pro-life on the basis of the Talmud?

What I concluded was that there was bad faith here on the part of prochoice people who, because they disagreed with the conclusion of religiously motivated prolife citizens of America, disparaged the religious motivations that undergirded them. There was no such uproar about Reverend King's religious motivations for civil rights. They were a part of making civil rights a holy crusade.

I saw and I see no reason why religious Americans should feel constrained to express their religious view and urge that those views become public policy. I am still uncertain about how my view on abortion ought to be translated, if at all, into public policy, but I know that the killing of a fetus is not a morally neutral act that ought to be covered by some privacy doctrine whether invented or discovered in the Constitution.

God is not finished with me, but I know now that the Judaism which has been with me since I came to maturity speaks not only in the room where I light shabbat candles, but also and essentially to the world that shivers outside the glow of those candles.

Inculcating Humility

RUTH R. WISSE

Not long ago, on the campus of my university, I was talking to one of our activists, a professor who devotes much of her time to defending the rights of various academic constituencies. It is here relevant to note that this professor is an American and a non-Jewish Jew — that is, someone identifiably Jewish who underscores her disaffiliation from both the religious and the national content of Jewishness.

I was deploring what seemed a marked increase in the use of the classroom as a pulpit. Students were complaining of the promotion of political causes during regular class hours, a practice that had been mercifully slow in overtaking McGill. She nodded agreement: She herself, having lately complained to the building director about the presence in the lobby of a "Christian exhibit," had asked him to remove the offensive material. I was dumbfounded by this turn in the conversation. "How can you object to an exhibit?" I asked. "What was offensive about the material?" "It was religious material," she said. "That was offensive to me!"

I am not an American, and I cannot properly address the constitutional issues of church and state, but this chance conversation may help to explain why my thinking on the role of religion in public life has, indeed, changed. I had once assumed that liberalism was the guarantor of rights, only to discover that an illiberal liberalism could become the denier of rights. My objection to the doctrinaire university classroom, an objection influenced by the great Old Liberal Sidney Hook, takes for granted the right of everyone to promote his views, as long as the promoter is not empowered to deny the same freedom to others. But the New Liberal (my fellow professor to the core) defines freedom as the right to promote her views, and oppression as the attempt of others to express theirs. She regards religion as her special enemy, since its claim to speak in the name of ultimate Truth is the most serious challenge to her identical claim for irreligion.

Thus my defense of religion in public life is first and foremost a defense of religion against the illiberal liberal who would deny it the right of free speech. If religion enjoys no privileged place in American life, it should certainly be accorded its competitive place, its right of influence as well as of worship.

I would go even further. The way I judge ideas is not through their highest claim, but through their lowest perversion. It is for this reason that Judaism seems to me a superior religion. Focused inward on containing man's capacity for evil through a pattern of small habits, it runs the risk of atrophying into dry ritual rather than enriching civilized life to the fullest — but that is the worst it does. I leave it to others to make their comparisons.

By the same token, I have come to trust the religious faith in God more than the liberal faith in Reason. At its best, the belief in a higher-than-human power breeds humility, which is the spiritual guarantor of tolerance. And even at its worst, every God-centered religion is at least open to the appeal to its highest transcendent principles. Contrarily, the evidence of our century suggests that the totalitarian impulse is implicit rather than accidental in doctrinaire irreligion which adores its shrunken vision of humankind. The difference between my illiberal colleague and a Communist commissar is only one of degree.

I am convinced that the uniquely democratic American Constitution could not have been conceived save under the aegis of God. Nor do I believe that American democracy can flourish without a sense of the God who inspired the Founders. It may seem bizarre, both to those who are religiously gifted and to those who deny the existence of God, to suggest that faith in the God of our ancestors can be a substitute for faith of one's own, but if the closest one can come to God is through what was fashioned in His Spirit, it is still sufficiently humbling. The appeal to God in the oath of allegiance, the oath of office, in benedictions on ceremonial occasions, and even on the coin of the realm, is an attenuated but still vital reminder of the source of the American idea of freedom. I very much doubt that American freedom can survive without it.

Tacit Understandings

MIDGE DECTER

Many years ago, someone complained to the then British prime minister, Sir Harold Macmillan, that the people of Britain had lost their sense of purpose. "If they want a sense of purpose," he replied, "let them go to their bishops."

This was a deeply civilized thing to say — he was a deeply civilized man — and a response whose appositeness it seems not too snooty to suppose few of his interlocutors were likely to have understood. There would be even fewer among us today, when every *i* and *t* in the realm of the spirit must be legalistically dotted and crossed, every apprehension converted to a proposition, every tacit understanding translated to a slogan scrawled on public walls. This is a time, to name but one example, when the iron-and-gossamer connection of husband to wife and of both to child has been turned into something called "family values" and is thus both coarsened and weakened. In the same way, to be forced, as we unquestionably now are, to make a topic of public discussion of the relation between church and state means precisely that we are members of a society which has lost its hold — Harold Macmillan's hold — on the meaning of both.

As for my thinking on this subject, it has not changed; it has only just, haltingly, begun. What should be the role of religion in American public life? Why, to keep us humble, to keep us mindful that we are not a better people than God's other children but are beyond any measure luckier, and perhaps above all to instruct the citizens of a democracy where beyond state and government and policy-making the true transcendence that every one of us at least sometimes looks for is to be found.

But this is a far cry indeed from the public controversies that our current epidemic of so-called realist atheism has given rise to, such as whether it is permissible to pray or celebrate Christmas in schools and other public institutions, or to grant government support of one kind or another to private religious education. What to do about these? I wish I knew. Not as a Jew — that's easy: whatever unease Jews felt in an American culture dominated by Christianity ain't nothin' compared with the anxiety for Jews and everybody else in a culture dominated by ravening atheists (sometimes mistakenly called "humanists"), including, be it noted, for the atheists themselves. Still, it is not easy as an American to know how far we may go before we damage the pluralism that is essential to the special nature of this society, where, to use Richard Neuhaus' metaphor, we are to draw the outer boundaries, and how we are to furnish our presently desperately naked square.

But would not God Himself enjoin us to be modest and even a little fearful in our deliberations about how best to go about beseeching Him to restore our sense of purpose?

A Decorous Judaism

HADLEY ARKES

Many years ago I heard an interview on radio with a Unitarian minister who was trying to explain the tenets of his church. "Let me put it this way," he said to the interviewer. "The only time the words 'Jesus Christ' are heard in our church is when the janitor falls down the stairs."

American Jews have hardly been more sluggish in traveling the path of modernity and emancipating themselves from the texts and fables that were fashioned for more primitive minds in those days before religion became theology. Most of the people in America who count themselves as Jewish are content these days to live lives, shall we say, that are not overburdened with theology. They come together to mark the Jewish calendar, they preserve the memory of the Holocaust and the worst trials of our people, and they are prepared to be summoned at any mo-

ment to the defense of Israel. Their life as a Jewish community is conse-
crated to the preservation of a Jewish people.

But the meaning of a Jewish people is increasingly detached from
any notion of a people that finds its character in a covenant with God or
a dedication to His laws. In fact, any serious discussion about God or
matters theological is often regarded as rather indecorous and unsettling. In my own community, in a congregation filled with academics, it
has even been easier to bring people together in working on a Jewish
cookbook than in considering the theses or the doctrinal points that define the Jewishness of the congregation.

A dozen years ago, in a national meeting of the American Jewish
Committee, I made the case for restraining a band of Nazis from march-
ing through a Jewish community in Skokie, Illinois. The response I received that morning was buoyant and confirming, and yet the American
Jewish Community finally backed away from the project of restraining
the Nazis. The reasons were evident in the meeting and in the responses
of Jews throughout the country: There were, in Skokie, many survivors
of the Holocaust, but the passion for protecting those survivors was
overborne by a deeper uneasiness over the prospect of restricting political speech. The concern to protect "our own" was modified or translated into the sense of a Jewish stake in the First Amendment. But this
fastidiousness has not prevented American Jews from going to the rescue of other groups, to protect them from the symbols of assault. The
same large-souled people who would not restrain the brandishing of
swastikas apparently have no trouble in sustaining prosecutions for the
burning of crosses — or even in using injunctions and restraining thugs
in advance from the burning of crosses.

In the transfiguration of Judaism in America, it is the First
Amendment and the Constitution that have become "our own." And
we seem to have made them our own more than any other group; for
more than any other group, we seem more earnestly concerned about
injuries to the Constitution than injuries to our own people. Other
groups may not experience the same conflict because they do not read
the Constitution in the same way — in the way, for example, that
makes no moral discrimination among the kinds of speech or the
kinds of political factions that the Constitution was meant to protect.
From the public face of American Judaism, we would infer that for
many American Jews, the Constitution has become incorporated in

the character of Judaism as a source of principles that may even override the texts of the Pentateuch.

But not, of course, the Constitution in its original texts — not the Constitution that offered protections for slavery and no votes for women — and not even the understanding of natural rights and "self-evident" moral truths that underlay the Constitution. What has become authoritative is the Constitution in its most modern, *liberal* rendering, and the most liberal rendering of all is the rendition that accords with the agenda of political liberalism.

After all, what is one to make of the passages that fill that embarrassing book of Deuteronomy:

> Then Sihon came out against us, he and all his people, into battle at Jahaz. And the Lord our God delivered him up before us; and we smote him, and his sons, and all his people. And we took all his cities at that time, and utterly destroyed every city, the men, and the women, and the little ones; we left none remaining. (Deuteronomy 2:32-34)

Passages of this kind we decorously put aside as no longer consistent with what are called "Jewish values." And from what are those "values" drawn, those values that reject the notion of visiting punishment and death upon people without making discriminations between the innocent and guilty? Apparently, those "values" are drawn from a moral understanding, cultivated over centuries, and from a tradition of reflection that has been affected by Christianity and the Enlightenment.

The Constitution is preeminently the product of that tradition; but the liberal rendering of the Constitution marks an "advance" — a further radical step which has a more recent beginning. The training school of liberalism is now in the schools of law, and for liberal jurisprudence, the new age in the law begins in 1965 with *Griswold v. Connecticut,* the decision on contraception and privacy, the decision that prepared the ground for *Roe v. Wade* and the "right to an abortion." Those decisions are now taken as the touchstone for liberal jurisprudence. As one professor was heard to remark, no theory of jurisprudence that gives the "wrong" result in *Roe v. Wade* could possibly be a valid theory of the law.

If the Constitution has become more authoritative than the Bible for many Jews and if the Constitution has become identified with the liberalism of the left, the defining issue for the politics and jurisprudence of liberalism has become the issue of abortion. That point became clear beyond cavil with the hearings over Robert Bork. The Democrats had lost their constituency for redistribution and an expansion of the welfare state. The Democrats had become the party of the courts; their mission now was simply to protect the courts as the judges imposed policies on abortion, busing, and the environment that could not gather support at the polls. What was at stake in the Bork hearings was the defense of *Roe v. Wade* — and how else to account for the interest of the American Jewish Committee in taking a position on this nomination to the Court? What distinctly Jewish interests were engaged in the appointment of Robert Bork?

The teachings of Jewish law have been set quite emphatically in opposition to abortion. On that point, the Orthodox have never suffered serious doubts, even though Jewish teaching has been far more equivocal and shaded with far more stray confusions than the teachings of Catholicism on this matter. Hence, the curious persistence of those assertions in the Talmud that the embryo in the first forty days is "mere liquid," and that the embryo does not form until forty days. But these passages may be dismissed more readily by grownups who understand that the science of embryology has moved now well beyond the level of Aristotle's biology. Of more lingering mischief is the kind of teaching found, say, in Nachmanides: that a fetus attached to the mother is not yet a life with a standing of its own, with a claim to be protected by the law because the child is not self-sufficient. That ancient mistake of moral reasoning seems to claim a more enduring credulity.

Still, as I say, the teaching of Jewish law has been set mainly, strongly, in opposition to the killing of unborn children, just as it has been set in opposition to euthanasia. But now, of course, the "privacy interest" in abortion has been made the ground for new claims of rights — to end the lives of aged, infirm patients and to withdraw medical care from newborn, retarded infants. In each of these instances, the same moral premises are engaged and the same parties understand that the defense of *Roe v. Wade* is at stake.

And so each case rounds up the usual suspects: the same advocacy groups, the same facile lawyers from the ACLU, the same clusters of doctors and ministers. Each of these delegations finds a prominent Jewish presence in offering the brief and fueling the movement, and we can expect that these positions too will soon gather support among Jewish civic organizations. But the movement is sufficiently advanced already to make the point. The Jewish presence in our politics has now been associated with moral ends that find little tethering in the documents and the traditions distinct to Judaism, and the defense of Jewish interests is waged now in the name of policies that may be utterly at odds with the commands of Jewish law.

In my own congregation in Amherst (or the congregation that used to be mine), I discovered years ago one forbidden subject. I was often invited to speak to the congregation on questions of affirmative action or any other matter of public interest. But it became clear that I could not speak on the question of abortion without straining the community and dividing the congregation. Out of prudence, I held back, but the understanding seemed to settle upon me: that the price of my membership in the congregation was to preserve my silence in the synagogue on the issue that I regarded, more surely with each passing year, as the gravest question of moral consequence before us. That unease would not be felt within every Jewish congregation. But it marks the tension that puts some of us in an adversary position right now to understandings that define — unmistakably and unbendingly — the Jewish community in America.

The report was offered to me of a Catholic friend who was measuring, quite soberly, the depth of ignorance as large numbers of Catholics were going untutored in the teachings of their own religion. "Half of the Church is in heresy," he said, "and the other half do not know enough to know it." The melancholy commentary that may be offered now on the state of Jewish understanding in America is that we may count it as a notable advance if we could attain even this condition, the condition that is counted among our Catholic friends as a grievous misfortune.

ALAN L. MITTLEMAN

A Jewish Civil Religion

ALAN L. MITTLEMAN

The Zionist thinker Ahad Ha'am distinguished between the "problem of the Jews" and the "problem of Judaism." Political Zionism — the attempt to secure a homeland through diplomatic means for oppressed Jewry — aimed solely, in Ahad Ha'am's view, at a solution of the problem of the Jews. The broader, and to him more insistent issue, was the vitality of Jewish tradition, spiritual life, and culture, that is, the problem of Judaism. For Ahad Ha'am, the religious-cultural question had to come first. Without a great renascence of Jewish spirit and communal life, neither political activity as such nor the ends it might achieve could be sustained.

I find the distinction between the problem of Judaism and the problem of the Jews serviceable for the present discussion. As I reflect on how my views about the relation of religion and public life have changed, I find that I have grown more concerned about the problem of American Judaism and less worried about the problem of American Jews. By the latter term I mean the concern to sustain an open society in which Jews suffer no discrimination simply because they are Jews. By the problem of Judaism I mean concern for the kind and quality of Jewish life which Jews in fact lead in the open society.

Most Jewish considerations of the nexus of religion and public life are fixated on the problem of the Jews. Will diversity be compromised or openness diminished by the "intrusion" of religious values into public life? Will Jews become second-class citizens in a more publicly Christian society?

These are the typical Jewish questions, yet other questions, I believe, ought to be asked. What kind of religious life is correlated with the judgment that public affairs ought to be wholly separate from religious values? Is it true, as Jewish spokesmen often argue, that public secularity almost miraculously supports private religious intensity? Or is it the case that public secularity begets, reflexively, the secularization of religious communities which advocate a secularizing strategy? In my view, this is precisely what has happened to Judaism in America.

A strategy of uncompromising secularization directed toward the public realm has become a defining condition of the internal Jewish world. Consequently, a renewal of Jewish life requires a fresh consideration of the connections between religion and public affairs. The renewal of Jewish life and the reappraisal of Jewish social thought are tightly correlated.

How has the problem of Judaism developed? Judaism is not a sectarian or otherworldly religion. While always a religion of the study hall, it is also a religion of marketplaces, courts, and operating rooms. Since the Emancipation, when Jews gave up whatever communal autonomy was left to them in favor of citizenship rights in modern states, these applications of Judaism have withered into academic topics. Even in Israel, the applicability of traditional Jewish approaches to public matters remains quite limited. Judaism, however, resists confessionalization. While some extreme versions of Reform in Germany and the U.S. did precisely that, most Jews compensated for the loss of a public dimension by embracing modern, surrogate forms of historical action such as Zionism and liberalism.

These concerns point in rather different directions. Zionism is survivalist. Liberalism is universalist. The one asserts the primacy of action for the Jewish good. The other appeals to considerations of the common good. Yet both amount phenomenologically to a Jewish public discourse. Both compensate for the loss of a once all-encompassing Jewish world by providing a rationale for action in history and a self-definition of the Jew as an active, political being. Both, in a sense, have become Judaism.

Judaism in America has become a religion, as Jonathan Woocher put it, of "sacred survival" on the one hand and, I would add, social gospel on the other. Judaism has become the civil religion of an American minority. The periphery has become the center. Values of tolerance, pluralism, fairness, equal rights, and so on have come to be located at the core. Not that these very agreeable values could not have been found to some extent at the core all along. They could have been and were. Rather, there is an artifice and disingenuousness about the process of their valorization. Jewish organizations, for example, antecedently convinced of a woman's right to abortion have combed Jewish sources for proof texts and then displayed the results as evidence of Judaism's defense of abortion rights. Indeed, Jewish law supports abortion in some (fairly restricted) cases. That is not the point. What is at issue is the meretricious or — more charitably — pathetic nature of the exercise.

I do not take issue here with where the process winds up, but with where it begins. If American Jews had a genuine public philosophy, they would not have to be reduced to adventitious proof-texting. Their consciences would be formed by their subtle and ramified legal tradition. They would argue for the applicability of that tradition to the common good in an appropriately public manner, as the Catholic bishops have tried to do. Instead, they imitate the progressive, yet apodictic pronouncements of Protestant church bodies. Elevated, self-assured moralism substitutes for disciplined argument. And what is said is no different from what might have been said by others. Whatever is distinctive about Judaism has been left out of account either because it does not accord with the liberal consensus or because Jews lack a public philosophy of adequate complexity to mediate the values of their tradition to the culture at large. The result is not a lively tension between a distinctive Judaism and the public realm, but a redundant repetition by Jews of the culture's (liberal) common sense.

I have argued that the quality and credibility of Judaism are in some sense inseparable from Judaism's engagement with public questions. Because the mode of that engagement heretofore has been dictated by imperatives from the general culture rather than Jewish tradition, Judaism has acquired the cast of a civil religion. Renewal requires that authentic Jewish perspectives be allowed to penetrate our thinking about public matters. As I want to see other groups engage in their own renewal, I welcome their involvement in public discourse. I do not see how authenticity — or simple self-respect — permits anything less.

Dabru 'Emet: *A Jewish Statement on Christians and Christianity*

Dabru 'Emet ("Speak the Truth"), signed by more than 150 rabbis and Jewish scholars, appeared in both the *New York Times* and the *Baltimore Sun* on September 10, 2000.

In recent years, there has been a dramatic and unprecedented shift in Jewish and Christian relations. Throughout the nearly two millennia of Jewish exile, Christians have tended to characterize Judaism as a failed religion or, at best, a religion that prepared the way for, and is completed in, Christianity. In the decades since the Holocaust, however, Christianity has changed dramatically. An increasing number of official church bodies, both Roman Catholic and Protestant, have made public statements of their remorse about Christian mistreatment of Jews and Judaism. These statements have declared, furthermore, that Christian teaching and preaching can and must be reformed so that they acknowledge God's enduring covenant with the Jewish people and celebrate the contribution of Judaism to world civilization and to Christian faith itself.

We believe these changes merit a thoughtful Jewish response. Speaking only for ourselves — an interdenominational group of Jewish scholars — we believe it is time for Jews to learn about the efforts of Christians to honor Judaism. We believe it is time for Jews to reflect on what Judaism may now say about Christianity. As a first step, we offer eight brief statements about how Jews and Christians may relate to one another.

Jews and Christians worship the same God. Before the rise of Christianity, Jews were the only worshipers of the God of Israel. But Christians also worship the God of Abraham, Isaac, and Jacob, creator of heaven and earth. While Christian worship is not a viable religious choice for Jews, as Jewish theologians we rejoice that, through Christianity, hundreds of millions of people have entered into relationship with the God of Israel.

Jews and Christians seek authority from the same book — the Bible (what Jews call "Tanakh" and Christians call the "Old Testament"). Turning to it for religious orientation, spiritual enrichment, and communal education, we each take away similar lessons: God created and sustains the universe; God established a covenant with the people Israel; God's revealed word guides Israel to a life of righteousness; and God will ultimately redeem Israel and the whole world. Yet Jews and Christians interpret the Bible differently on many points. Such differences must always be respected.

Christians can respect the claim of the Jewish people upon the land of Israel. The most important event for Jews since the Holocaust has been the reestablishment of a Jewish state in the Promised Land. As members of a biblically based religion, Christians appreciate that Israel was promised — and given — to Jews as the physical center of the covenant between them and God. Many Christians support the State of Israel for reasons far more profound than mere politics. As Jews, we applaud this support. We also recognize that Jewish tradition mandates justice for all non-Jews who reside in a Jewish state.

Jews and Christians accept the moral principles of Torah. Central to the moral principles of Torah is the inalienable sanctity and dignity of every human being. All of us were created in the image of God. This shared moral emphasis can be the basis of an improved relationship between our two communities. It can also be the basis of a powerful witness to all humanity for improving the lives of our fellow human beings and for standing against the immoralities and idolatries that harm and degrade us. Such witness is especially needed after the unprecedented horrors of the past century.

Nazism was not a Christian phenomenon. Without the long history of Christian anti-Judaism and Christian violence against Jews, Nazi ideology could not have taken hold nor could it have been carried out. Too many Christians participated in, or were sympathetic to, Nazi atrocities against Jews. Other Christians did not protest sufficiently against these atrocities. But Nazism itself was not an inevitable outcome of Christianity. If the Nazi extermination of the Jews had been fully successful, it would have turned its murderous rage more directly to Christians. We recognize with gratitude those Christians who risked or sacrificed their lives to save Jews during the Nazi regime. With that in mind, we encourage the continuation of recent efforts in Christian theology to repudiate unequivocally contempt of Judaism and the Jewish people. We applaud those Christians who reject this teaching of contempt, and we do not blame them for the sins committed by their ancestors.

The humanly irreconcilable difference between Jews and Christians will not be settled until God redeems the entire world as promised in Scripture. Christians know and serve God through Jesus Christ and the Christian tradition. Jews know and serve God through Torah and the Jewish tradition. That difference will not be settled by one community insisting that it has interpreted Scripture more accurately than the other, nor by exercising political power over the other. Jews can respect Christians' faithfulness to their revelation just as we expect Christians to respect our faithfulness to our revelation. Neither Jew nor Christian should be pressed into affirming the teaching of the other community.

A new relationship between Jews and Christians will not weaken Jewish practice. An improved relationship will not accelerate the cultural and religious assimilation that Jews rightly fear. It will not change traditional Jewish forms of worship, nor increase intermarriage between Jews and non-Jews, nor persuade more Jews to convert to Christianity, nor create a false blending of Judaism and Christianity. We respect Christianity as a faith that originated within Judaism and that still has significant contacts with it. We do not see it as an extension of Judaism. Only if we cherish our own traditions can we pursue this relationship with integrity.

Jews and Christians must work together for justice and peace.
Jews and Christians, each in their own way, recognize the unredeemed state of the world as reflected in the persistence of persecution, poverty, and human degradation and misery. Although justice and peace are finally God's, our joint efforts, together with those of other faith communities, will help bring the kingdom of God for which we hope and long. Separately and together, we must work to bring justice and peace to our world. In this enterprise, we are guided by the vision of the prophets of Israel: "It shall come to pass in the end of days that the mountain of the Lord's house shall be established at the top of the mountains and be exalted above the hills, and the nations shall flow unto it . . . and many peoples shall go and say, 'Come ye and let us go up to the mountain of the Lord to the house of the God of Jacob and He will teach us of His ways and we will walk in His paths'" (Isaiah 2:2-3).

"*Dabru 'Emet:* A Jewish Statement on Christians and Christianity," organized under the auspices of the Baltimore-based Institute on Christian and Jewish Studies, was drafted by Dr. David Novak of the University of Toronto, Dr. Tikva Frymer-Kensky of the University of Chicago, Dr. Peter Ochs of the University of Virginia, and Dr. Michael Signer of the University of Notre Dame. A partial list of the other signatories includes:

Dr. David Blumenthal
Emory University

Dr. Eugene B. Borowitz
Hebrew Union College — Jewish Institute of Religion

Rabbi Gary Bretton-Granatoor
Stephen Wise Free Synagogue
New York, New York

A Jewish Statement on Christians and Christianity

Rabbi Nina Beth Cardin
Baltimore, Maryland

Dr. Robert Chazan
New York University

Dr. Norman Cohen
Hebrew Union College — Jewish Institute of Religion

Rabbi Barry Cytron
The Jay Phillips Center for Jewish-Christian Learning

Dr. Elliot Dorff
University of Judaism

Rabbi Yechiel Eckstein
International Fellowship of Christians and Jews

Rabbi Joseph H. Ehrenkranz
Center for Christian-Jewish Understanding

Rabbi Jerome Epstein
United Synagogue of Conservative Judaism

Rabbi Seymour L. Essrog
Adat Chaim Congregation
Reisterstown, Maryland

Rabbi Harvey Fields
Wilshire Boulevard Temple
Los Angeles, California

Rabbi Barry Freundel
Kesher Israel Congregation
Washington, D.C.

Rabbi Albert H. Friedlander
Leo Baeck College
London, England

Rabbi Laura Geller
Temple Emanuel
Beverly Hills, California

Dr. Robert Gibbs
University of Toronto

Dr. Neil Gillman
Jewish Theological Seminary of America

Dr. David Gordis
University of Judaism

Rabbi Irving Greenberg
Jewish Life Network

Dr. Susannah Heschel
Dartmouth College

Dr. Lawrence Hoffman
Hebrew Union College — Jewish Institute of Religion

Rabbi Leon Klenicki
Anti-Defamation League

Rabbi Charles A. Kroloff
Central Conference of American Rabbis

Rabbi Ronald Kronish
Interreligious Coordinating Council in Israel

Rabbi Harold Kushner
Natick, Massachusetts

Rabbi Simeon J. Maslin
Congregation Keneseth Israel
Elkins Park, Pennsylvania

Dr. Paul Mendes-Flohr
Hebrew University/University of Chicago

A Jewish Statement on Christians and Christianity

Rabbi Paul J. Menitoff
Central Conference of American Rabbis

Rabbi Joel Meyers
The Rabbinical Assembly

Dr. Alan L. Mittleman
Muhlenberg College

Rabbi Hayim Goren Perelmuter
*Bernardin Center for Christian and Jewish Studies
at Catholic Theological Union*

Rabbi W. Gunther Plaut
*Holy Blossom Temple
Toronto, Ontario, Canada*

Dr. Ronald Price
Institute of Traditional Judaism

Dr. Hilary Putnam
Harvard University

Rabbi Jeffrey Salkin
*The Community Synagogue
Port Washington, New York*

Rabbi David Sandmel
Institute on Christian and Jewish Studies

Dr. Marc Saperstein
George Washington University

Rabbi Sandy Eisenberg Sasso & Rabbi Dennis Sasso
*Congregation Beth-El Zedeck
Indianapolis, Indiana*

Rabbi Chaim Seidler-Feller
*Hillel Jewish Student Center
Los Angeles, California*

Rabbi Ronald B. Sobel
Congregation Emanu-El
New York, New York

Rabbi Jacob Staub
Reconstructionist Rabbinical College

Dr. David A. Teusch
Reconstructionist Rabbinical College

Rabbi Lennard Thal
Union of American Hebrew Congregations

Rabbi Arnold Jacob Wolf
K.A.M. Isaiah Israel Congregation
Chicago, Illinois

Dr. Elliot Wolfson
New York University

Rabbi David Wolpe
Sinai Temple
Los Angeles, California

Rabbi Eric H. Yoffie
Union of American Hebrew Congregations

Rabbi Sheldon Zimmerman
Hebrew Union College — Jewish Institute of Religion

Christians, Jews, and Anti-Semitism

THE EDITORS OF *FIRST THINGS*

When, in 1992, William F. Buckley published *In Search of Anti-Semitism,* an unsettled and unsettling set of questions was once again brought to the fore. That has to be done from time to time. One may be inclined to think that there is nothing new to be said about anti-Semitism, and there is something to that. Many Americans, Jews and Christians alike, are weary of the subject, and that, too, is understandable, in part. Nonetheless, unsettled and unsettling questions need a careful public airing on occasion, or else they fester in the shadowed corners of our culture, breeding resentments and suspicions that corrode our common life.

Mr. Buckley's reflections on contemporary anti-Semitism are excruciatingly careful, and his conclusions meticulously firm. Most news reports focused on his criticisms of Patrick Buchanan, media commentator and presidential candidate. That is not surprising in an election year. Buckley pays equal attention, however, to Joseph Sobran, former senior editor of *National Review,* James Freedman, the president of Dartmouth College, and novelist Gore Vidal, who vents his blatantly anti-Semitic fevers in the pages of the *Nation.* Buckley's conclusions, in sum, are: Sobran is so "obsessed" with Jews and Israel that he cannot write on these subjects except in a manner that reasonable people might describe as anti-Semitic; Buchanan, while not an anti-Semite, has given frequent voice to sentiments that reasonable people must describe as anti-Semitic; Freedman, in his war against the conservative *Dartmouth Review,* is a demagogue who has shamelessly used the charge of anti-

Semitism to enforce conformity to political correctness; and Vidal, well, when it comes to Gore Vidal, Mr. Buckley is manifestly exercising heroic restraint. (He notes that Vidal complains that he has been lied about, that people have misrepresented his views. Buckley observes, "Anyone who lies about Mr. Vidal is doing him a kindness.")

Our purpose is not to review Mr. Buckley's essay, which readers can readily obtain for themselves. It is indeed a public service and will, in our judgment, deservedly become an important reference in a discussion that will not be settled any time soon. Our purpose, rather, is to inquire into some of the issues raised by the discussion of anti-Semitism. These are concerns that go to the heart of the *raison d'être* of our journal *First Things* and its publisher, the Institute on Religion and Public Life. Ours is a determinedly Christian-Jewish enterprise.

That is so because our constituting purpose — to advance a religiously informed public philosophy for a society of freedom and virtue — requires a secure partnership between Christians and Jews. (There are many reasons — frequently discussed in these pages — why such a partnership is required. Suffice it for the present that we are convinced that it is so.) Even more important, ours is a Christian-Jewish enterprise because we believe that, in ways that elude our complete understanding, God has covenantly entangled Jews and Christians. That entanglement, and the imperatives that it entails, will, it seems, continue until the final consummation of messianic promise. Happily, the resulting partnership is not only a matter of duty but also of delight in a company of Christians and Jews joined by common resolve.

To say that ours is a Christian-Jewish enterprise does not mean that it is some hybrid "third way" called Christian-Jewish, distinct from the ways of Judaism and Christianity. As we understand it, the Christian-Jewish partnership requires that Jews be Jews and Christians be Christians. It is precisely as Jews that Jews are, at the most serious level, entangled with Christians, and vice versa. True pluralism, as we intend never to tire of saying, is not pretending that our differences make no difference. True pluralism is honestly engaging the differences that make a very great difference in this world, and perhaps in the next. In full awareness of the differences, we do believe that it is appropriate, indeed necessary, to speak of a Judeo-Christian tradition.

A common Judeo-Christian tradition is not a common faith. To be sure, Christian faith is inexplicable apart from Judaism, and a growing number of Jewish thinkers are convinced that Jewish self-understanding must encompass an understanding of Christianity in the divinely ordered scheme of history. It is at this level of discerning God's intention that Jews and Christians are most inescapably and intensively entangled with one another. Neither among Christians nor among Jews is there any settled consensus about the nature and outcome of that entanglement. The joint exploration of these questions is still a relatively new thing, and the future of this new thing rests almost entirely with Jews and Christians in America. That is why the Jewish-Christian dialogue, as it is called, comes in for regular attention in *First Things*.

When we speak of the Judeo-Christian tradition, however, the reference is usually to matters moral rather than theological, although the two are not easily separable. Christians embrace the "moral law" (as in, for instance, the Ten Commandments) revealed by the God of Abraham, who is also the One whom Jesus called Father. Jew and Christian alike can affirm that this moral law is consonant with morality constructed on the basis of natural law, general revelation, or even studiously "secular" reasoning. While similar moral conclusions can be reached by taking different routes, most Americans (more than 90 percent) claim to reach their moral conclusions by a route that they identify as religious. Of course there is no numerical balance between the Judeo and the Christian, since only a little over 2 percent of Americans identify themselves as Jews. Moreover, the imbalance is accentuated by the fact that 60 percent of Jews do not belong or contribute to any Jewish organizations, religious or otherwise, whereas well over 60 percent of non-Jews are church members.

These factors further underscore the importance of affirming a Judeo-Christian tradition. The phrase reminds Christians of their dependence upon Judaism and the respect they owe its living representatives. It reminds Jews of the religious foundations of their security in an overwhelmingly non-Jewish society, and of the need to cultivate moral commonalities. Regrettably and dangerously, many Jews believe that their safety in this society is secured exclusively by positive law and secular reason, even when these are posited against the moral sensibilities of the Christian majority. Equally regrettable and dangerous, many Christians believe that this is a "Christian nation" in which the presence of Jews can be dismissed as an anomaly or, when it cannot be so easily dismissed, is resented as an intrusion. Against both errors, it is important to insist that our public moral order rests upon a Judeo-Christian tradition.

Those who care about that tradition must give sustained attention to the evil of anti-Semitism. Some Christians immediately respond that too much attention is already given anti-Semitism. What, they ask, about Jewish anti-Christianism? There is no denying that some Jews give every appearance of being anti-Christian, or at least of wanting to expunge every evidence of Christianity from our public life. The propensities of the dominantly Jewish leadership of the American Civil Liberties Union come immediately to mind. At the same time, a growing number of Jewish thinkers are arguing, not least of all in the pages of *First Things,* that the posture of groups such as the ACLU is misguided, dangerous, and just plain dumb. In any event — given the numerical imbalance between Jews and Christians in this society, and given the still recent horrors experienced by Jews in other societies where the majority claimed to be Christian — it should not be necessary to persuade Christians that there is not a moral or consequential equivalence between anti-Semitism and anti-Christianism.

As aforesaid, the question of anti-Semitism must be revisited from time to time. It is a salutary exercise for Christians and Jews to better understand one of the more loathsome diseases of the modern era. In addition, the forms and motor forces of anti-Semitism are not stable but assume at times new configurations. Ours is such a time, as we shall see. Admittedly, it is frustratingly difficult to define anti-Semitism, and the very term has been recklessly debased by its facile use in order to silence critics (see the reference above to Freedman of Dartmouth). It is not anti-Semitism if one, all in all, does not like Jews very much, just as there is no moral culpability if, all in all, one has a dislike for Italians. To eliminate from human society generalized distastes and preferences — including those that engage ethnicity, religion, nation, language, and race — is neither possible nor desirable, although there is a style of liberalism that erroneously insists that it is both.

A person who, all in all, does not like Jews raises a reasonable suspicion of anti-Semitism if he makes a public point of it. (If some of his best friends are Jews, it counts in his favor, although it may simply indicate that he is confused about his prejudices.) And if he makes a public point of it in a way that suggests that Jews are a public problem and that something should be done about them, he is almost demanding that he be viewed as an anti-Semite. After innumerable unsuccessful tries by others, we do not entertain the conceit that we will come up with a definition of anti-Semitism that will meet with universal agreement. But, for what it is worth, we propose this: An anti-Semite is someone who declares that certain vices and character flaws are specifically Jewish, or who would, for whatever reason, deny to Jews rights and privileges readily accorded to others.

It is always appropriate to ask whether anti-Semitism so defined is on the rise in our society. If we consult the polls and other survey research data, the answer is that anti-Semitism has steadily and dramatically declined. In the modern era, and perhaps in all of history, Jews have never been so secure as they are at present in the United States of America. (They are certainly not so secure in the Middle East.) And yet Mr. Buckley opines that the likes of Pat Buchanan and Gore Vidal would have been more severely and generally censured for their anti-Semitic delinquencies, say, ten years ago. He may well be right.

This does not necessarily indicate an increase of anti-Semitism. Recent years have witnessed a general assault upon, and consequent weakening of, societal taboos. There was no reason to expect that the taboo against anti-Semitism, backed by the now fading memory of the Holocaust, would be spared. The defiance of taboos is deemed to be liberating, and a certain cachet of daring is attached to the speaking of the unspeakable. Liberation and liberalism are related more than phonetically, which is one reason why anti-Semitism is increasingly more evident on the Left rather than the Right. While the public expression of anti-Semitism need not indicate an increase of anti-Semitism, it could, if it goes unchecked, create a climate conducive to such an increase. It must not, therefore, go unchecked.

Restoring the taboo against anti-Semitism is made more difficult precisely because Jews are so very much part of American life. Most Americans — and it is well to remember that most Americans have no more than a passing acquaintance with any Jews — are puzzled by the suggestion that Jews are to be viewed as somehow endangered. For the next generation — if not for young people today — Auschwitz will be invoked with all the historical resonance of Appomattox. In short, Jews less and less possess that moral attribute so treasured in our culture, victim status. On the contrary, they are viewed as a particularly prominent part of "the establishment" that it is the duty of the right-minded, meaning the left-minded, to excoriate. Nobody advocates quotas or affirmative action for Jews, unless it be to limit their access to positions of influence. Jews are no longer a certified "minority."

Inveterate anti-Semites have long treated the disproportionate influence of Jews — especially in the academy, journalism, and entertainment — as a dirty little secret to which it is their duty to alert an unsuspecting public. The assumption is that numerically disproportionate means inordinate, as in excessive and dangerously out of control. It is self-defeating and simply silly to pretend that Jews are not disproportionately represented in many sectors of societal leadership. One may attribute this to various factors: superior intelligence and energy, habits of diligence and enterprise, or maybe it had something to do with being chosen by God. Anti-Semites attribute it to a Jewish conspiracy. Their claims to the contrary, anti-Semites are not distinguished by their candor in recognizing the influence of Jews. Their deplorable distinction is in the reason they give to explain that influence, and the consequent threat they perceive in it.

The disproportionate influence of Jews is not without problems. The chief problem is that most Jews are not very Jewish. Or, as a number of Jewish observers have put it, those Jews who are Jewish are interested in Jewishness but not in Judaism. In other words, they affirm Jewishness as ethnicity or folkway but have no use for Judaism as religion. One result is that Jews tend to have a disproportionate and, yes, inordinate secularizing influence in our culture. In addition, some religious Jews join the secularists in subscribing to the doctrine that the more secular the culture is the safer it will be Jews. Not surprisingly, this leads — as in the instances of the ACLU and the American Jewish Congress — to an extremist notion of the separation of church and state that is tantamount to the separation of religion from public life.

As becomes increasingly obvious, that notion is not democratically sustainable. And a good thing, too, for a public square that is devoid of religiously grounded imperatives and inhibitions is a very dangerous place for a very small and very prominent population that is very importantly different. The questions of secularization and the Judeo-Christian tradition have everything to do with the culture wars in which our society is embroiled. The conflict has produced tacit alliances on some public issues between, on the one hand, Orthodox Jews and Conservative Jews who are religiously conservative and, on the other, culturally assertive Christians, notably Roman Catholics and evangelicals. Especially encouraging are the renewed Christian urgency in reappropriating the Jewish shape of Christianity and the emergence of a new generation of Jewish intellectual leadership prepared to argue for a culture firmly secured by the Judeo-Christian tradition.

And now we have come so far with nary a mention of the State of Israel. The anti-Semitism that occasioned the Buckley discussion that occasioned this discussion has everything to do with Israel. In the Christian-Jewish enterprise of which *First Things* is part, Israel matters and matters enormously. A few brief observations are in order. American support for Israel is coming under growing attack from isolationists on both the left and the right of our political culture. The attack from the left, representing itself as anti-Zionism or pro-Palestinianism, is the more virulent. In the view from the left, Israel, which has won too many wars, has become the Goliath oppressing the Palestinian David, and, in addition, bears the onus of being backed by the necessarily oppressive power of the United States. Israel is depicted as a garrison state, it being conveniently forgotten that one rational response to being surrounded by declared enemies is to erect a garrison.

Other dynamics contribute to the enervating of American commitment to Israel. The idea of a Jewish homeland as a partial reparation for an unspeakable injustice ineluctably loses its force as the immediacy of the Holocaust recedes into the past. The end of the Cold War nullifies Israel's role as an ally in the contest against Communism. A greater awareness of the political culture of the Middle East makes less plausible the claim that Israel serves as the vanguard of democracy in that part of the world. These previously persuasive reasons for backing Israel will no longer work. Like it or not, the special relationship with Israel increasingly depends upon the strength of the Jewish-Christian entanglement we discussed at the beginning. The deluded ideologists of *Realpolitik* notwithstanding, the "hard" realities of American-Israel relations are ideas about chosenness, destiny, messianic promise, and a people that, however imperfectly, participates in the holiness of the land that Christians call holy.

To care about Jews and Judaism is to care about Israel. That is because to care about others is to participate in what they care about. That is because the communal, psychological, and spiritual consequences of the demise of Israel are too ghastly to contemplate. To care about Israel is to take care not only that Israel survive but that Israel flourish. Caring about Israel does not preclude disagreements about Israel. We may even disagree over whether the establishment of the state in 1948 was just or justly done, never mind divinely ordained. The infrangible fact is that it is there, adamantly, relentlessly, steadfastly there — and with it is invested a large part of the biblical mystery that is Judaism. We may certainly disagree over policies and actions of the Israeli government, not least its control and treatment of people it has conquered, albeit in a defensive war. And there is sure to be continuing disagreement over what the U.S. can or should do to secure a greater measure of peace in that region of the world.

But at the end of the day, when all the arguments have been made, those involved in the Christian-Jewish effort to restore moral sanity to a world manifestly going mad will be able to tell the difference between those who do and those who do not care whether Israel will survive and flourish. And from there it is not a long step to understanding who does and who does not care about Jews and Judaism. And that being determined, we will likely have a firmer fix on what is and what is not anti-Semitism in our time.

Contributors

Elliot Abrams, former President of the Washington-based Ethics and Public Policy Center, is a member of the National Security Council.

Hadley Arkes is the Edward Ney Professor of Jurisprudence and American Institutions at Amherst College. He is the author of *First Things,* the book, and *Beyond the Constitution.*

Matthew Berke, former Managing Editor of *First Things,* is a fellow at the Madison Center of Princeton University.

Midge Decter is a former Distinguished Fellow of the Institute on Religion and Public Life.

Marc Gellman is Rabbi of Temple Beth Torah in Dix Hills, New York, and the author of *Does God Have a Big Toe? Stories About Stories in the Bible.*

Milton Himmelfarb is a former Director of Research for the American Jewish Committee and a former Editor of the *American Jewish Year Book.* He is author of *The Jews of Modernity.*

Clifford E. Librach is Rabbi of Temple Sinai (Reformed) in Sharon, Massachusetts.

Stephen Miller has written numerous essays on political and cultural questions.

Alan L. Mittleman teaches in the Religion Department at Muhlenberg College.

Richard John Neuhaus is Editor-in-Chief of *First Things*.

David Novak, a member of the Editorial Board of *First Things,* holds the Dorothy Shiff Chair of Jewish Studies at the University of Toronto.

Jakob J. Petuchowski was a Reform rabbi and the Sol and Arlene Bronstein Professor of Judaeo-Christian Studies and Research Professor of Jewish Theology and Liturgy at the Hebrew Union College in Cincinnati.

Isaac C. Rottenberg is a minister of the Reformed Church of America.

Jonathan D. Sarna is the Joseph H. and Belle R. Braun Professor of American Jewish History at Brandeis University and author of *American Jews and Church-State Relations.*

Edward S. Shapiro is Professor of History at Seton Hall University and the author of *A Time for Healing: American Jewry After World War II.*

David Singer is Editor of the *American Jewish Yearbook.*

Marc D. Stern is Co-Director of the Commission on Law and Social Action for the American Jewish Congress.

Aaron Wildavsky is Professor of Political Science and Public Policy at the University of California, Berkeley.

Ruth R. Wisse is Professor of Yiddish Literature and of Comparative Literature at Harvard University.

Nicholas Wolfson is the Ellen Ash Peters Professor of Law, University of Connecticut School of Law, and author of *First Amendment Rights and the SEC.*

Acknowledgments and Works Reproduced

Elliot Abrams, "Judaism or Jewishness?" *First Things* (June/July 1997): 18-25.

Midge Decter, "A Jew in Anti-Christian America," *First Things* (October 1995): 25-31.

Alan L. Mittleman, "The Modern Jewish Condition," *First Things* (October 1994): 30-34.

David Singer, "The Orthodox Jew as Intellectual Crank," *First Things* (August/September 1990): 44-48.

Matthew Berke, "God and Gender in Judaism," *First Things* (June/July 1996): 33-38.

Alan L. Mittleman, "Pluralism v. Multiculturalism," *First Things* (December 1996): 14-17. First published as "Jews in Multicultural America."

Edward S. Shapiro, "Blacks and Jews Entangled," *First Things* (August/September 1994): 29-35.

David Novak, "When Jews Are Christians," *First Things* (November 1991): 42-46.

Isaac C. Rottenberg, "Those Troublesome Messianic Jews," *First Things* (December 1992): 26-32. First published as "Messianic Jews: Troubling Presence."

David Novak, "Jews and Catholics: Beyond Apologies," *First Things* (January 1999): 20-25.

Stephen Miller, "Confessions of a Rootless Cosmopolitan Jew," *First Things* (February 1992): 41-44.

Marc Gellman, "The Demon in the Jewish Soul," *First Things* (October 1990): 7-10.

Clifford E. Librach, "The Fragmented Faith of American Jews," *First Things* (February 1997): 19-21.

Aaron Wildavsky, "Why Egalitarianism Is Not Good for the Jews," *First Things* (November 1991): 7-9. First published as "Is Egalitarianism Good for the Jews?"

Jakob J. Petuchowski, "A Rabbi's Christmas," *First Things* (December 1991): 8-10.

Richard John Neuhaus, "Anti-Semitism and Our Common Future," *First Things* (March 1992): 58-63.

The following were then-untitled contributions to "Judaism and American Public Life: A Symposium," published by *First Things* in March of 1991.

Marc D. Stern, "Beguiled by the Public Square," *First Things* (March 1991): 17-19.

Nicholas Wolfson, "The Dominating Majority," *First Things* (March 1991): 20-21.

Milton Himmelfarb, "Mordecai's Hope," *First Things* (March 1991): 21-23.

Jonathan D. Sarna, "On an Equal Footing," *First Things* (March 1991): 24.

Marc Gellman, "Shabbat Candles for Life," *First Things* (March 1991): 25-26.

Ruth R. Wisse, "Inculcating Humility," *First Things* (March 1991): 26-27.

Midge Decter, "Tacit Understandings," *First Things* (March 1991): 28.

Hadley Arkes, "A Decorous Judaism," *First Things* (March 1991): 31-33.

Alan L. Mittleman, "A Jewish Civil Religion," *First Things* (March 1991): 35-36.